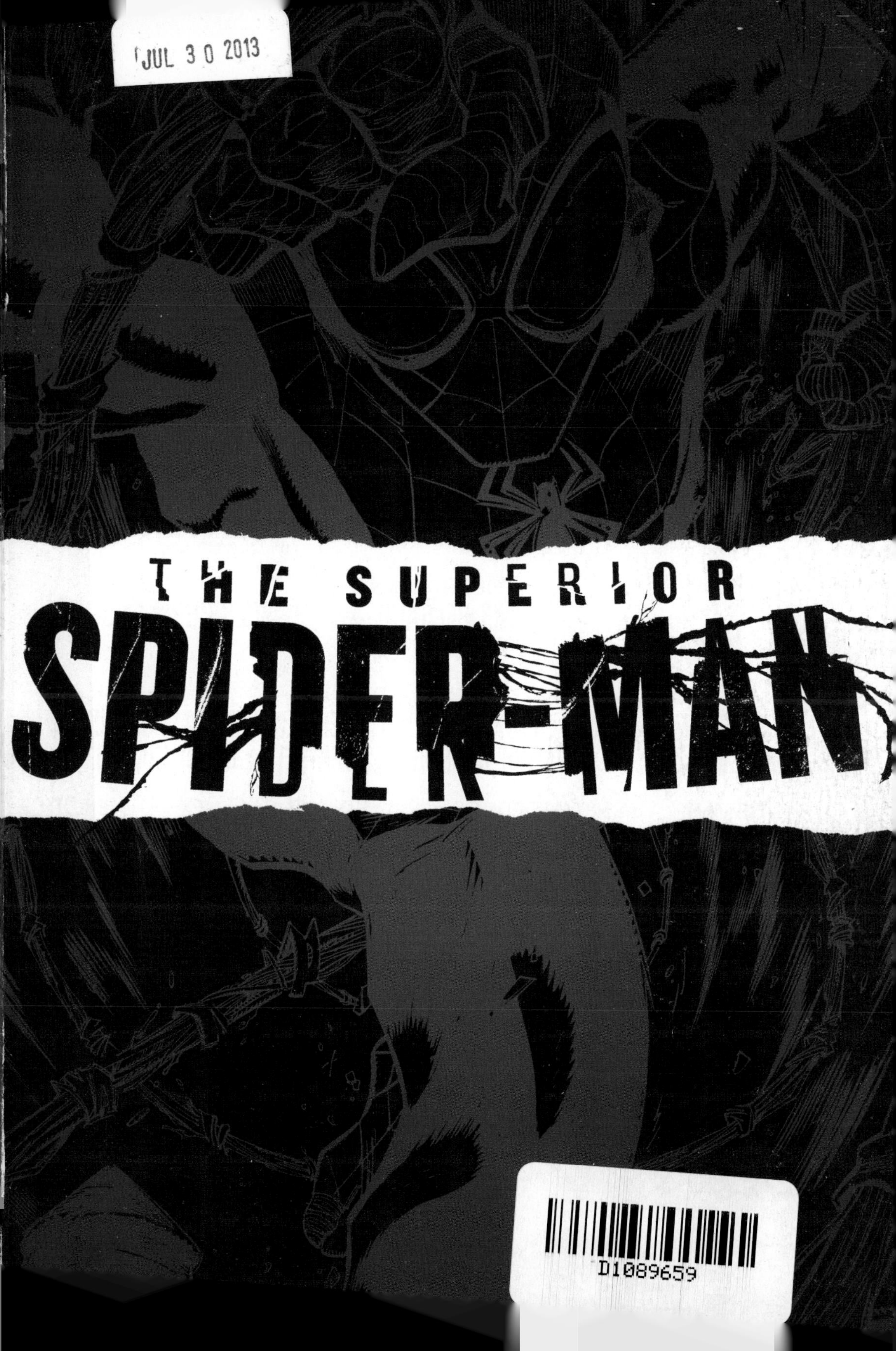
THE SUPERIOR
SPIDER-MAN

THE SUPERIOR SPIDER-MAN

MY OWN WORST ENEMY

WRITER
DAN SLOTT

ARTIST, #1-3
RYAN STEGMAN

PENCILER, #4-5
GIUSEPPE CAMUNCOLI

INKER, #4-5
JOHN DELL WITH
GIUSEPPE CAMUNCOLI (#5)

COLOR ARTIST
EDGAR DELGADO WITH
ANTONIO FABELA (#5)

LETTERER
VC'S CHRIS ELIOPOULOS

COVER ART
RYAN STEGMAN & EDGAR DELGADO (#1-3); **GIUSEPPE CAMUNCOLI, JOHN DELL & EDGAR DELGADO** (#4); AND **GIUSEPPE CAMUNCOLI, JOHN DELL & JIM CHARALAMPIDIS** (#5)

LOGO DESIGN
NESSIM HIGSON

ASSISTANT EDITOR
ELLIE PYLE

EDITOR
STEPHEN WACKER

EXECUTIVE EDITOR
TOM BREVOORT

Collection Editor: **Jennifer Grünwald** • Assistant Editors: **Alex Starbuck & Nelson Ribeiro** • Editor, Special Projects: **Mark D. Beazley**
Senior Editor, Special Projects: **Jeff Youngquist** • SVP of Print & Digital Publishing Sales: **David Gabriel** • Book Design: **Jeff Powell**

Editor in Chief: **Axel Alonso** • Chief Creative Officer: **Joe Quesada** • Publisher: **Dan Buckley** • Executive Producer: **Alan Fine**

SUPERIOR SPIDER-MAN VOL. 1: MY OWN WORST ENEMY. Contains material originally published in magazine form as SUPERIOR SPIDER-MAN #1-5. First printing 2013. ISBN# 978-0-7851-6704-4. Published by MARVEL WORLDWIDE, INC., a subsidiary of MARVEL ENTERTAINMENT, LLC. OFFICE OF PUBLICATION: 135 West 50th Street, New York, NY 10020. **Printed in the U.S.A.** ALAN FINE, EVP - Office of the President, Marvel Worldwide, Inc. and EVP & CMO Marvel Characters B.V.; DAN BUCKLEY, Publisher & President - Print, Animation & Digital Divisions; JOE QUESADA, Chief Creative Officer; TOM BREVOORT, SVP of Publishing; DAVID BOGART, SVP of Operations & Procurement, Publishing; C.B. CEBULSKI, SVP of Creator & Content Development; DAVID GABRIEL, SVP of Print & Digital Publishing Sales; JIM O'KEEFE, VP of Operations & Logistics; DAN CARR, Executive Director of Publishing Technology; SUSAN CRESPI, Editorial Operations Manager; ALEX MORALES, Publishing Operations Manager; STAN LEE, Chairman Emeritus. For information regarding advertising in Marvel Comics or on Marvel.com, please contact Niza Disla, Director of Marvel Partnerships, at ndisla@marvel.com. For Marvel subscription inquiries, please call 800-217-9158. **Manufactured between 4/10/2013 and 5/13/2013 by QUAD/GRAPHICS, VERSAILLES, KY, USA.**

10 9 8 7 6 5 4 3 2 1

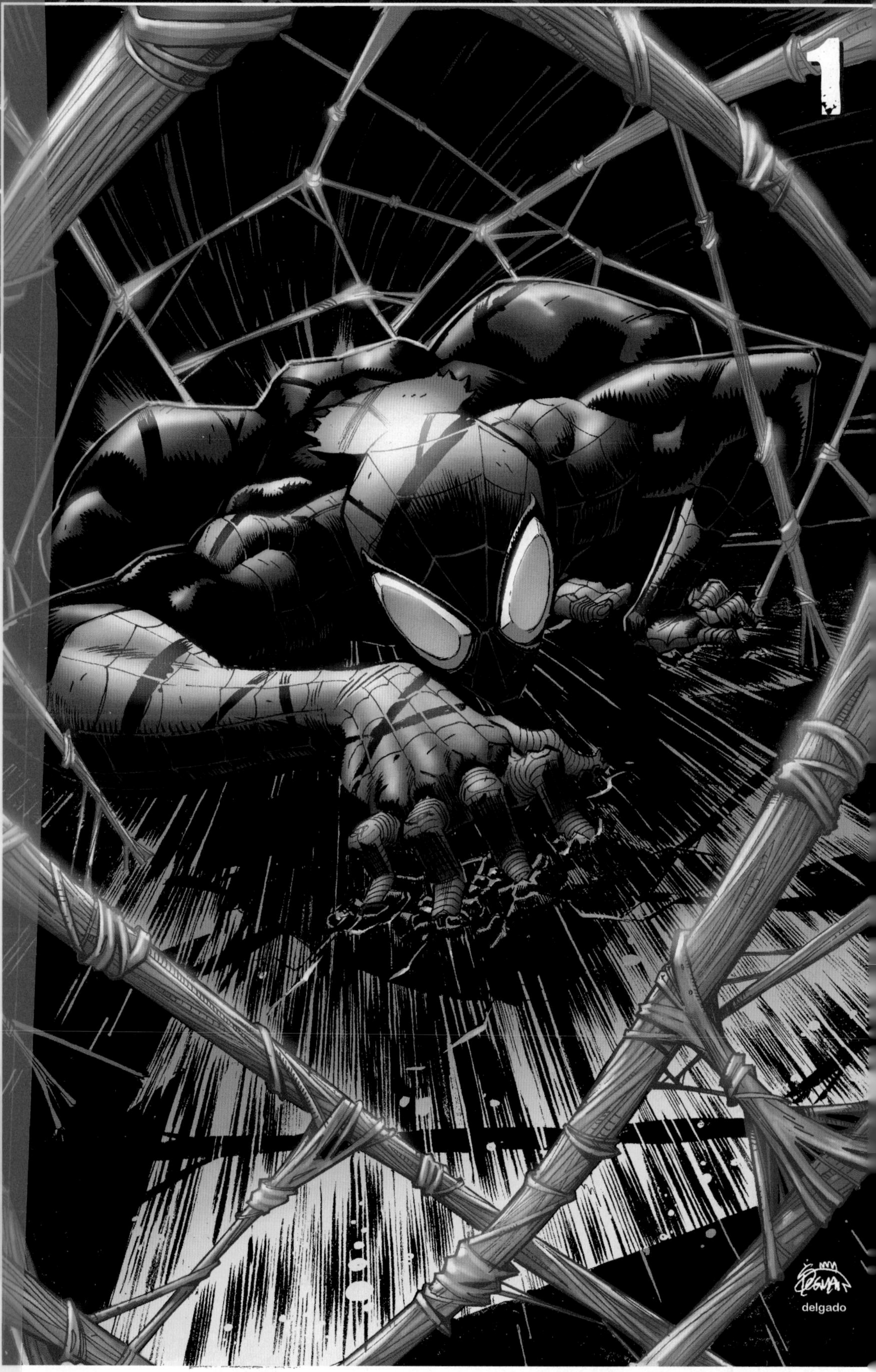
1
delgado

HERO OR MENACE?

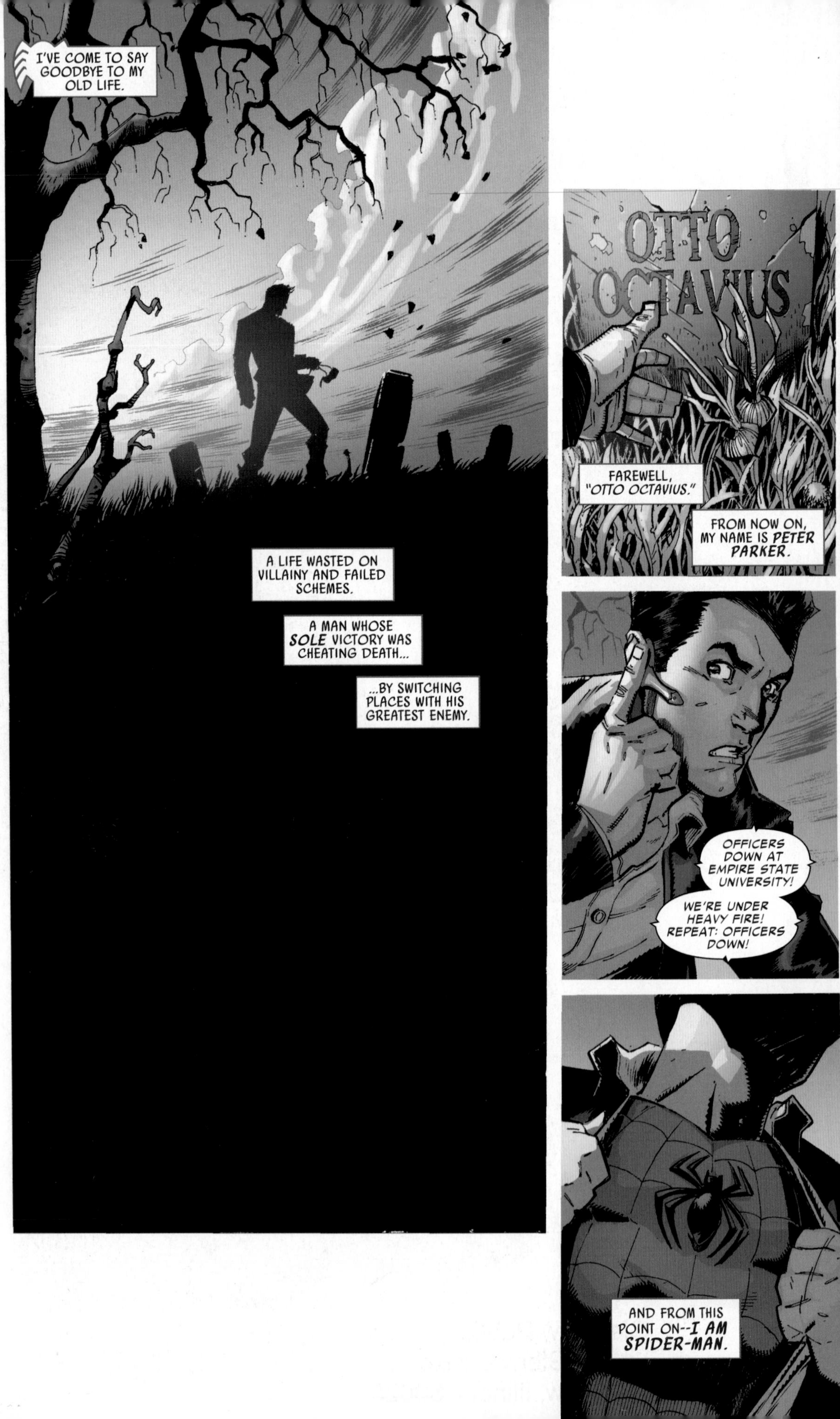
I'VE COME TO SAY GOODBYE TO MY OLD LIFE.
A LIFE WASTED ON VILLAINY AND FAILED SCHEMES.
A MAN WHOSE SOLE VICTORY WAS CHEATING DEATH...
...BY SWITCHING PLACES WITH HIS GREATEST ENEMY.
OTTO OCTAVIUS
FAREWELL, "OTTO OCTAVIUS."
FROM NOW ON, MY NAME IS PETER PARKER.
OFFICERS DOWN AT EMPIRE STATE UNIVERSITY!
WE'RE UNDER HEAVY FIRE! REPEAT: OFFICERS DOWN!
AND FROM THIS POINT ON--I AM SPIDER-MAN.

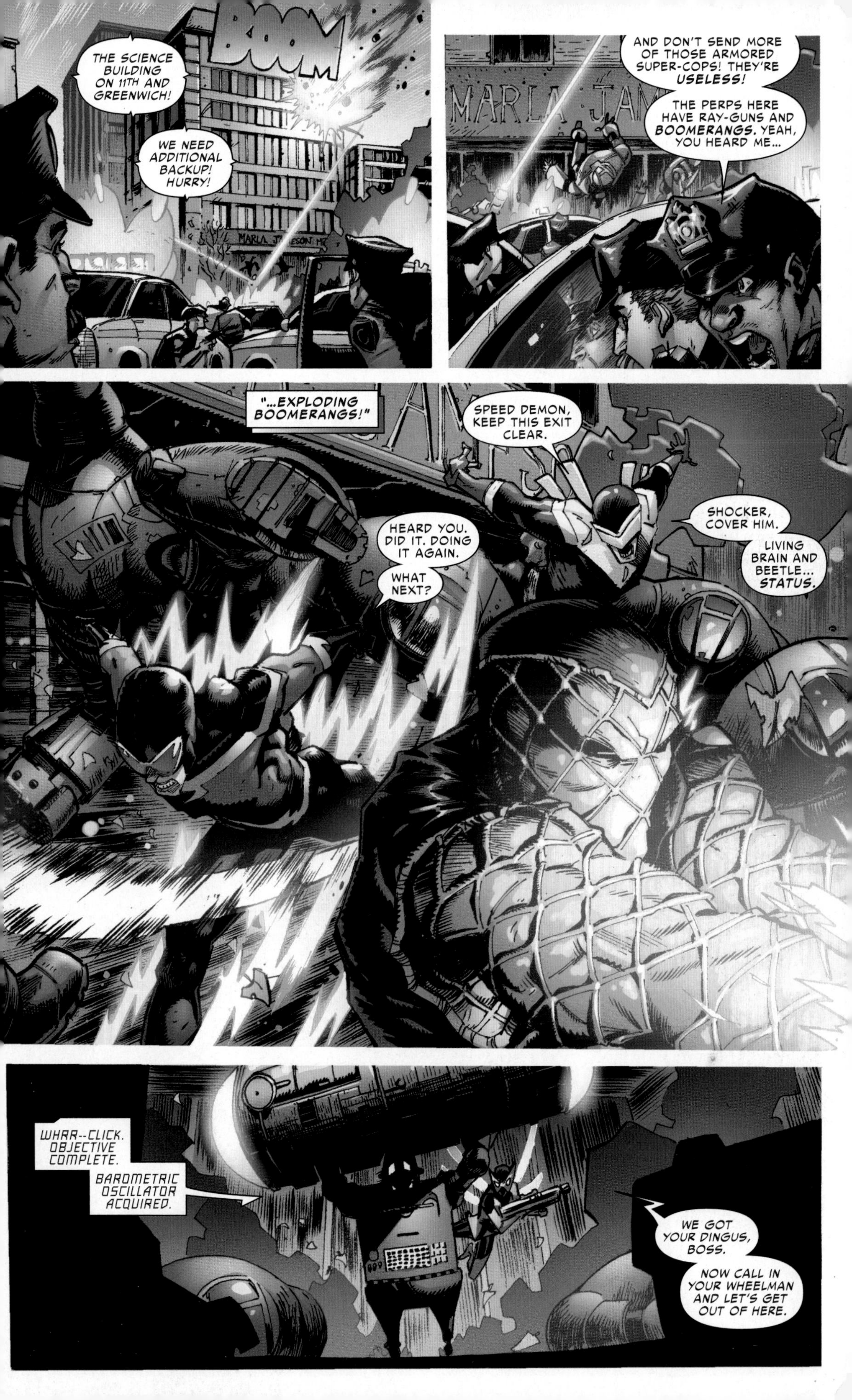
BOOM
THE SCIENCE BUILDING ON 11TH AND GREENWICH!
WE NEED ADDITIONAL BACKUP! HURRY!
MARLA JAMESON
AND DON'T SEND MORE OF THOSE ARMORED SUPER-COPS! THEY'RE USELESS!
THE PERPS HERE HAVE RAY-GUNS AND BOOMERANGS. YEAH, YOU HEARD ME...
"...EXPLODING BOOMERANGS!"
SPEED DEMON, KEEP THIS EXIT CLEAR.
HEARD YOU. DID IT. DOING IT AGAIN.
WHAT NEXT?
SHOCKER, COVER HIM.
LIVING BRAIN AND BEETLE... STATUS.
WHRR--CLICK. OBJECTIVE COMPLETE.
BAROMETRIC OSCILLATOR ACQUIRED.
WE GOT YOUR DINGUS, BOSS.
NOW CALL IN YOUR WHEELMAN AND LET'S GET OUT OF HERE.

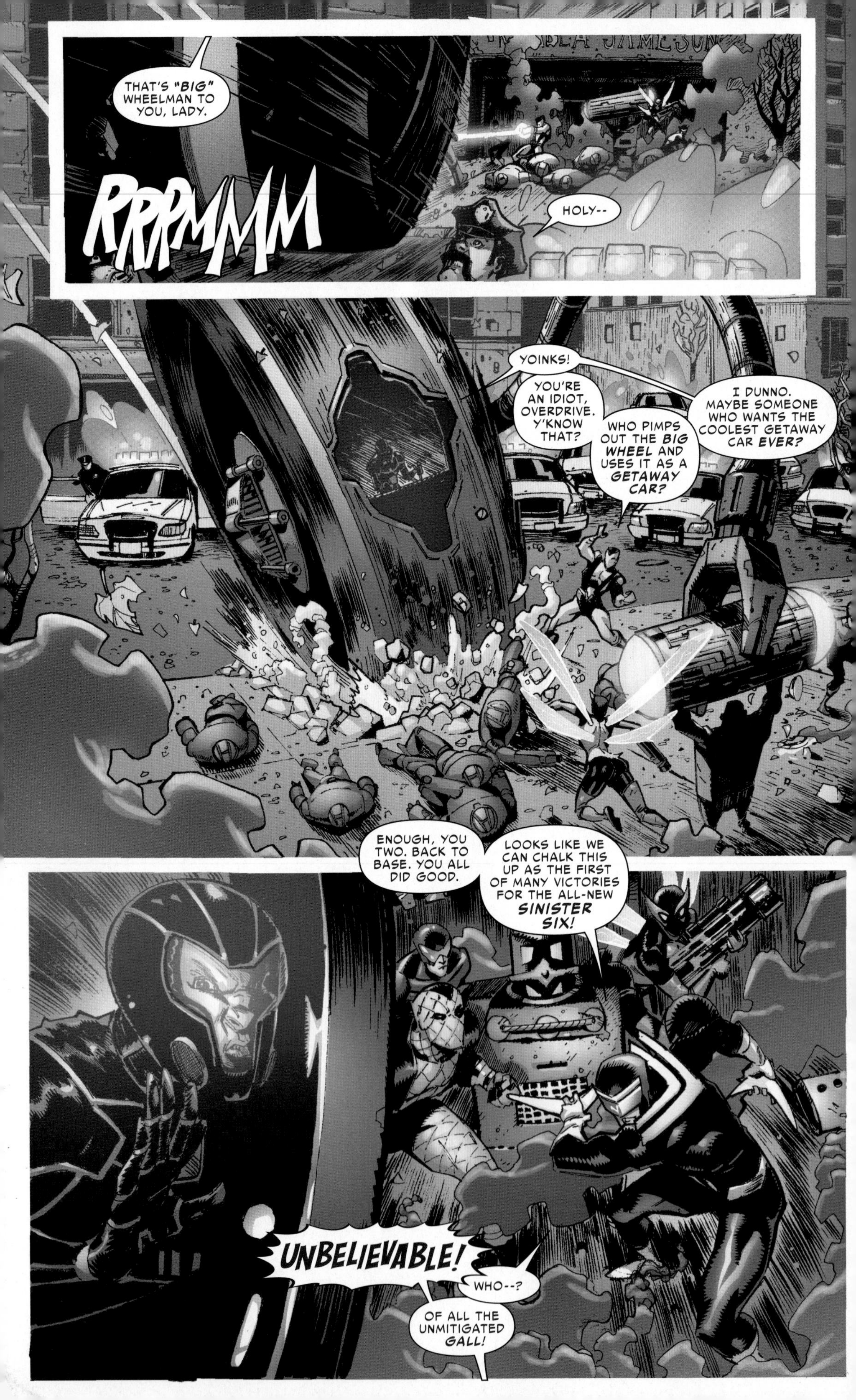

THAT'S "*BIG*" WHEELMAN TO YOU, LADY.
RRPMMM
HOLY--
YOINKS!
YOU'RE AN IDIOT, OVERDRIVE. Y'KNOW THAT?
WHO PIMPS OUT THE *BIG WHEEL* AND USES IT AS A *GETAWAY CAR?*
I DUNNO. MAYBE SOMEONE WHO WANTS THE COOLEST GETAWAY CAR *EVER?*
ENOUGH, YOU TWO. BACK TO BASE. YOU ALL DID GOOD.
LOOKS LIKE WE CAN CHALK THIS UP AS THE FIRST OF MANY VICTORIES FOR THE ALL-NEW **SINISTER SIX!**
UNBELIEVABLE!
WHO--?
OF ALL THE UNMITIGATED *GALL!*

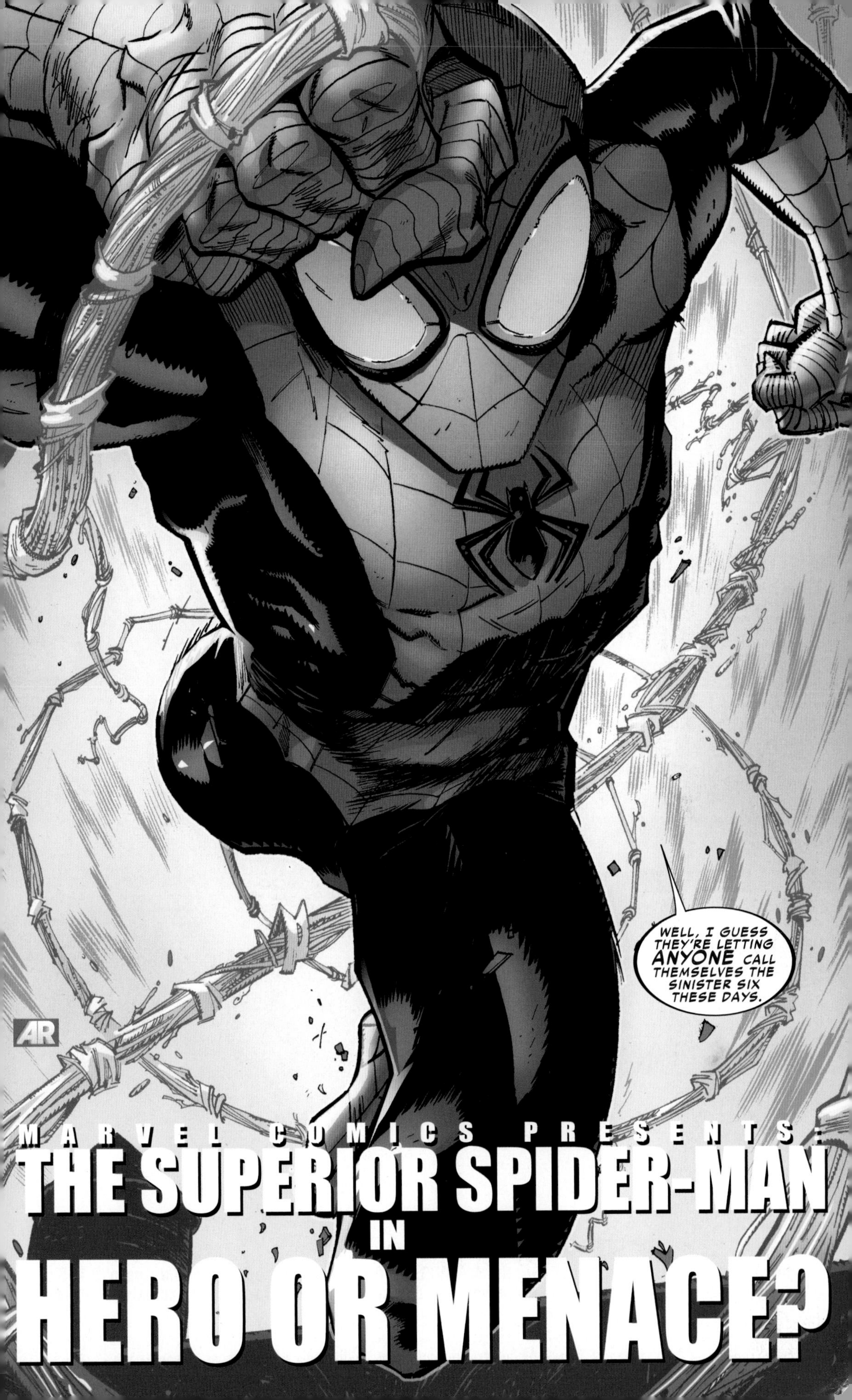
WELL, I GUESS THEY'RE LETTING ANYONE CALL THEMSELVES THE SINISTER SIX THESE DAYS.
MARVEL COMICS PRESENTS:
THE SUPERIOR SPIDER-MAN
IN
HERO OR MENACE?

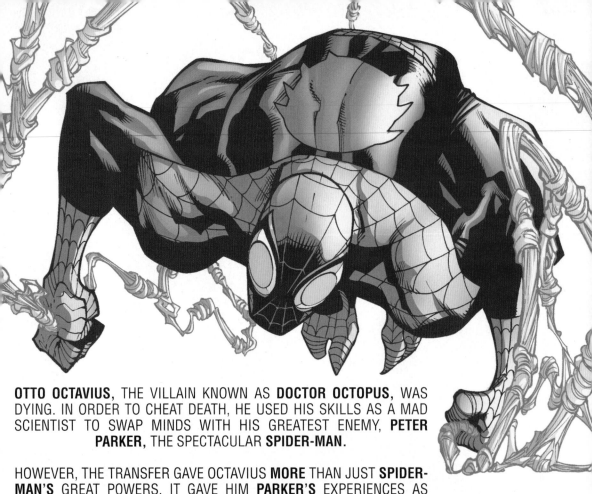

OTTO OCTAVIUS, THE VILLAIN KNOWN AS **DOCTOR OCTOPUS,** WAS DYING. IN ORDER TO CHEAT DEATH, HE USED HIS SKILLS AS A MAD SCIENTIST TO SWAP MINDS WITH HIS GREATEST ENEMY, **PETER PARKER,** THE SPECTACULAR **SPIDER-MAN.**

HOWEVER, THE TRANSFER GAVE OCTAVIUS **MORE** THAN JUST **SPIDER-MAN'S** GREAT POWERS, IT GAVE HIM **PARKER'S** EXPERIENCES AS WELL...INCLUDING THE LESSON OF GREAT RESPONSIBILITY! NOW OTTO OCTAVIUS IS BEGINNING A **NEW** LIFE AS A HERO -- POSSIBLY THE GREATEST HERO OF ALL--

THE SUPERIOR SPIDER-MAN

When you see this: AR, open up the MARVEL AR APP (available on applicable Apple ® iOS or Android TM devices) and use your camera-enabled device to unlock extra-special exclusive features!*

* In fact, there is AR on this very page! Give it a try now! - Smart phone Stephen

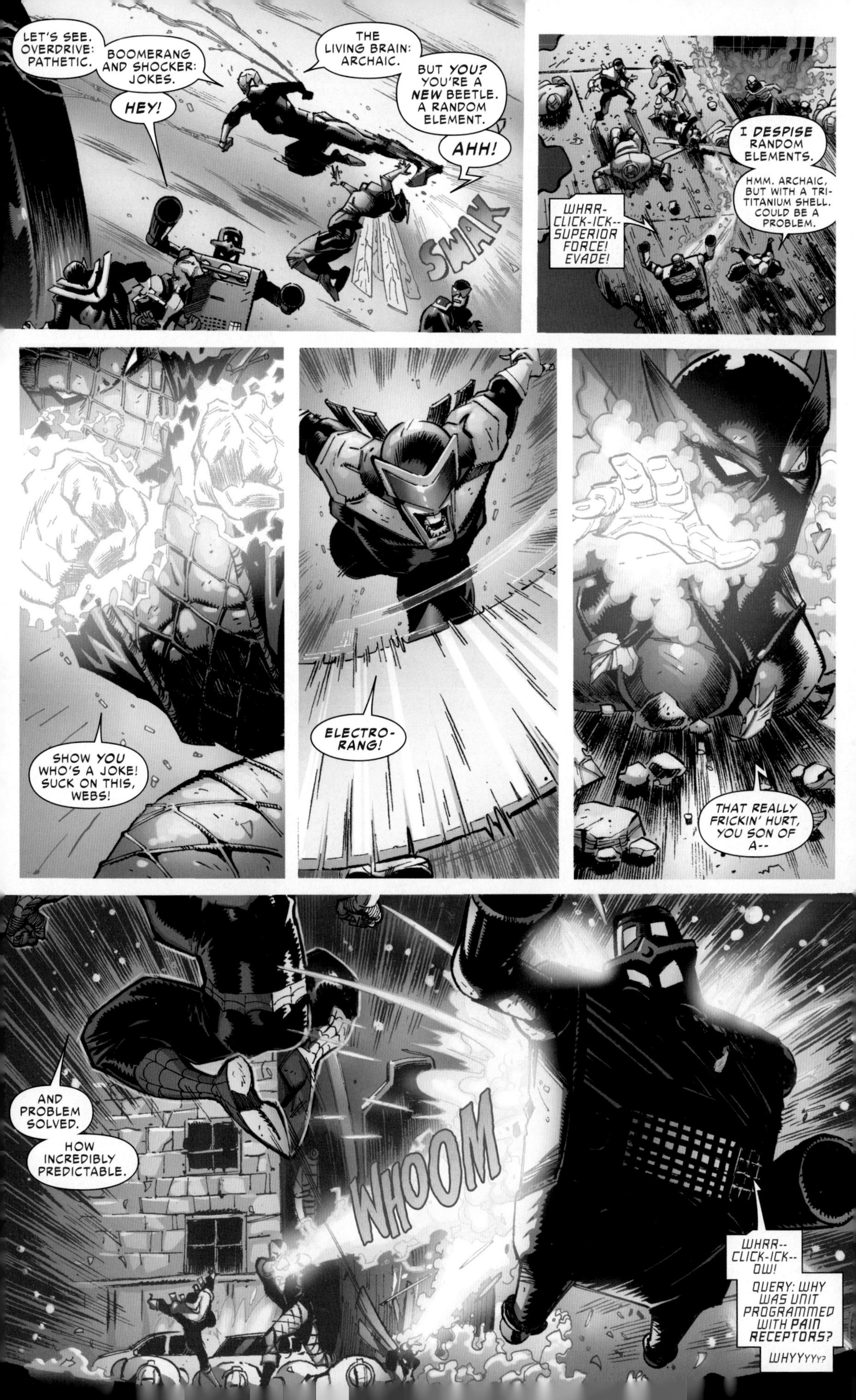
LET'S SEE. OVERDRIVE: PATHETIC.
BOOMERANG AND SHOCKER: JOKES.
HEY!
THE LIVING BRAIN: ARCHAIC.
BUT YOU? YOU'RE A NEW BEETLE. A RANDOM ELEMENT.
AHH!
SWAK
I DESPISE RANDOM ELEMENTS.
HMM. ARCHAIC, BUT WITH A TRI-TITANIUM SHELL. COULD BE A PROBLEM.
WHRR-CLICK-ICK--SUPERIOR FORCE! EVADE!
SHOW YOU WHO'S A JOKE! SUCK ON THIS, WEBS!
ELECTRO-RANG!
THAT REALLY FRICKIN' HURT, YOU SON OF A--
AND PROBLEM SOLVED.
HOW INCREDIBLY PREDICTABLE.
WHOOM
WHRR--CLICK-ICK--OW!
QUERY: WHY WAS UNIT PROGRAMMED WITH PAIN RECEPTORS?
WHYYYYY?

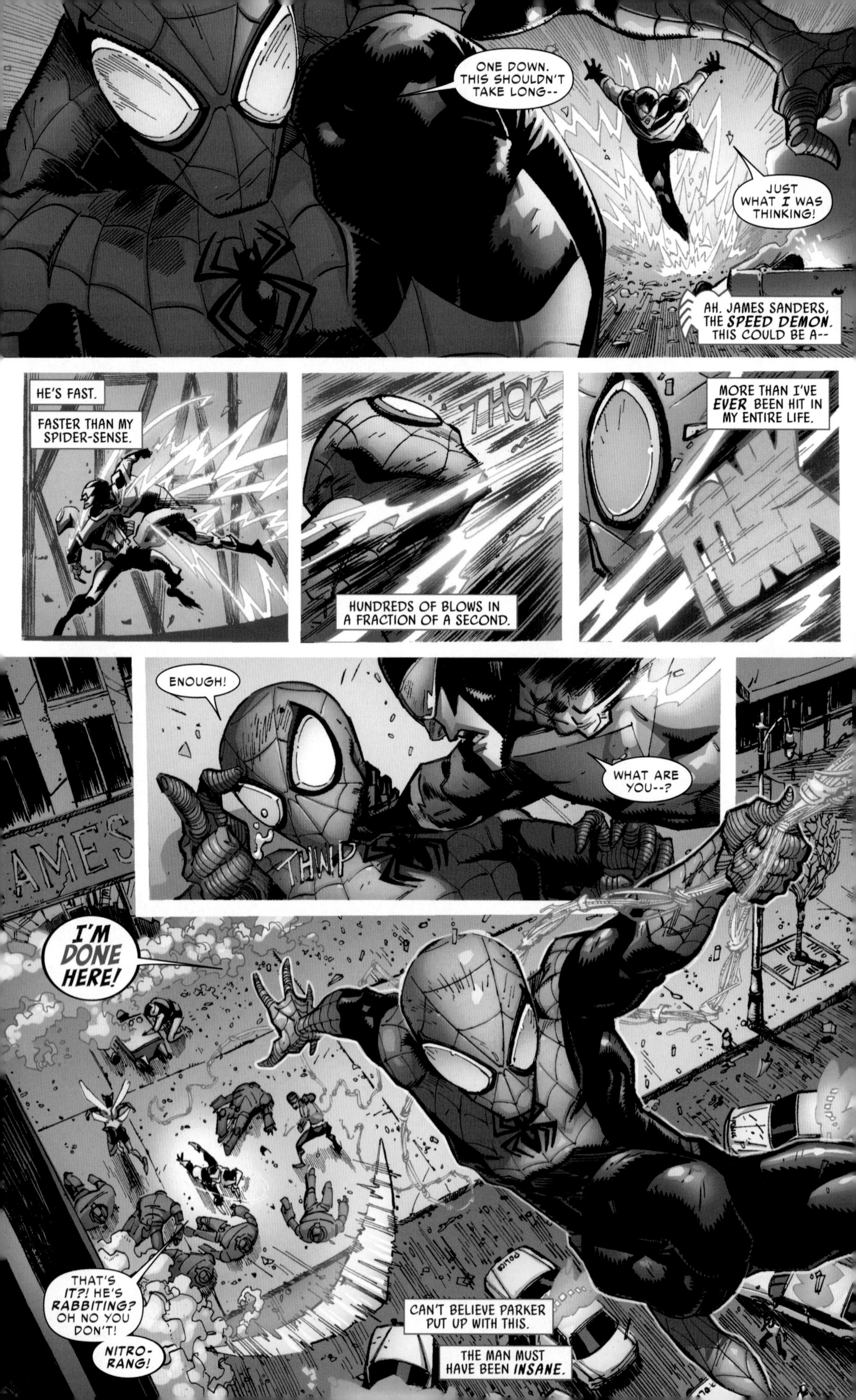

ONE DOWN. THIS SHOULDN'T TAKE LONG--
JUST WHAT *I* WAS THINKING!
AH. JAMES SANDERS, THE ***SPEED DEMON.*** THIS COULD BE A--
HE'S FAST.
FASTER THAN MY SPIDER-SENSE.
THOK
HUNDREDS OF BLOWS IN A FRACTION OF A SECOND.
MORE THAN I'VE ***EVER*** BEEN HIT IN MY ENTIRE LIFE.
ENOUGH!
WHAT ARE YOU--?
THWIP
AMES
I'M DONE HERE!
THAT'S *IT?!* HE'S ***RABBITING?*** OH NO YOU DON'T!
NITRO-RANG!
CAN'T BELIEVE PARKER PUT UP WITH THIS.
THE MAN MUST HAVE BEEN ***INSANE.***

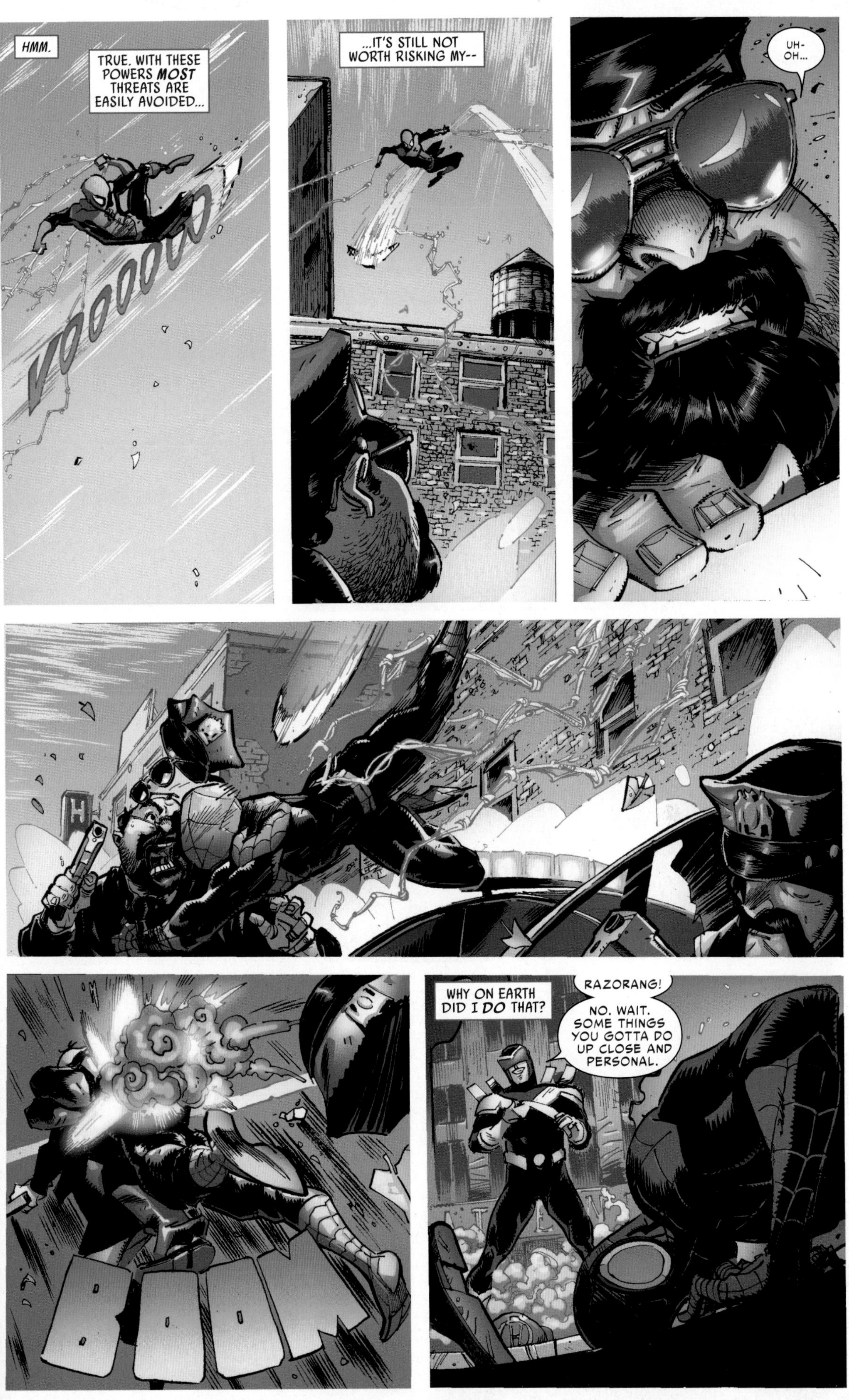
HMM.
TRUE. WITH THESE POWERS MOST THREATS ARE EASILY AVOIDED...
VOOOOO
...IT'S STILL NOT WORTH RISKING MY--
UH-OH...
WHY ON EARTH DID I DO THAT?
RAZORANG!
NO. WAIT. SOME THINGS YOU GOTTA DO UP CLOSE AND PERSONAL.

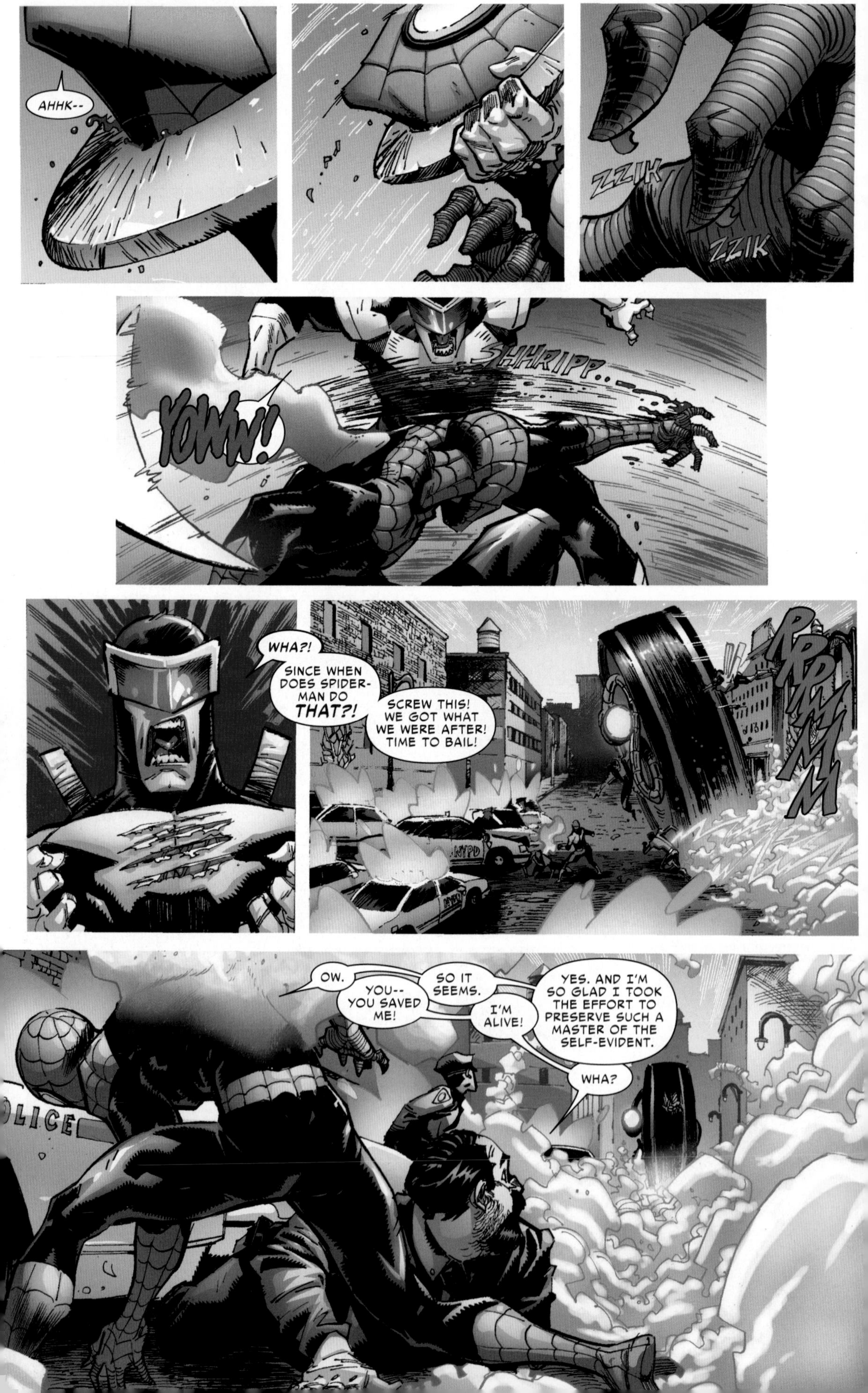
AHHK--
ZZIK
ZZIK
SHHRIPP...
YOWW!
WHA?!
SINCE WHEN DOES SPIDER-MAN DO THAT?!
SCREW THIS! WE GOT WHAT WE WERE AFTER! TIME TO BAIL!
RRRMMM
NYPD
OW.
YOU-- YOU SAVED ME!
SO IT SEEMS.
I'M ALIVE!
YES. AND I'M SO GLAD I TOOK THE EFFORT TO PRESERVE SUCH A MASTER OF THE SELF-EVIDENT.
WHA?
POLICE

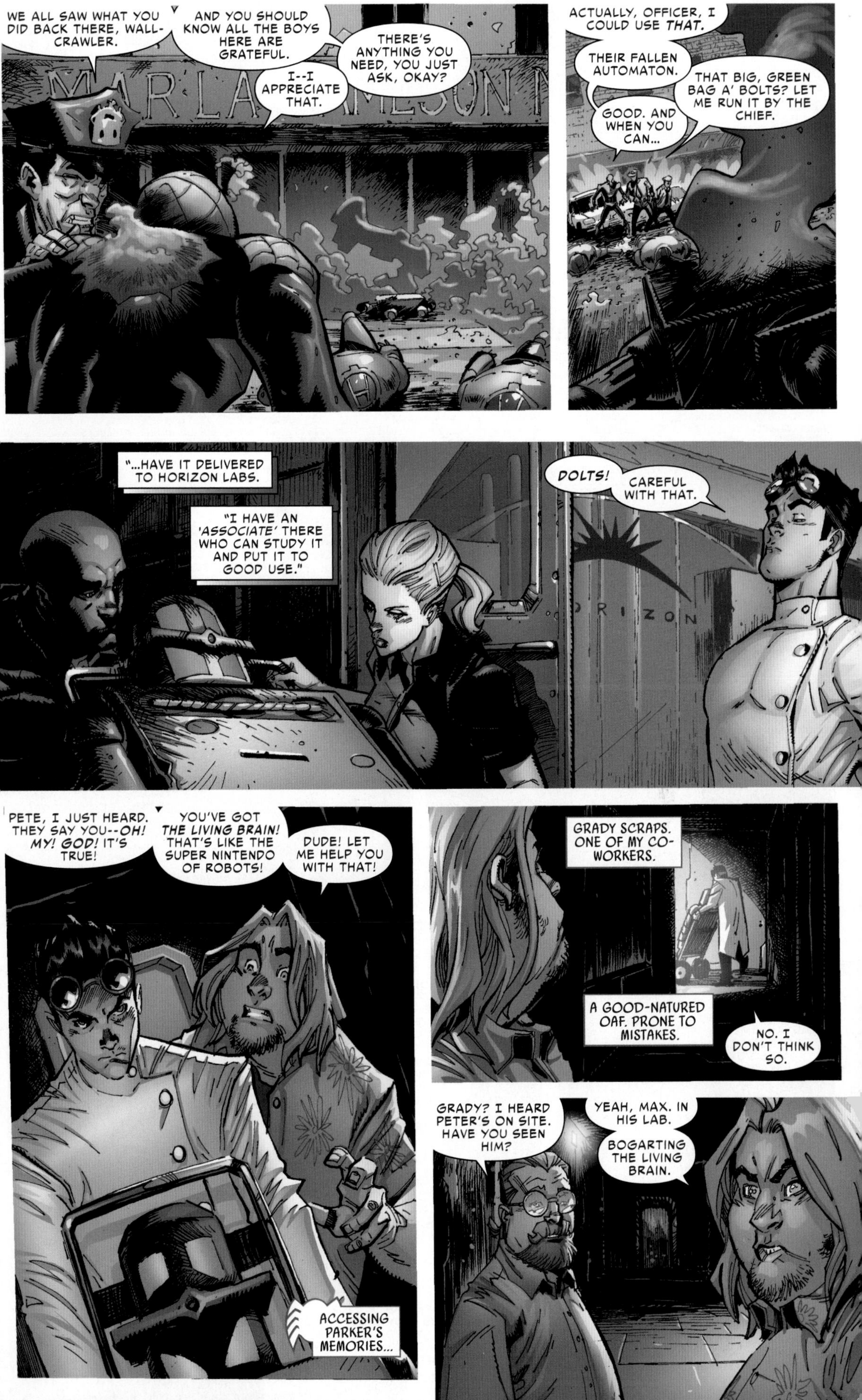
WE ALL SAW WHAT YOU DID BACK THERE, WALL-CRAWLER.
AND YOU SHOULD KNOW ALL THE BOYS HERE ARE GRATEFUL.
THERE'S ANYTHING YOU NEED, YOU JUST ASK, OKAY?
I--I APPRECIATE THAT.
ACTUALLY, OFFICER, I COULD USE THAT.
THEIR FALLEN AUTOMATON.
THAT BIG, GREEN BAG A' BOLTS? LET ME RUN IT BY THE CHIEF.
GOOD. AND WHEN YOU CAN...
"...HAVE IT DELIVERED TO HORIZON LABS.
"I HAVE AN 'ASSOCIATE' THERE WHO CAN STUDY IT AND PUT IT TO GOOD USE."
DOLTS!
CAREFUL WITH THAT.
HORIZON
PETE, I JUST HEARD. THEY SAY YOU--OH! MY! GOD! IT'S TRUE!
YOU'VE GOT THE LIVING BRAIN! THAT'S LIKE THE SUPER NINTENDO OF ROBOTS!
DUDE! LET ME HELP YOU WITH THAT!
ACCESSING PARKER'S MEMORIES...
GRADY SCRAPS. ONE OF MY CO-WORKERS.
A GOOD-NATURED OAF. PRONE TO MISTAKES.
NO. I DON'T THINK SO.
GRADY? I HEARD PETER'S ON SITE. HAVE YOU SEEN HIM?
YEAH, MAX. IN HIS LAB.
BOGARTING THE LIVING BRAIN.

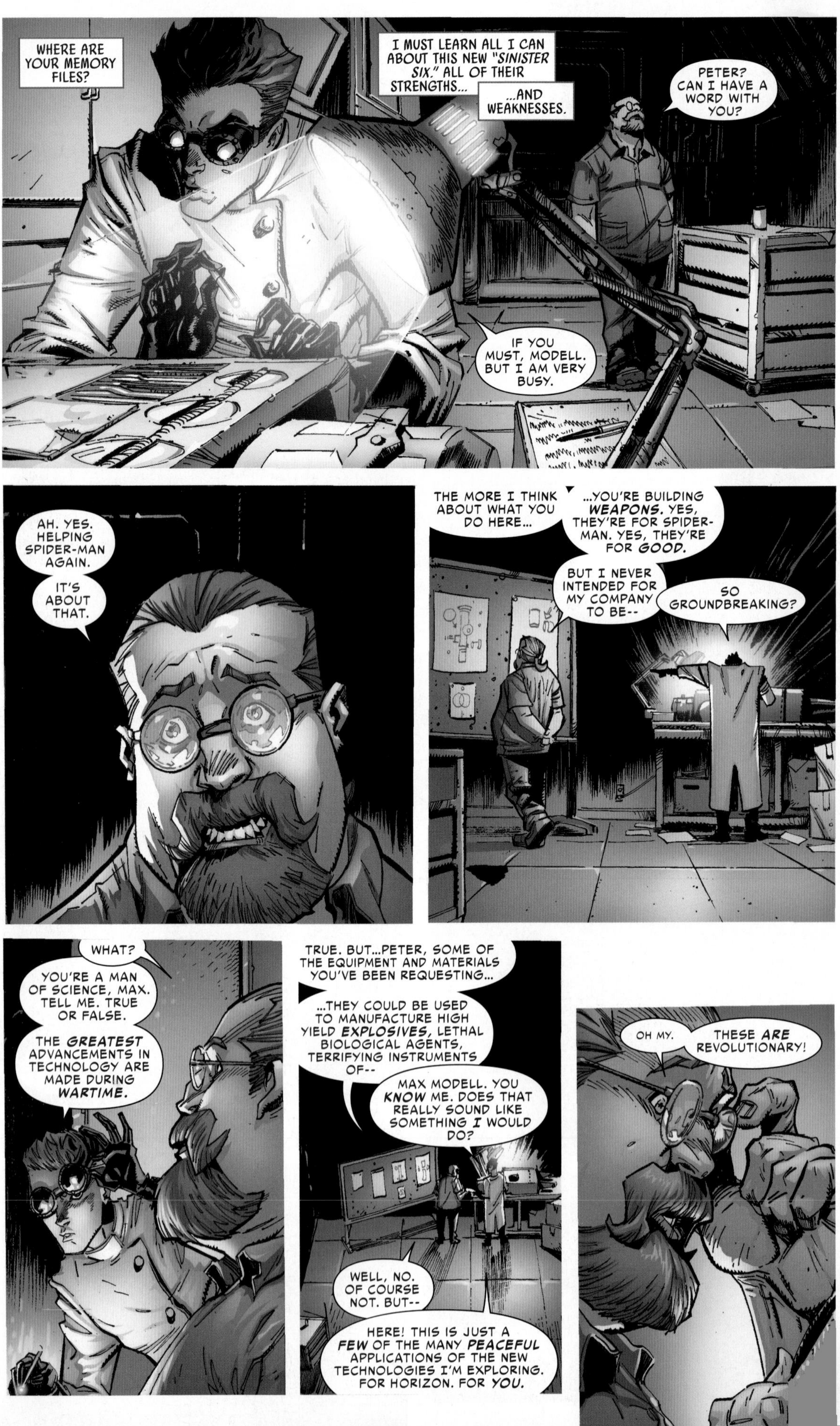
WHERE ARE YOUR MEMORY FILES?
I MUST LEARN ALL I CAN ABOUT THIS NEW "SINISTER SIX." ALL OF THEIR STRENGTHS...
...AND WEAKNESSES.
PETER? CAN I HAVE A WORD WITH YOU?
IF YOU MUST, MODELL. BUT I AM VERY BUSY.
AH. YES. HELPING SPIDER-MAN AGAIN.
IT'S ABOUT THAT.
THE MORE I THINK ABOUT WHAT YOU DO HERE...
...YOU'RE BUILDING WEAPONS. YES, THEY'RE FOR SPIDER-MAN. YES, THEY'RE FOR GOOD.
BUT I NEVER INTENDED FOR MY COMPANY TO BE--
SO GROUNDBREAKING?
WHAT?
YOU'RE A MAN OF SCIENCE, MAX. TELL ME. TRUE OR FALSE.
THE GREATEST ADVANCEMENTS IN TECHNOLOGY ARE MADE DURING WARTIME.
TRUE. BUT...PETER, SOME OF THE EQUIPMENT AND MATERIALS YOU'VE BEEN REQUESTING...
...THEY COULD BE USED TO MANUFACTURE HIGH YIELD EXPLOSIVES, LETHAL BIOLOGICAL AGENTS, TERRIFYING INSTRUMENTS OF--
MAX MODELL. YOU KNOW ME. DOES THAT REALLY SOUND LIKE SOMETHING I WOULD DO?
WELL, NO. OF COURSE NOT. BUT--
HERE! THIS IS JUST A FEW OF THE MANY PEACEFUL APPLICATIONS OF THE NEW TECHNOLOGIES I'M EXPLORING. FOR HORIZON. FOR YOU.
OH MY.
THESE ARE REVOLUTIONARY!

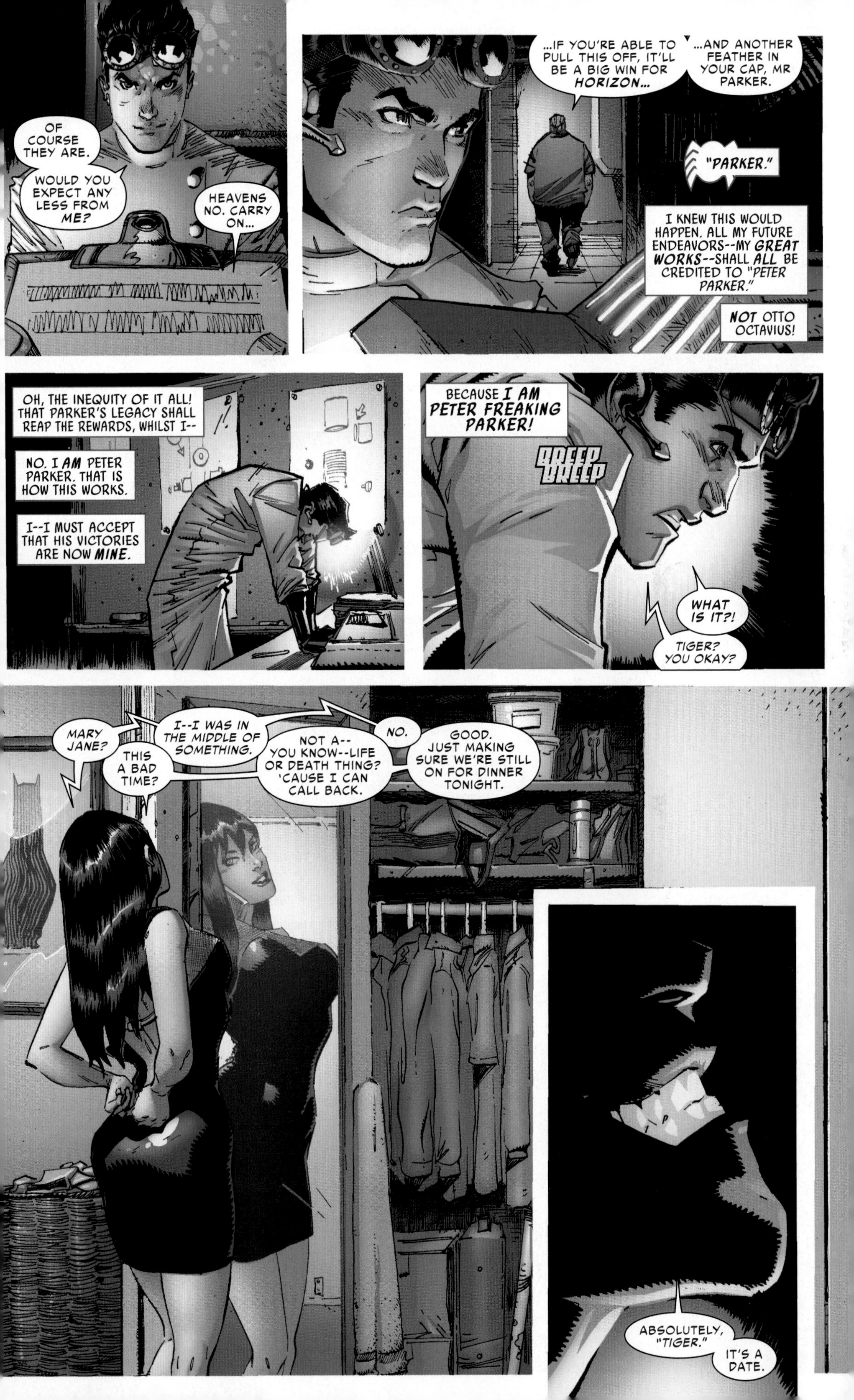
OF COURSE THEY ARE.
WOULD YOU EXPECT ANY LESS FROM ME?
HEAVENS NO. CARRY ON...
...IF YOU'RE ABLE TO PULL THIS OFF, IT'LL BE A BIG WIN FOR HORIZON...
...AND ANOTHER FEATHER IN YOUR CAP, MR PARKER.
"PARKER."
I KNEW THIS WOULD HAPPEN. ALL MY FUTURE ENDEAVORS--MY GREAT WORKS--SHALL ALL BE CREDITED TO "PETER PARKER."
NOT OTTO OCTAVIUS!
OH, THE INEQUITY OF IT ALL! THAT PARKER'S LEGACY SHALL REAP THE REWARDS, WHILST I--
NO. I AM PETER PARKER. THAT IS HOW THIS WORKS.
I--I MUST ACCEPT THAT HIS VICTORIES ARE NOW MINE.
BECAUSE I AM PETER FREAKING PARKER!
BREEP BREEP
WHAT IS IT?!
TIGER? YOU OKAY?
MARY JANE?
I--I WAS IN THE MIDDLE OF SOMETHING.
THIS A BAD TIME?
NOT A-- YOU KNOW--LIFE OR DEATH THING? 'CAUSE I CAN CALL BACK.
NO.
GOOD. JUST MAKING SURE WE'RE STILL ON FOR DINNER TONIGHT.
ABSOLUTELY, "TIGER."
IT'S A DATE.

I *AM* PETER PARKER. AND THAT'S NOT SUCH A BAD THING AT ALL.

RUNNING A NIGHTCLUB.

SUPER-POWERS. JUST YOUTH. VIGOR. ARTS. HEALTH CODES. SAFETY CHECKS.

HIGH PAYING JOB. STATE OF THE ART LAB. KEEPING UP STAFF MORALE.

AND THEN THERE'S *THIS* LOVELY CREATURE. CUSTOMER WHO WAS MAKING A SCENE--

YES. PETER PARKER'S LIFE WILL SUIT ME JUST FINE.

AND THE *BEST* PART ABOUT IT?

PETER?

THE VIEW.

PETER? ARE YOU EVEN LISTENING TO ME?

SORRY. I WAS DISTRACTED.

DO YOU HAVE TO WEAR THAT HEADSET WHILE WE'RE EATING?

YES, ACTUALLY. I'M MONITORING SOMETHING THAT'S SPIDER-MAN RELATED.

OH! THE POLICE BAND? IS THERE AN EMERGENCY? DO YOU HAVE TO--

NO. NOTHING LIKE THAT. I'M LISTENING IN ON THE SINISTER SIX.

THEY'RE PLOTTING THEIR NEXT ATTACK.

WHAT?!

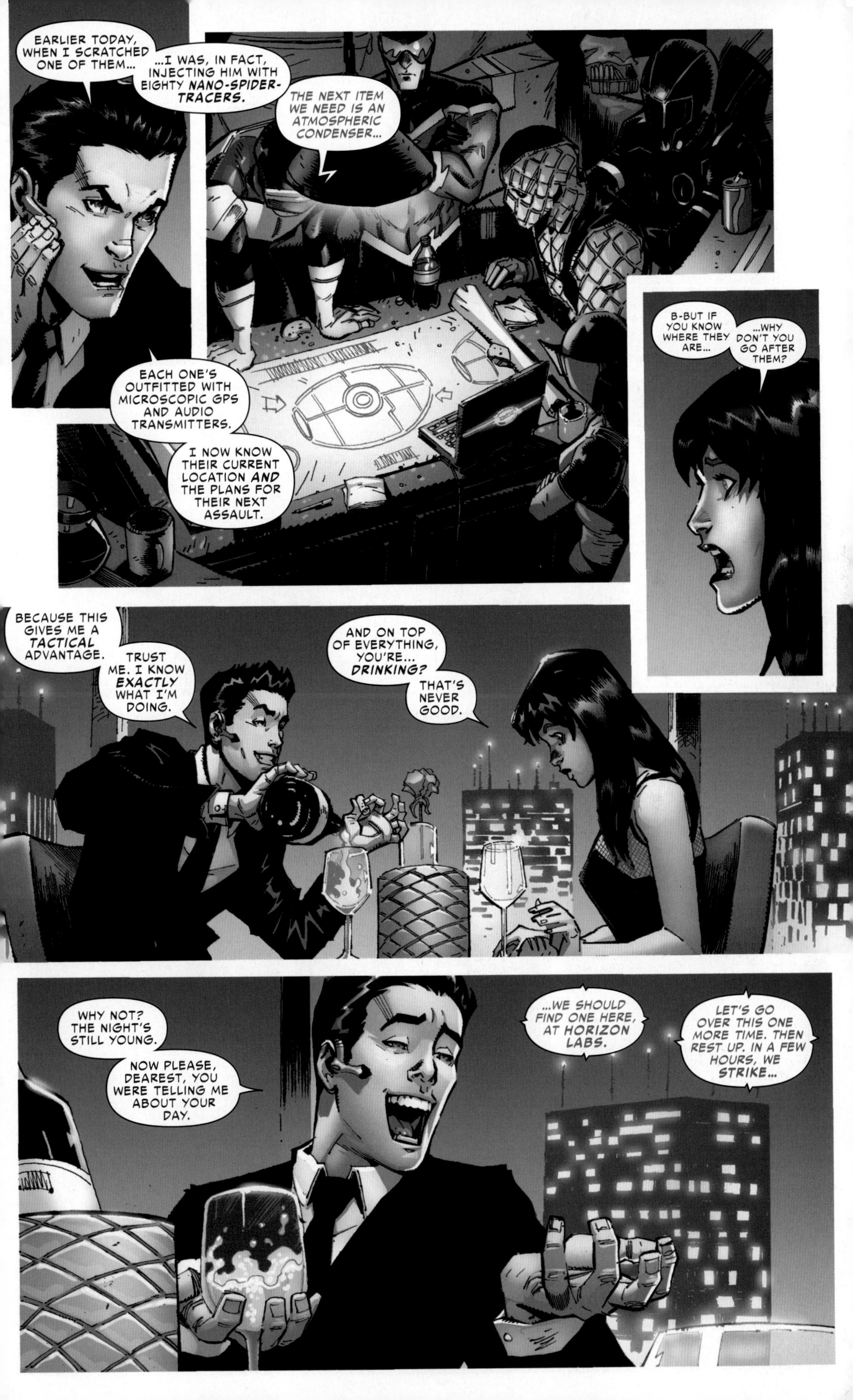
EARLIER TODAY, WHEN I SCRATCHED ONE OF THEM...
...I WAS, IN FACT, INJECTING HIM WITH EIGHTY NANO-SPIDER-TRACERS.
THE NEXT ITEM WE NEED IS AN ATMOSPHERIC CONDENSER...
EACH ONE'S OUTFITTED WITH MICROSCOPIC GPS AND AUDIO TRANSMITTERS.
I NOW KNOW THEIR CURRENT LOCATION AND THE PLANS FOR THEIR NEXT ASSAULT.
B-BUT IF YOU KNOW WHERE THEY ARE...
...WHY DON'T YOU GO AFTER THEM?
BECAUSE THIS GIVES ME A TACTICAL ADVANTAGE.
TRUST ME. I KNOW EXACTLY WHAT I'M DOING.
AND ON TOP OF EVERYTHING, YOU'RE... DRINKING?
THAT'S NEVER GOOD.
WHY NOT? THE NIGHT'S STILL YOUNG.
NOW PLEASE, DEAREST, YOU WERE TELLING ME ABOUT YOUR DAY.
...WE SHOULD FIND ONE HERE, AT HORIZON LABS.
LET'S GO OVER THIS ONE MORE TIME. THEN REST UP. IN A FEW HOURS, WE STRIKE...

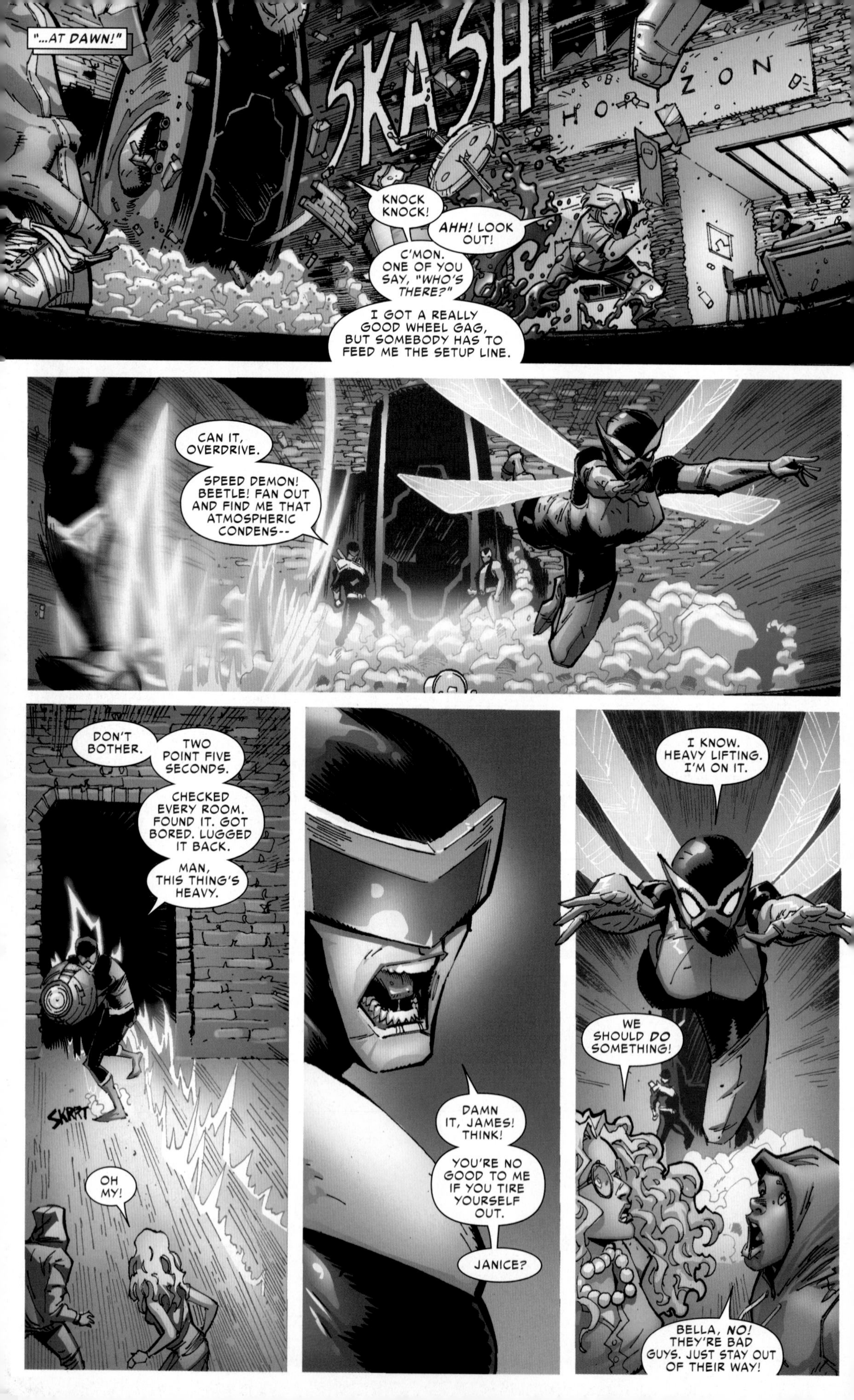
"...AT DAWN!"
SKASH
HORIZON
KNOCK KNOCK!
AHH! LOOK OUT!
C'MON. ONE OF YOU SAY, "WHO'S THERE?"
I GOT A REALLY GOOD WHEEL GAG, BUT SOMEBODY HAS TO FEED ME THE SETUP LINE.
CAN IT, OVERDRIVE.
SPEED DEMON! BEETLE! FAN OUT AND FIND ME THAT ATMOSPHERIC CONDENS--
DON'T BOTHER.
TWO POINT FIVE SECONDS.
CHECKED EVERY ROOM. FOUND IT. GOT BORED. LUGGED IT BACK.
MAN, THIS THING'S HEAVY.
SKRRT
OH MY!
DAMN IT, JAMES! THINK!
YOU'RE NO GOOD TO ME IF YOU TIRE YOURSELF OUT.
JANICE?
I KNOW. HEAVY LIFTING. I'M ON IT.
WE SHOULD DO SOMETHING!
BELLA, NO! THEY'RE BAD GUYS. JUST STAY OUT OF THEIR WAY!

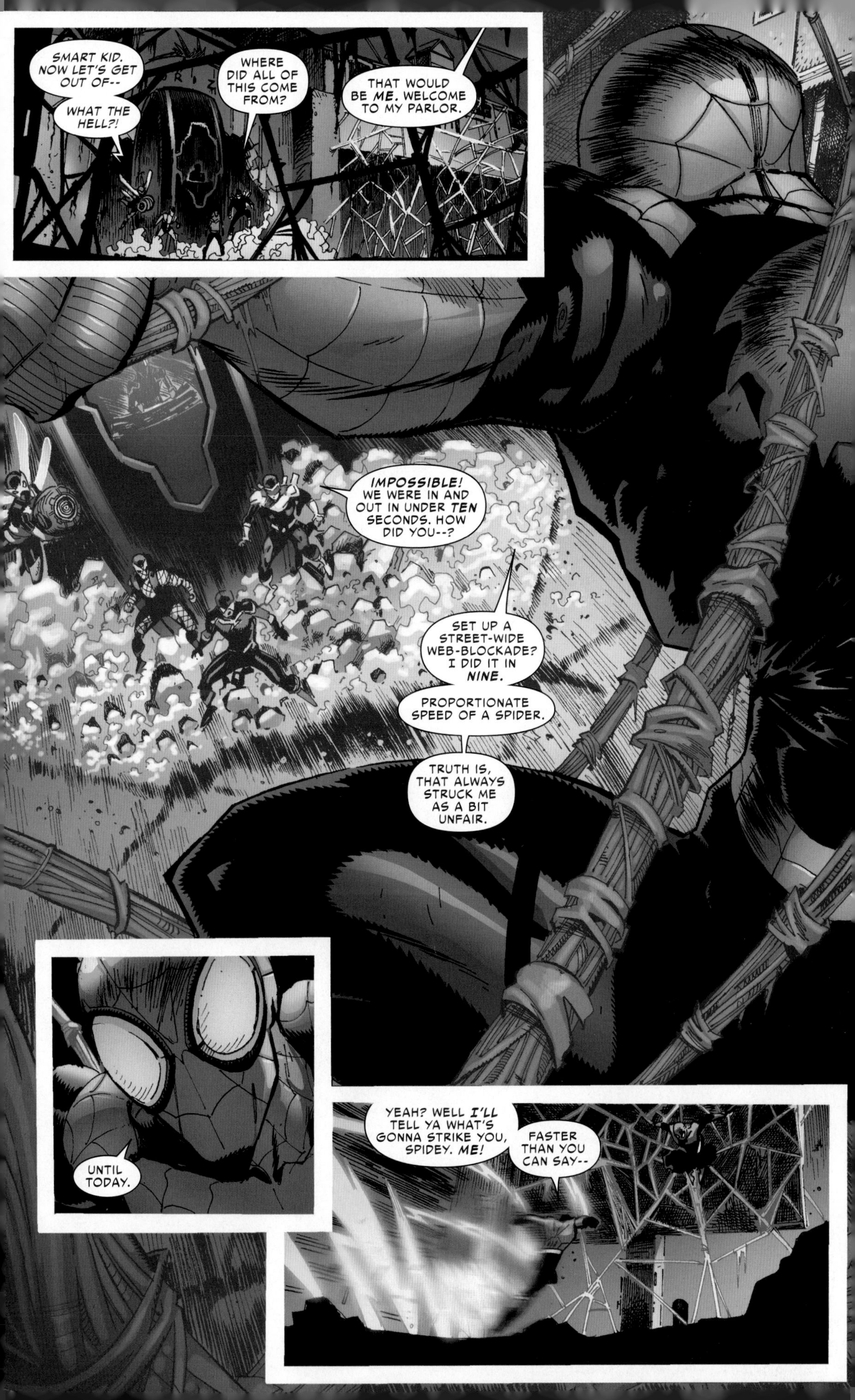
SMART KID. NOW LET'S GET OUT OF--
WHAT THE HELL?!
WHERE DID ALL OF THIS COME FROM?
THAT WOULD BE ME. WELCOME TO MY PARLOR.
IMPOSSIBLE! WE WERE IN AND OUT IN UNDER TEN SECONDS. HOW DID YOU--?
SET UP A STREET-WIDE WEB-BLOCKADE? I DID IT IN NINE.
PROPORTIONATE SPEED OF A SPIDER.
TRUTH IS, THAT ALWAYS STRUCK ME AS A BIT UNFAIR.
UNTIL TODAY.
YEAH? WELL I'LL TELL YA WHAT'S GONNA STRIKE YOU, SPIDEY. ME!
FASTER THAN YOU CAN SAY--

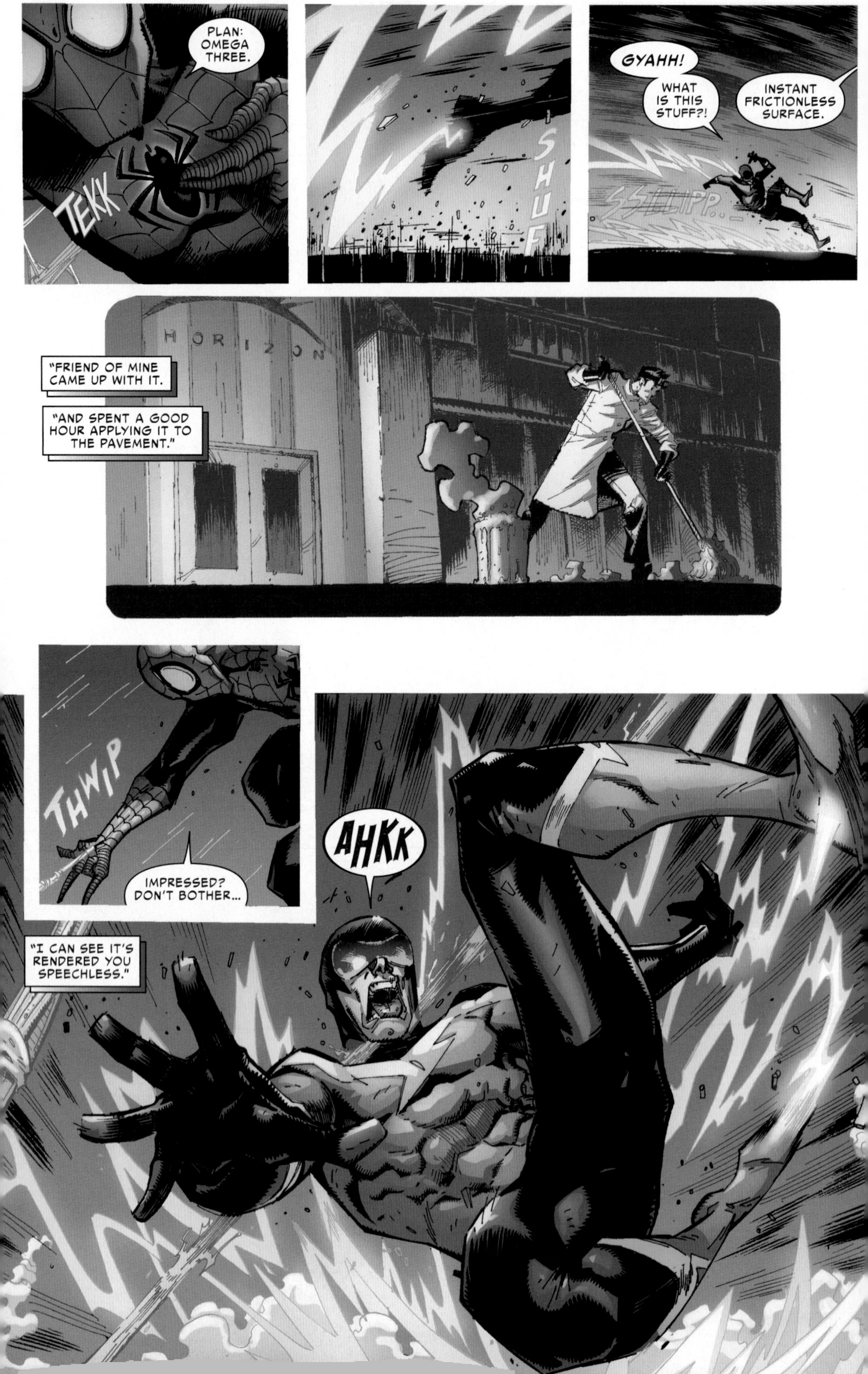
PLAN: OMEGA THREE.
TEKK
SHUF
GYAHH!
WHAT IS THIS STUFF?!
INSTANT FRICTIONLESS SURFACE.
SSLLIPP...
HORIZON
"FRIEND OF MINE CAME UP WITH IT.
"AND SPENT A GOOD HOUR APPLYING IT TO THE PAVEMENT."
THWIP
IMPRESSED? DON'T BOTHER...
AHKK
"I CAN SEE IT'S RENDERED YOU SPEECHLESS."

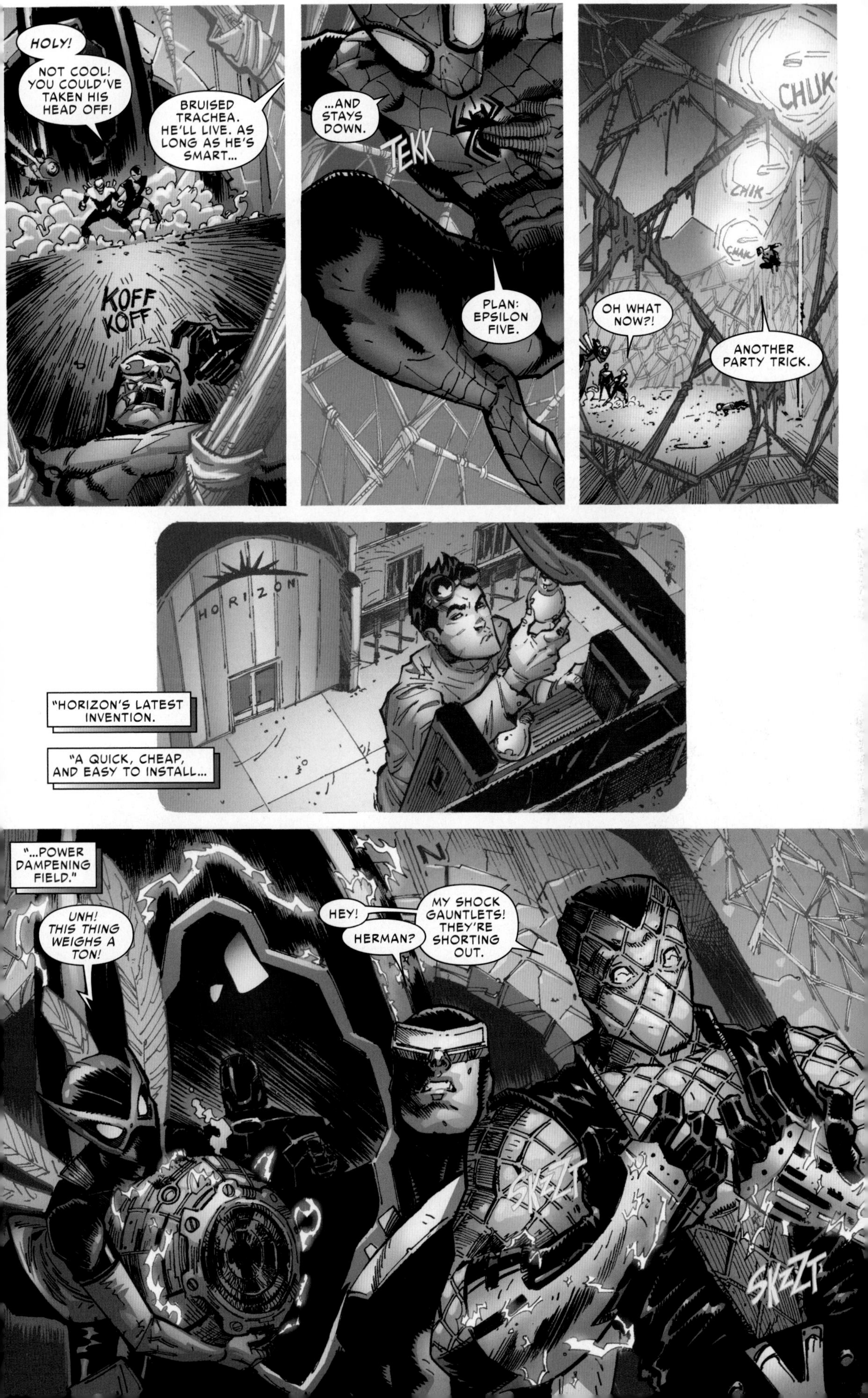
HOLY!
NOT COOL! YOU COULD'VE TAKEN HIS HEAD OFF!
BRUISED TRACHEA. HE'LL LIVE. AS LONG AS HE'S SMART...
KOFF KOFF
...AND STAYS DOWN.
TEKK
PLAN: EPSILON FIVE.
CHUK
CHIK
CHAK
OH WHAT NOW?!
ANOTHER PARTY TRICK.
HORIZON
"HORIZON'S LATEST INVENTION.
"A QUICK, CHEAP, AND EASY TO INSTALL...
"...POWER DAMPENING FIELD."
UNH! THIS THING WEIGHS A TON!
HEY!
HERMAN?
MY SHOCK GAUNTLETS! THEY'RE SHORTING OUT.
SKZZT
SKZZT

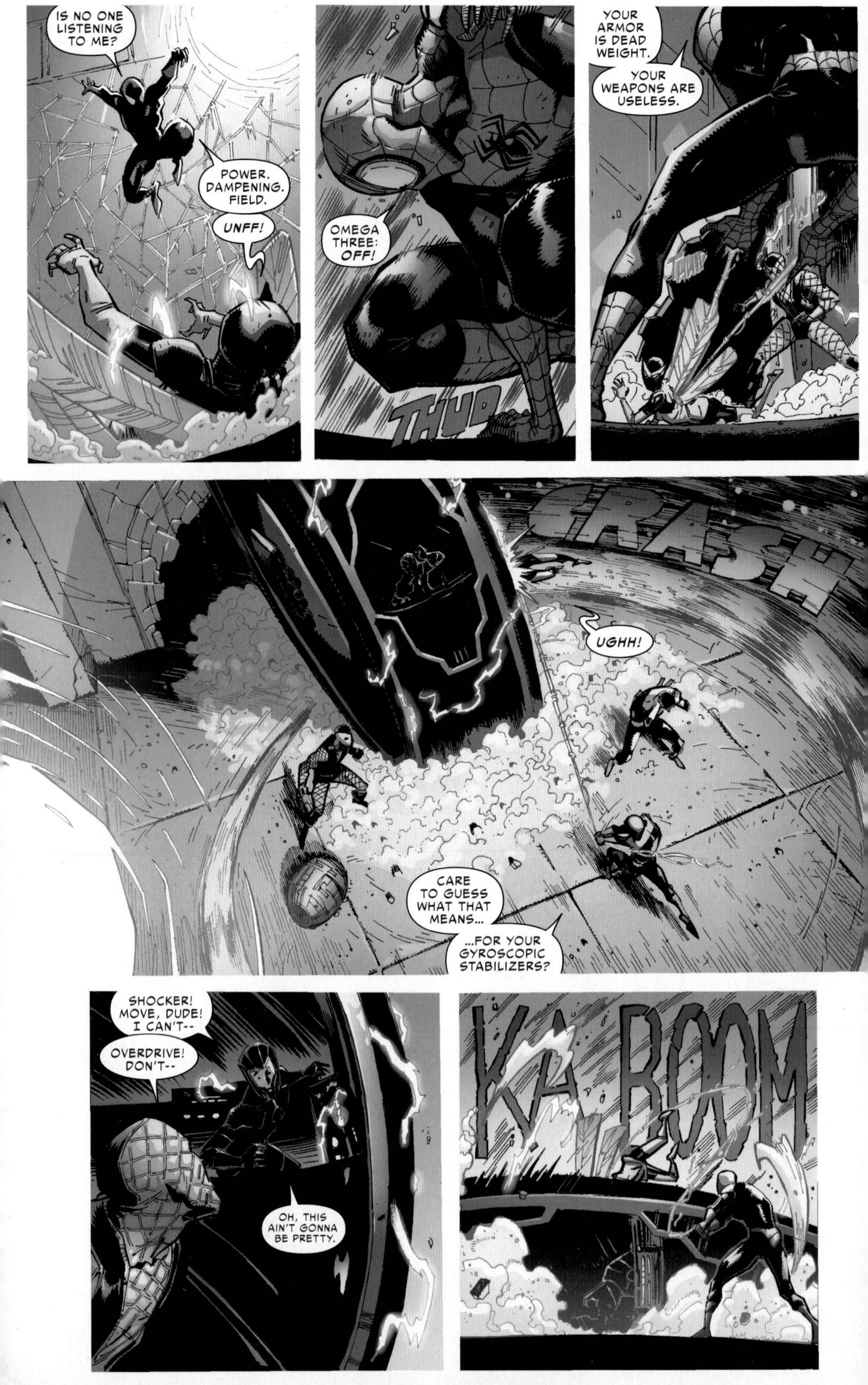
IS NO ONE LISTENING TO ME?
POWER. DAMPENING. FIELD.
UNFF!
OMEGA THREE: OFF!
THUD
YOUR ARMOR IS DEAD WEIGHT.
YOUR WEAPONS ARE USELESS.
CRASH
UGHH!
CARE TO GUESS WHAT THAT MEANS...
...FOR YOUR GYROSCOPIC STABILIZERS?
SHOCKER! MOVE, DUDE! I CAN'T--
OVERDRIVE! DON'T--
OH, THIS AIN'T GONNA BE PRETTY.
KA-BOOM

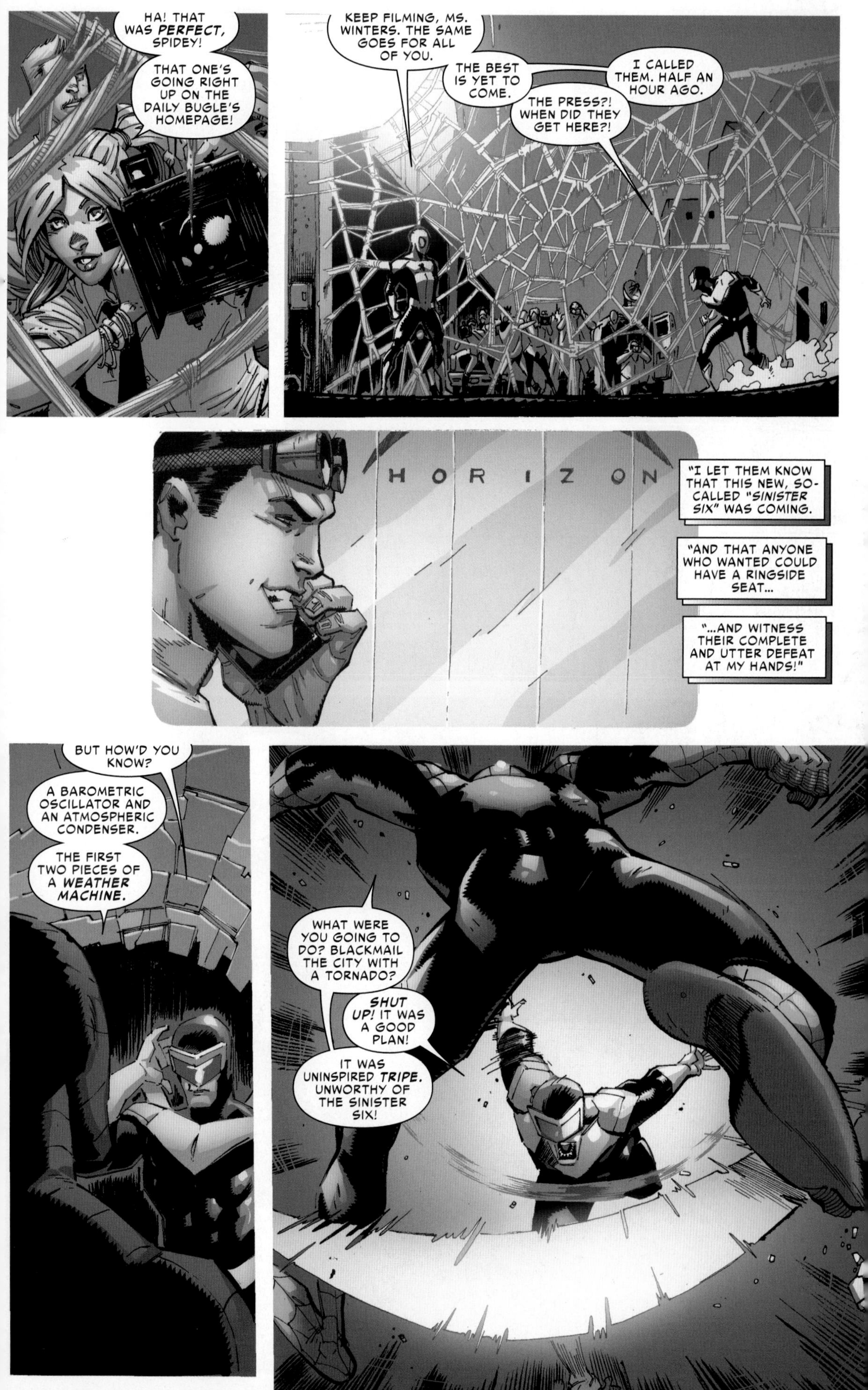

HA! THAT WAS PERFECT, SPIDEY!
THAT ONE'S GOING RIGHT UP ON THE DAILY BUGLE'S HOMEPAGE!
KEEP FILMING, MS. WINTERS. THE SAME GOES FOR ALL OF YOU.
THE BEST IS YET TO COME.
THE PRESS?! WHEN DID THEY GET HERE?!
I CALLED THEM. HALF AN HOUR AGO.
HORIZON
"I LET THEM KNOW THAT THIS NEW, SO-CALLED "SINISTER SIX" WAS COMING.
"AND THAT ANYONE WHO WANTED COULD HAVE A RINGSIDE SEAT...
"...AND WITNESS THEIR COMPLETE AND UTTER DEFEAT AT MY HANDS!"
BUT HOW'D YOU KNOW?
A BAROMETRIC OSCILLATOR AND AN ATMOSPHERIC CONDENSER.
THE FIRST TWO PIECES OF A WEATHER MACHINE.
WHAT WERE YOU GOING TO DO? BLACKMAIL THE CITY WITH A TORNADO?
SHUT UP! IT WAS A GOOD PLAN!
IT WAS UNINSPIRED TRIPE. UNWORTHY OF THE SINISTER SIX!

ALL RIGHT. I GIVE.
YOU WIN!
YES. I DO.
I GET TO WIN!
I'M BEATING THE SINISTER SIX!
AND EVERYONE IS GOING TO SEE IT!
AND THEY'LL GET THE MESSAGE!
THIS IS WHAT HAPPENS...
PLEASE...
...DON'T!
...WHEN YOU CROSS THIS SPIDER-MAN!

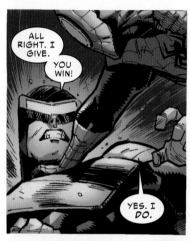

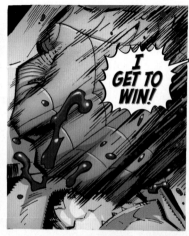

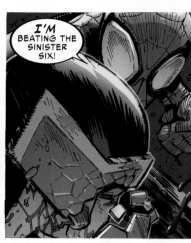

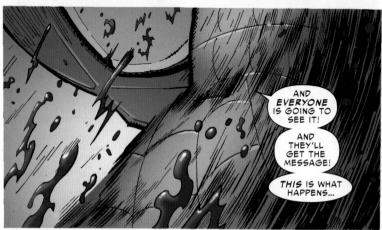

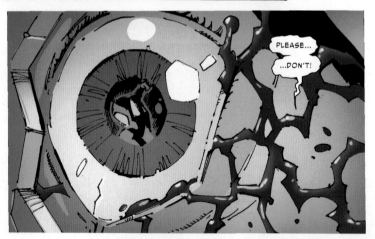

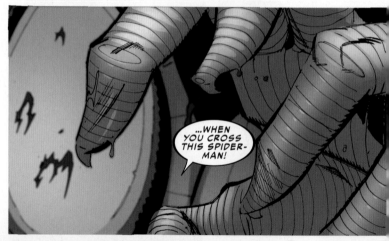

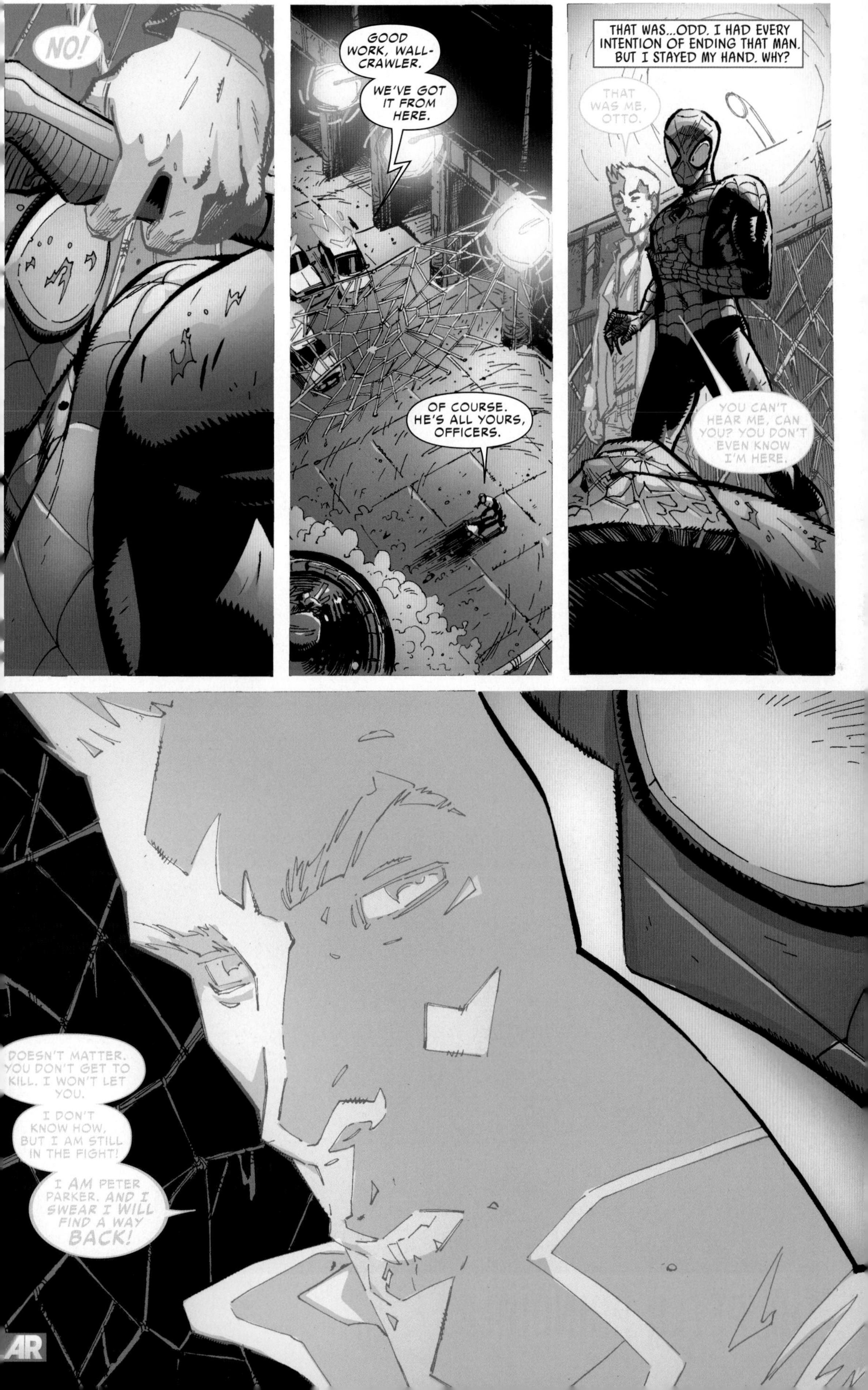
NO!
GOOD WORK, WALL-CRAWLER.
WE'VE GOT IT FROM HERE.
OF COURSE. HE'S ALL YOURS, OFFICERS.
THAT WAS...ODD. I HAD EVERY INTENTION OF ENDING THAT MAN. BUT I STAYED MY HAND. WHY?
THAT WAS ME, OTTO.
YOU CAN'T HEAR ME, CAN YOU? YOU DON'T EVEN KNOW I'M HERE.
DOESN'T MATTER. YOU DON'T GET TO KILL. I WON'T LET YOU.
I DON'T KNOW HOW, BUT I AM STILL IN THE FIGHT!
I AM PETER PARKER. AND I SWEAR I WILL FIND A WAY BACK!

2

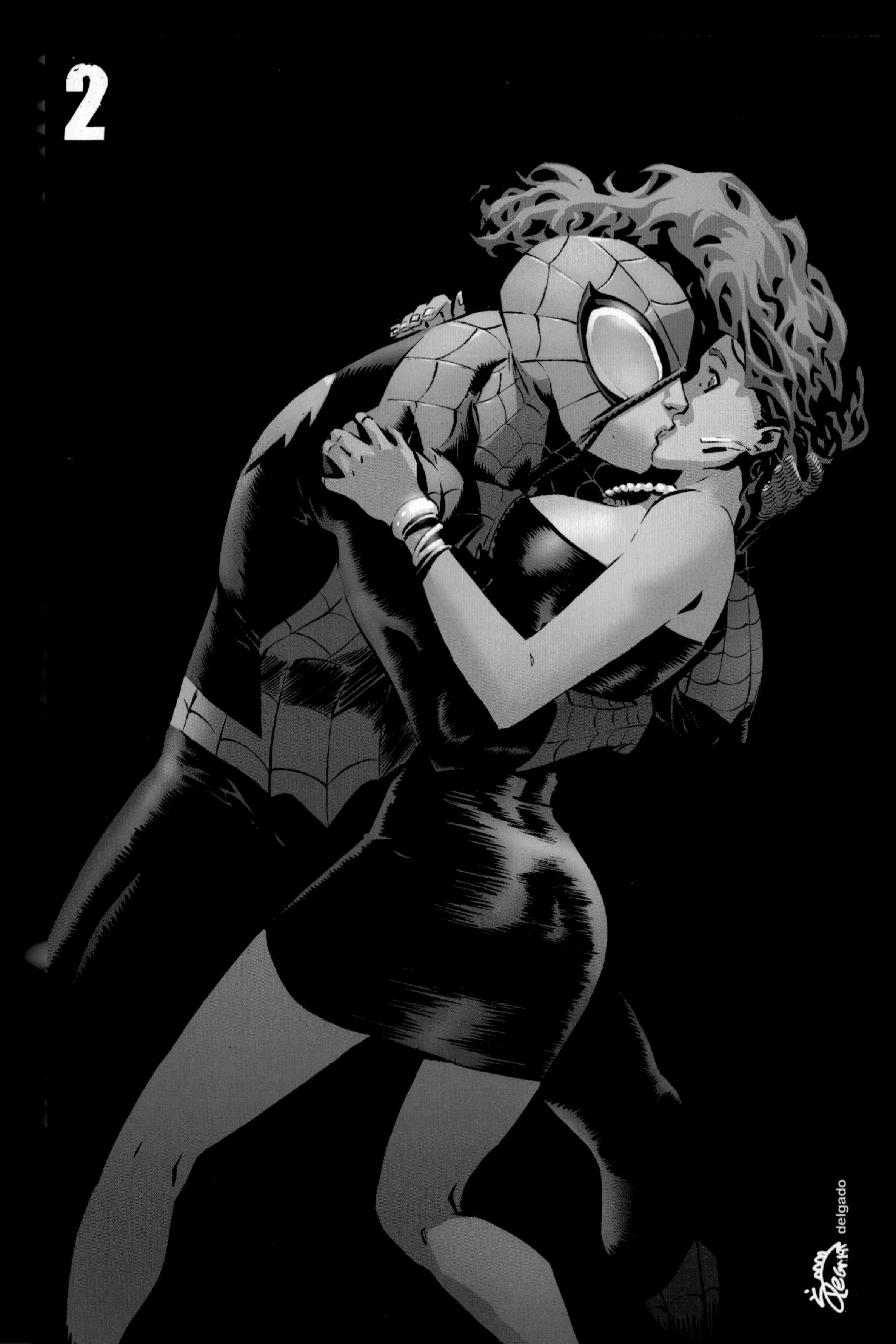
delgado

THE PETER PRINCIPLE

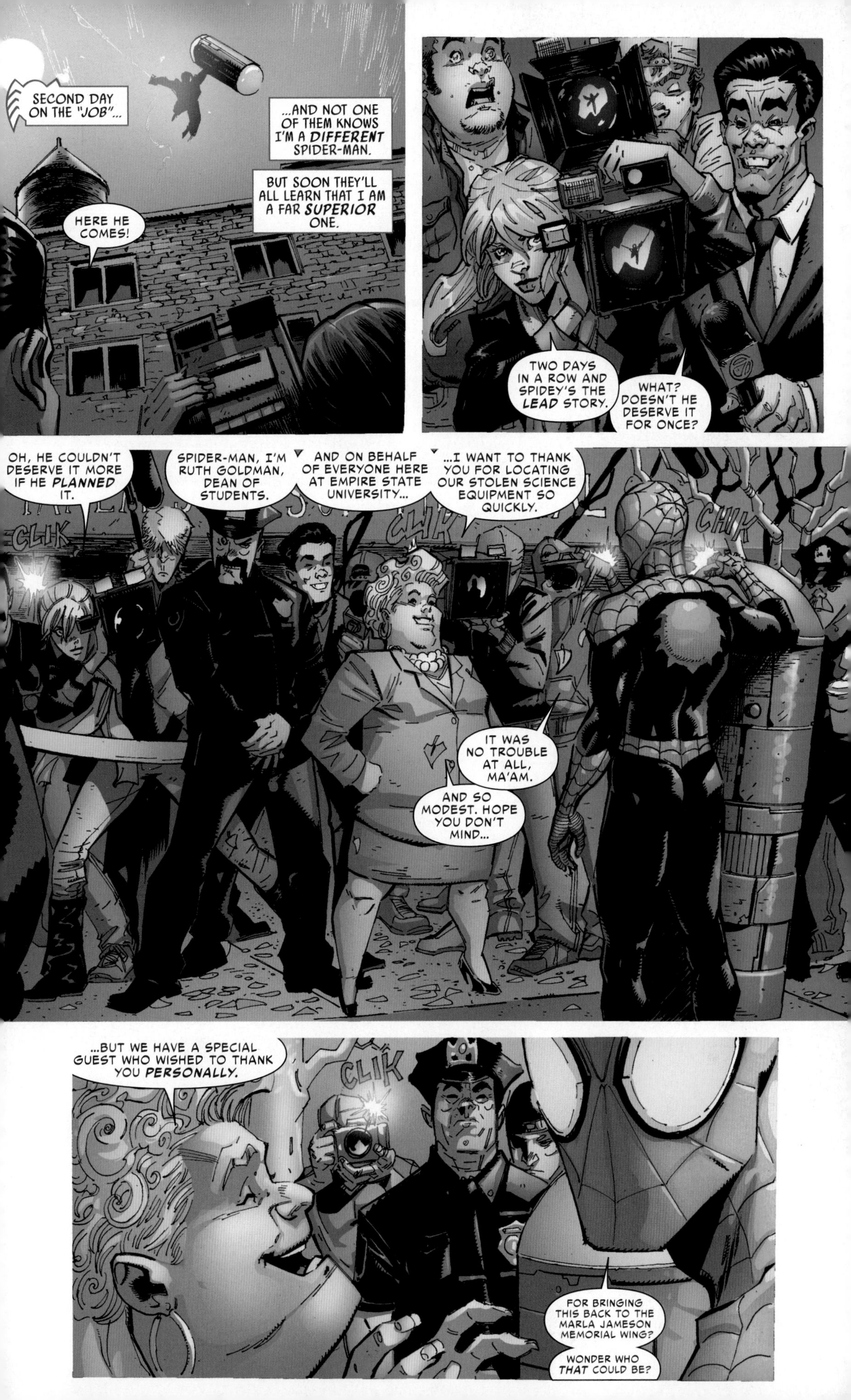

SECOND DAY ON THE "JOB"...
...AND NOT ONE OF THEM KNOWS I'M A DIFFERENT SPIDER-MAN.
BUT SOON THEY'LL ALL LEARN THAT I AM A FAR SUPERIOR ONE.
HERE HE COMES!
TWO DAYS IN A ROW AND SPIDEY'S THE LEAD STORY.
WHAT? DOESN'T HE DESERVE IT FOR ONCE?
OH, HE COULDN'T DESERVE IT MORE IF HE PLANNED IT.
SPIDER-MAN, I'M RUTH GOLDMAN, DEAN OF STUDENTS.
AND ON BEHALF OF EVERYONE HERE AT EMPIRE STATE UNIVERSITY...
...I WANT TO THANK YOU FOR LOCATING OUR STOLEN SCIENCE EQUIPMENT SO QUICKLY.
CLIK
CLIK
CHIK
IT WAS NO TROUBLE AT ALL, MA'AM.
AND SO MODEST. HOPE YOU DON'T MIND...
...BUT WE HAVE A SPECIAL GUEST WHO WISHED TO THANK YOU PERSONALLY.
CLIK
FOR BRINGING THIS BACK TO THE MARLA JAMESON MEMORIAL WING?
WONDER WHO THAT COULD BE?

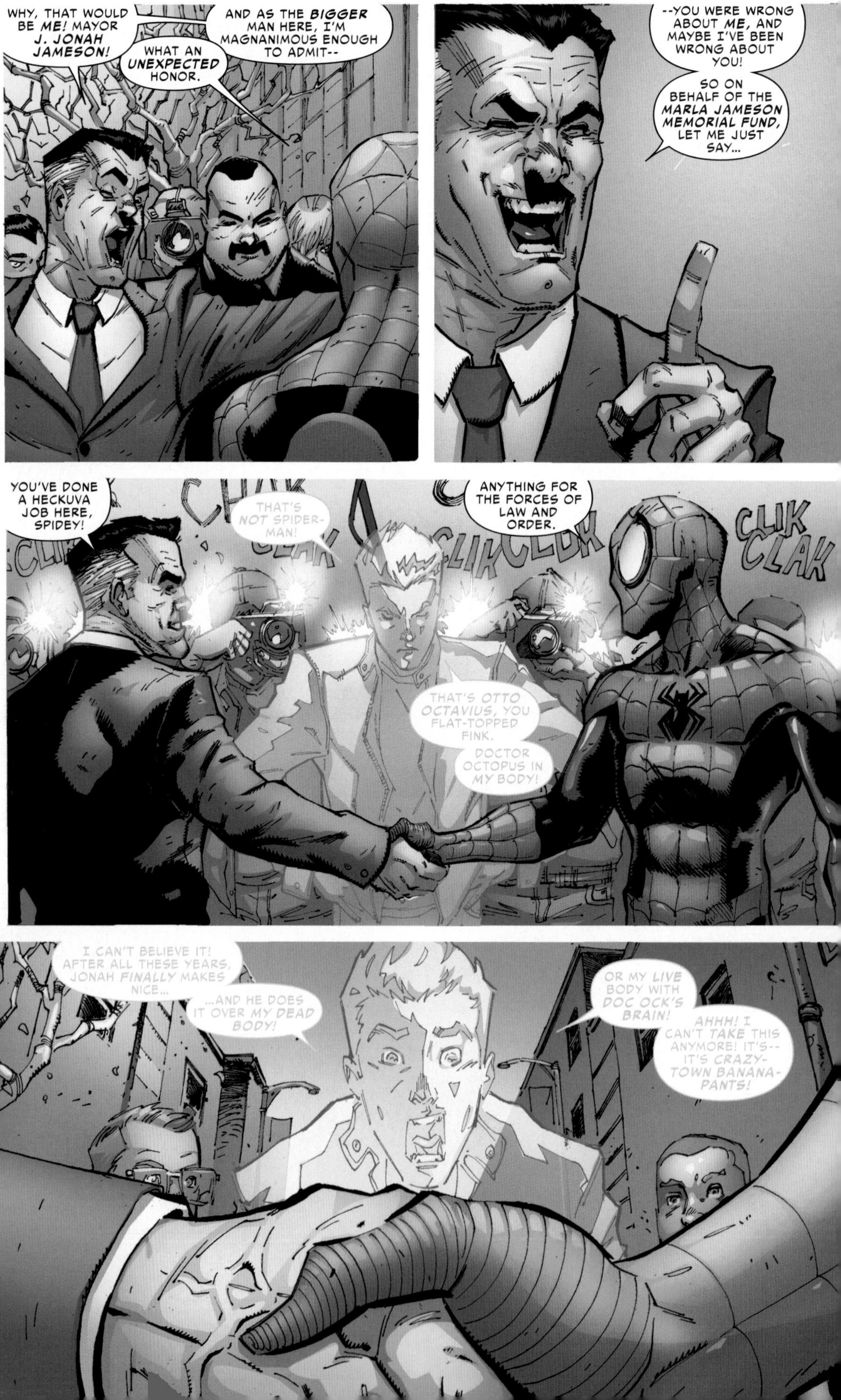
WHY, THAT WOULD BE *ME!* MAYOR *J. JONAH JAMESON!*
WHAT AN *UNEXPECTED* HONOR.
AND AS THE *BIGGER* MAN HERE, I'M MAGNANIMOUS ENOUGH TO ADMIT--
--YOU WERE WRONG ABOUT *ME,* AND MAYBE I'VE BEEN WRONG ABOUT YOU!
SO ON BEHALF OF THE *MARLA JAMESON MEMORIAL FUND,* LET ME JUST SAY...
YOU'VE DONE A HECKUVA JOB HERE, SPIDEY!
THAT'S *NOT* SPIDER-MAN!
ANYTHING FOR THE FORCES OF LAW AND ORDER.
CLIK CLAK
THAT'S *OTTO OCTAVIUS,* YOU FLAT-TOPPED FINK.
DOCTOR OCTOPUS IN *MY BODY!*
I CAN'T BELIEVE IT! AFTER ALL THESE YEARS, JONAH *FINALLY* MAKES NICE...
...AND HE DOES IT OVER *MY DEAD* BODY!
OR MY *LIVE* BODY WITH *DOC OCK'S BRAIN!*
AHHH! I CAN'T *TAKE* THIS ANYMORE! IT'S-- IT'S *CRAZY-TOWN BANANA-PANTS!*

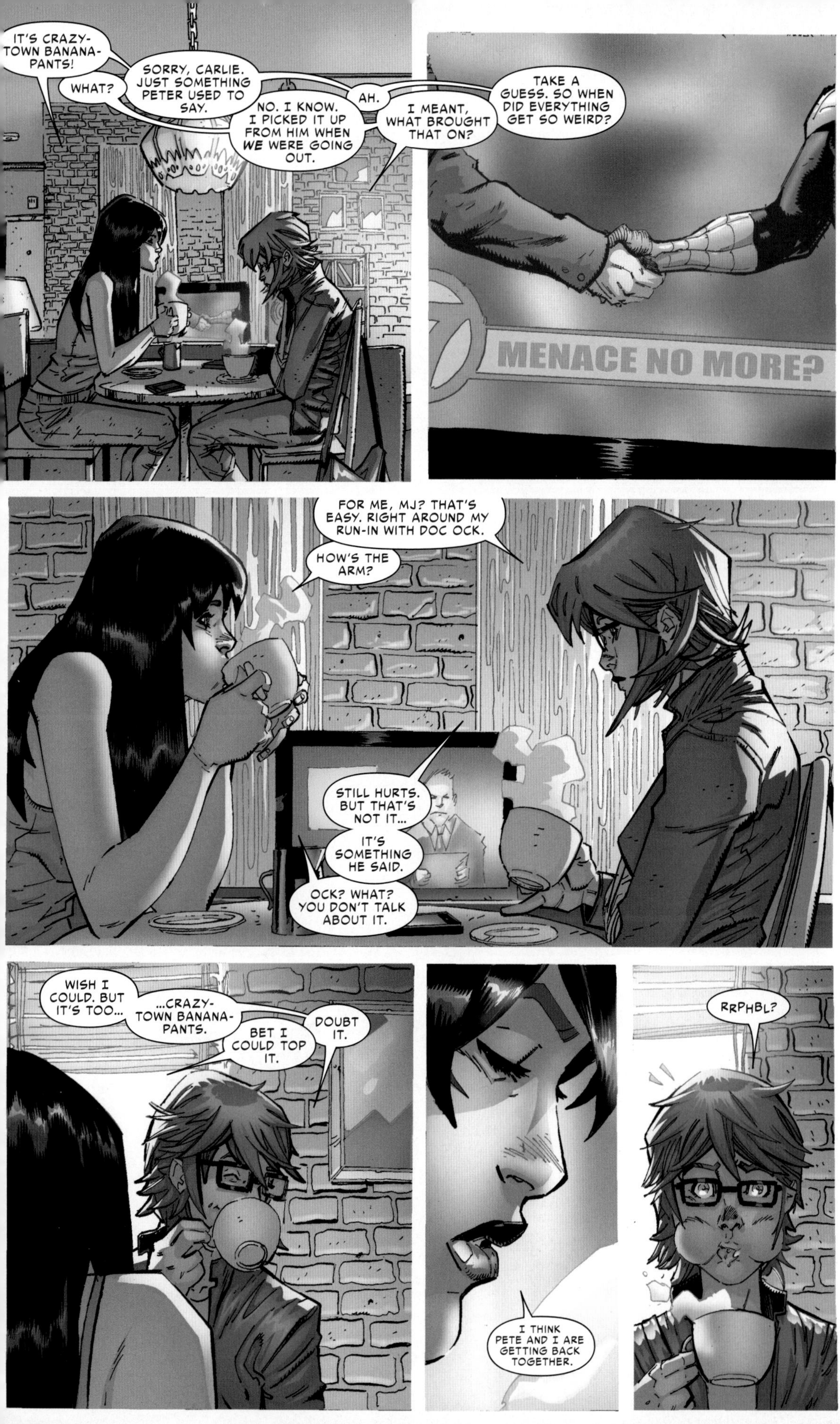
IT'S CRAZY-TOWN BANANA-PANTS!
WHAT?
SORRY, CARLIE. JUST SOMETHING PETER USED TO SAY.
AH.
NO. I KNOW. I PICKED IT UP FROM HIM WHEN WE WERE GOING OUT.
I MEANT, WHAT BROUGHT THAT ON?
TAKE A GUESS. SO WHEN DID EVERYTHING GET SO WEIRD?
MENACE NO MORE?
FOR ME, MJ? THAT'S EASY. RIGHT AROUND MY RUN-IN WITH DOC OCK.
HOW'S THE ARM?
STILL HURTS. BUT THAT'S NOT IT...
IT'S SOMETHING HE SAID.
OCK? WHAT? YOU DON'T TALK ABOUT IT.
WISH I COULD. BUT IT'S TOO...
...CRAZY-TOWN BANANA-PANTS.
BET I COULD TOP IT.
DOUBT IT.
I THINK PETE AND I ARE GETTING BACK TOGETHER.
RRPHBL?

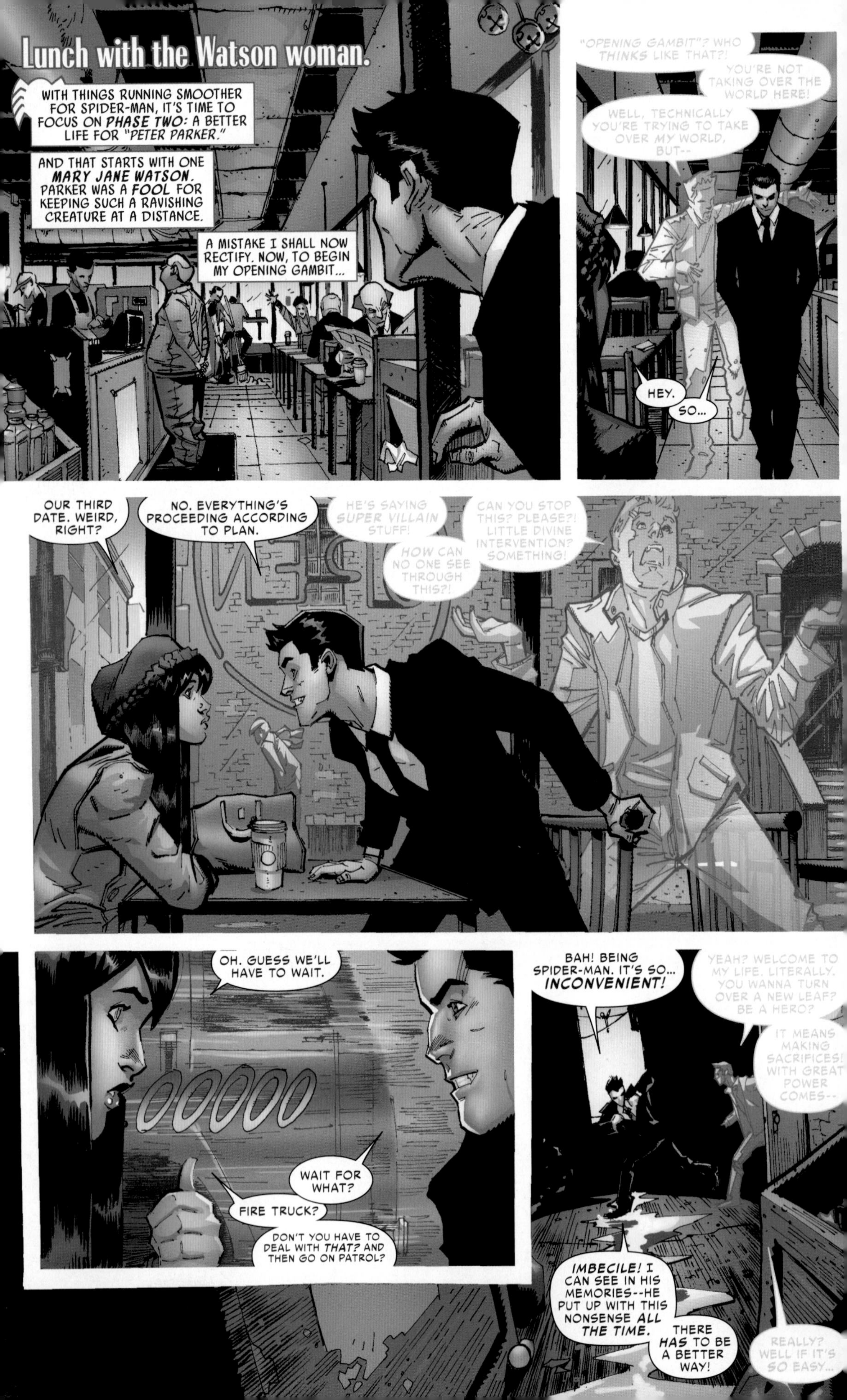
Lunch with the Watson woman.
WITH THINGS RUNNING SMOOTHER FOR SPIDER-MAN, IT'S TIME TO FOCUS ON PHASE TWO: A BETTER LIFE FOR "PETER PARKER."
AND THAT STARTS WITH ONE MARY JANE WATSON. PARKER WAS A FOOL FOR KEEPING SUCH A RAVISHING CREATURE AT A DISTANCE.
A MISTAKE I SHALL NOW RECTIFY. NOW, TO BEGIN MY OPENING GAMBIT...
"OPENING GAMBIT"? WHO THINKS LIKE THAT?!
YOU'RE NOT TAKING OVER THE WORLD HERE!
WELL, TECHNICALLY YOU'RE TRYING TO TAKE OVER MY WORLD, BUT--
HEY.
SO...
OUR THIRD DATE. WEIRD, RIGHT?
NO. EVERYTHING'S PROCEEDING ACCORDING TO PLAN.
HE'S SAYING SUPER VILLAIN STUFF!
HOW CAN NO ONE SEE THROUGH THIS?!
CAN YOU STOP THIS? PLEASE?! LITTLE DIVINE INTERVENTION? SOMETHING!
OH. GUESS WE'LL HAVE TO WAIT.
OOOOOO
WAIT FOR WHAT?
FIRE TRUCK?
DON'T YOU HAVE TO DEAL WITH THAT? AND THEN GO ON PATROL?
BAH! BEING SPIDER-MAN. IT'S SO... INCONVENIENT!
YEAH? WELCOME TO MY LIFE. LITERALLY. YOU WANNA TURN OVER A NEW LEAF? BE A HERO?
IT MEANS MAKING SACRIFICES! WITH GREAT POWER COMES--
IMBECILE! I CAN SEE IN HIS MEMORIES--HE PUT UP WITH THIS NONSENSE ALL THE TIME.
THERE HAS TO BE A BETTER WAY!
REALLY? WELL IF IT'S SO EASY...

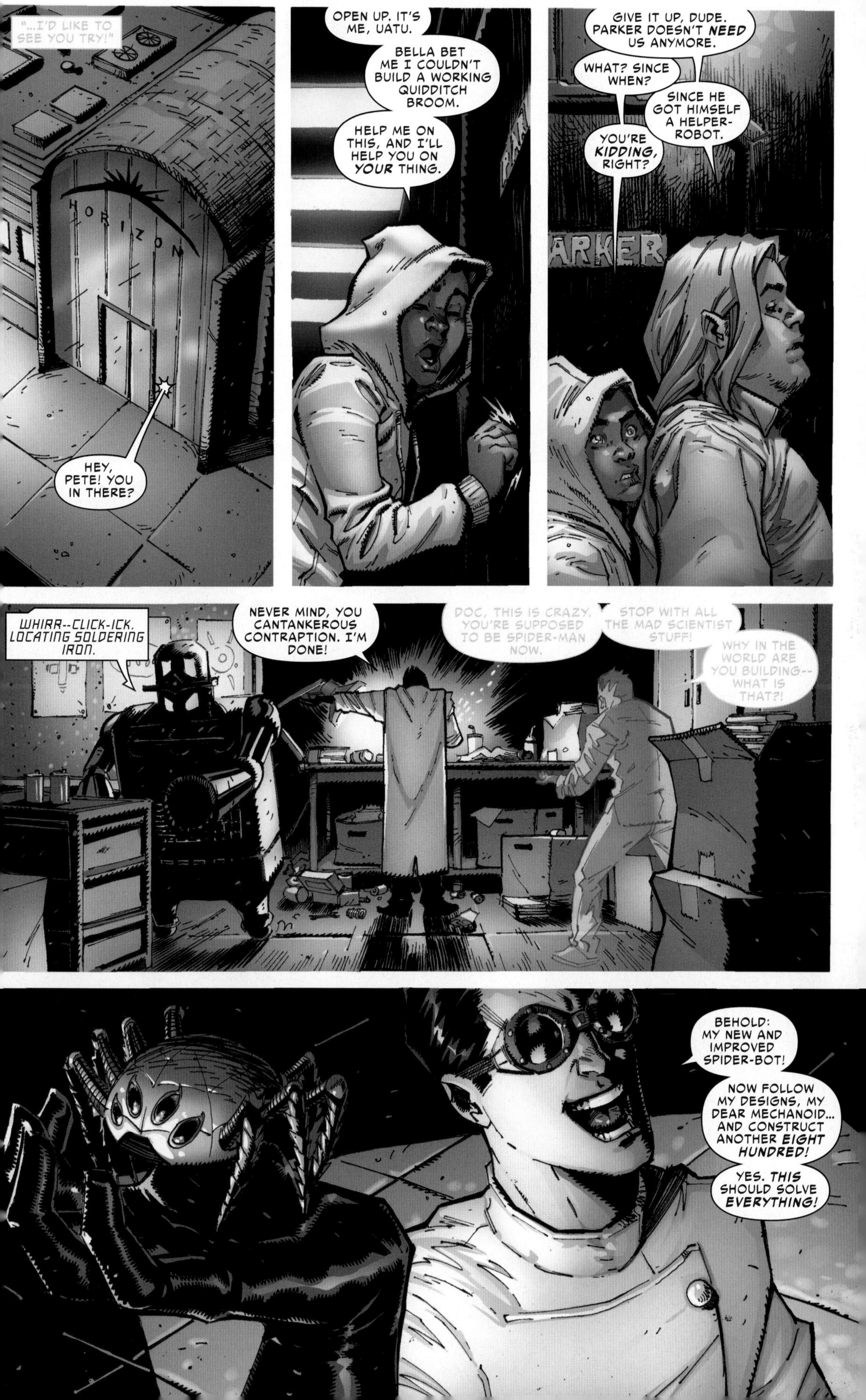
"...I'D LIKE TO SEE YOU TRY!"
HORIZON
HEY, PETE! YOU IN THERE?
OPEN UP. IT'S ME, UATU.
BELLA BET ME I COULDN'T BUILD A WORKING QUIDDITCH BROOM.
HELP ME ON THIS, AND I'LL HELP YOU ON YOUR THING.
GIVE IT UP, DUDE. PARKER DOESN'T NEED US ANYMORE.
WHAT? SINCE WHEN?
SINCE HE GOT HIMSELF A HELPER-ROBOT.
YOU'RE KIDDING, RIGHT?
ARKER
WHIRR--CLICK-ICK. LOCATING SOLDERING IRON.
NEVER MIND, YOU CANTANKEROUS CONTRAPTION. I'M DONE!
DOC, THIS IS CRAZY. YOU'RE SUPPOSED TO BE SPIDER-MAN NOW.
STOP WITH ALL THE MAD SCIENTIST STUFF!
WHY IN THE WORLD ARE YOU BUILDING-- WHAT IS THAT?!
BEHOLD: MY NEW AND IMPROVED SPIDER-BOT!
NOW FOLLOW MY DESIGNS, MY DEAR MECHANOID... AND CONSTRUCT ANOTHER EIGHT HUNDRED!
YES. THIS SHOULD SOLVE EVERYTHING!

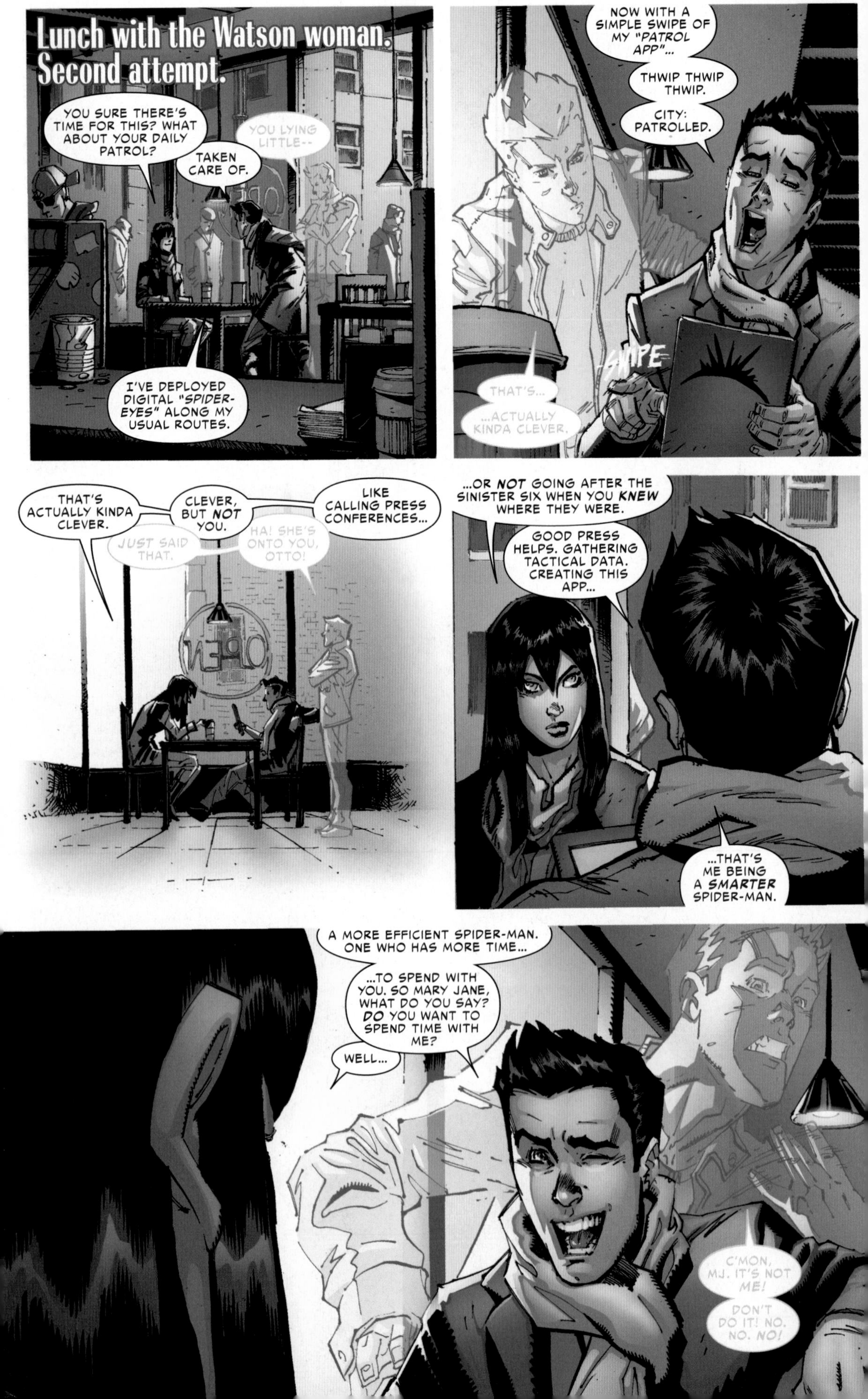
Lunch with the Watson woman. Second attempt.
YOU SURE THERE'S TIME FOR THIS? WHAT ABOUT YOUR DAILY PATROL?
TAKEN CARE OF.
YOU LYING LITTLE--
I'VE DEPLOYED DIGITAL "SPIDER-EYES" ALONG MY USUAL ROUTES.
NOW WITH A SIMPLE SWIPE OF MY "PATROL APP"...
THWIP THWIP THWIP.
CITY: PATROLLED.
SWIPE
THAT'S...
...ACTUALLY KINDA CLEVER.
THAT'S ACTUALLY KINDA CLEVER.
CLEVER, BUT NOT YOU.
JUST SAID THAT.
LIKE CALLING PRESS CONFERENCES...
HA! SHE'S ONTO YOU, OTTO!
...OR NOT GOING AFTER THE SINISTER SIX WHEN YOU KNEW WHERE THEY WERE.
GOOD PRESS HELPS. GATHERING TACTICAL DATA. CREATING THIS APP...
...THAT'S ME BEING A SMARTER SPIDER-MAN.
A MORE EFFICIENT SPIDER-MAN. ONE WHO HAS MORE TIME...
...TO SPEND WITH YOU. SO MARY JANE, WHAT DO YOU SAY? DO YOU WANT TO SPEND TIME WITH ME?
WELL...
C'MON, MJ. IT'S NOT ME!
DON'T DO IT! NO. NO. NO!

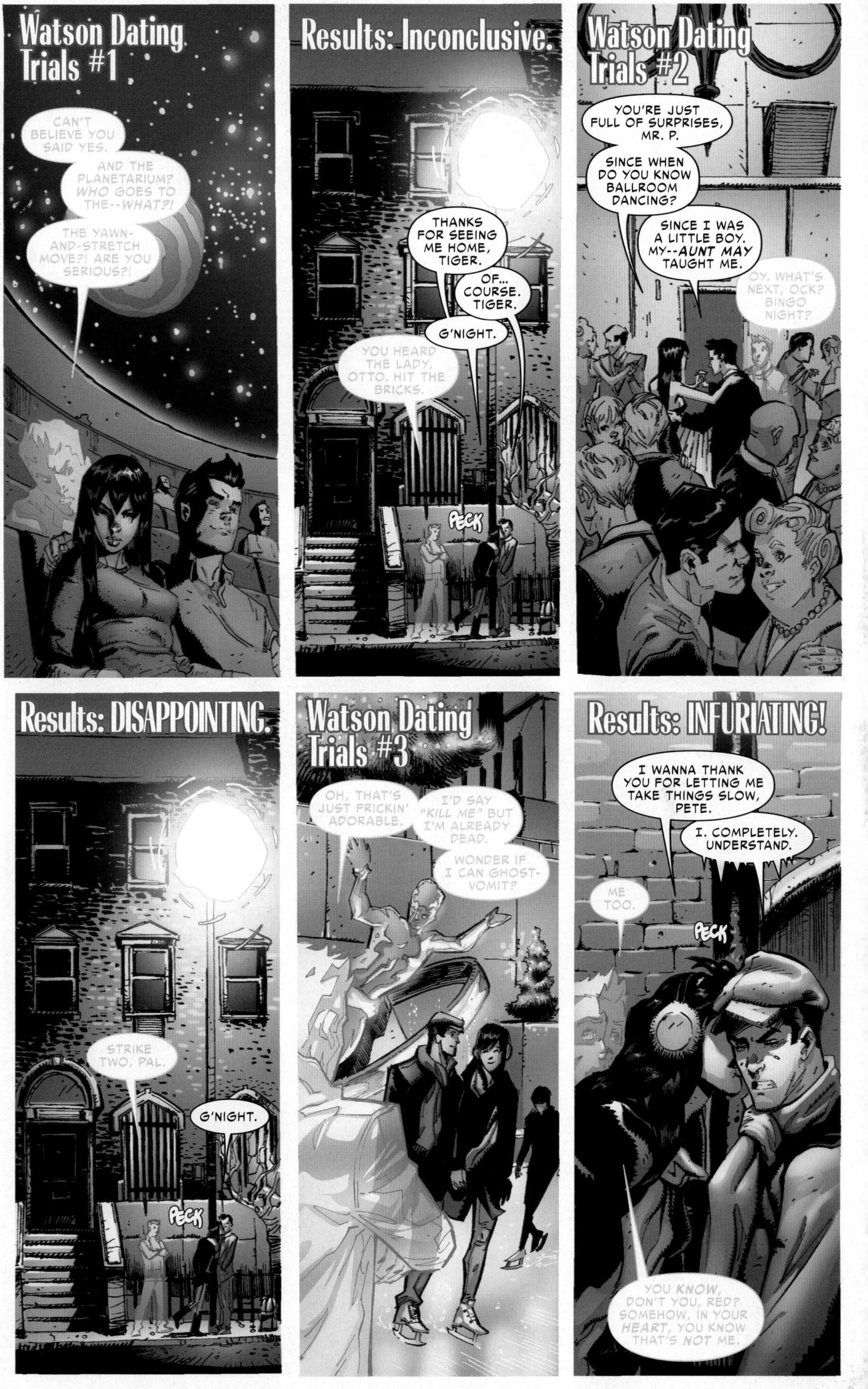
Watson Dating Trials #1
CAN'T BELIEVE YOU SAID YES.
AND THE PLANETARIUM? WHO GOES TO THE--WHAT?!
THE YAWN-AND-STRETCH MOVE?! ARE YOU SERIOUS?!
Results: Inconclusive.
THANKS FOR SEEING ME HOME, TIGER.
OF... COURSE. TIGER.
G'NIGHT.
YOU HEARD THE LADY, OTTO. HIT THE BRICKS.
PECK
Watson Dating Trials #2
YOU'RE JUST FULL OF SURPRISES, MR. P.
SINCE WHEN DO YOU KNOW BALLROOM DANCING?
SINCE I WAS A LITTLE BOY. MY--AUNT MAY TAUGHT ME.
OY. WHAT'S NEXT, OCK? BINGO NIGHT?
Results: DISAPPOINTING.
STRIKE TWO, PAL.
G'NIGHT.
PECK
Watson Dating Trials #3
OH, THAT'S JUST FRICKIN' ADORABLE.
I'D SAY "KILL ME" BUT I'M ALREADY DEAD.
WONDER IF I CAN GHOST-VOMIT?
Results: INFURIATING!
I WANNA THANK YOU FOR LETTING ME TAKE THINGS SLOW, PETE.
I. COMPLETELY. UNDERSTAND.
ME TOO.
PECK
YOU KNOW, DON'T YOU, RED? SOMEHOW, IN YOUR HEART, YOU KNOW THAT'S NOT ME.

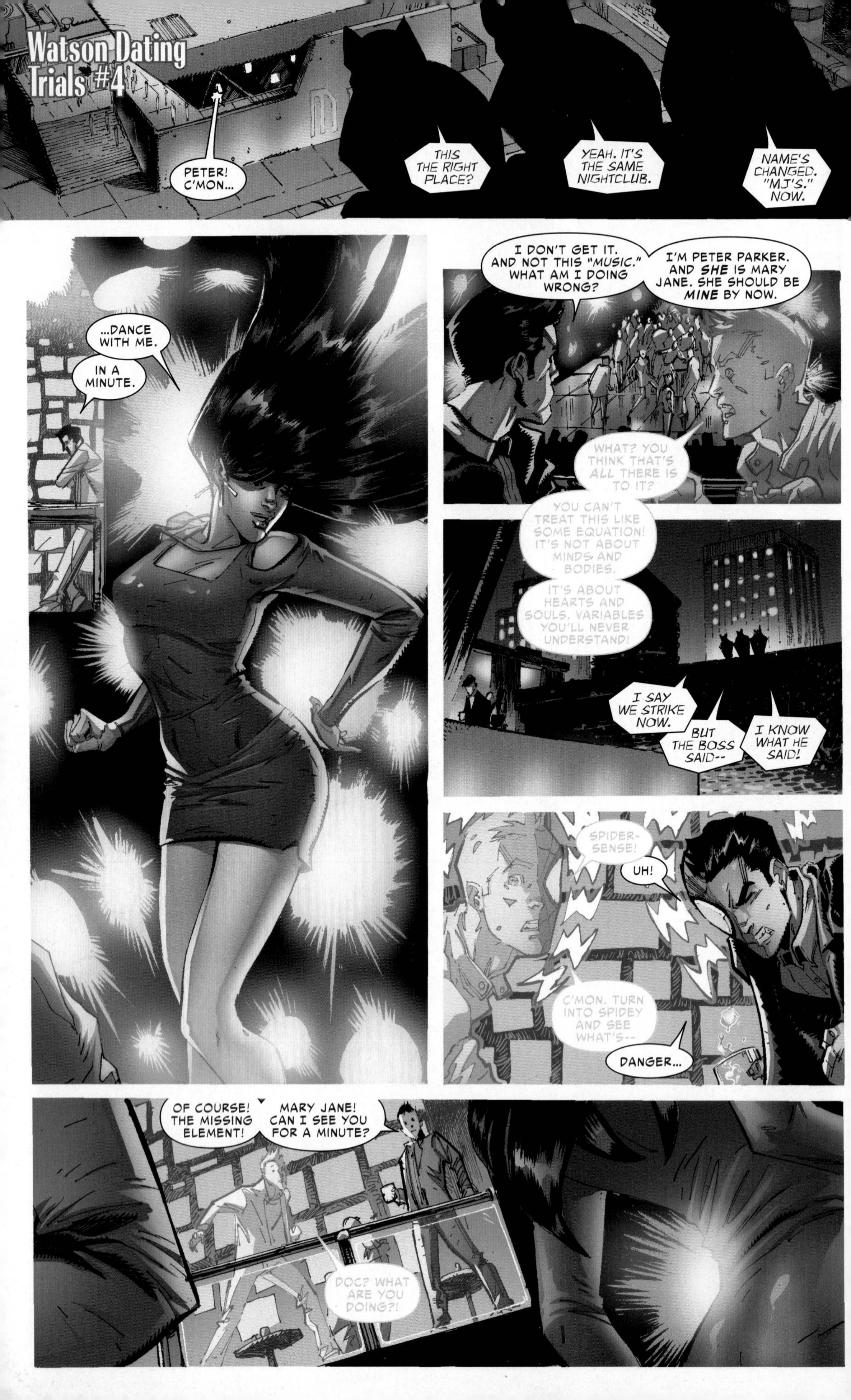
Watson Dating Trials #4
PETER! C'MON...
THIS THE RIGHT PLACE?
YEAH. IT'S THE SAME NIGHTCLUB.
NAME'S CHANGED. "MJ'S." NOW.
...DANCE WITH ME.
IN A MINUTE.
I DON'T GET IT. AND NOT THIS "MUSIC." WHAT AM I DOING WRONG?
I'M PETER PARKER. AND SHE IS MARY JANE. SHE SHOULD BE MINE BY NOW.
WHAT? YOU THINK THAT'S ALL THERE IS TO IT?
YOU CAN'T TREAT THIS LIKE SOME EQUATION! IT'S NOT ABOUT MINDS AND BODIES.
IT'S ABOUT HEARTS AND SOULS. VARIABLES YOU'LL NEVER UNDERSTAND!
I SAY WE STRIKE NOW.
BUT THE BOSS SAID--
I KNOW WHAT HE SAID!
SPIDER-SENSE!
UH!
C'MON. TURN INTO SPIDEY AND SEE WHAT'S--
DANGER...
OF COURSE! THE MISSING ELEMENT!
MARY JANE! CAN I SEE YOU FOR A MINUTE?
DOC? WHAT ARE YOU DOING?!

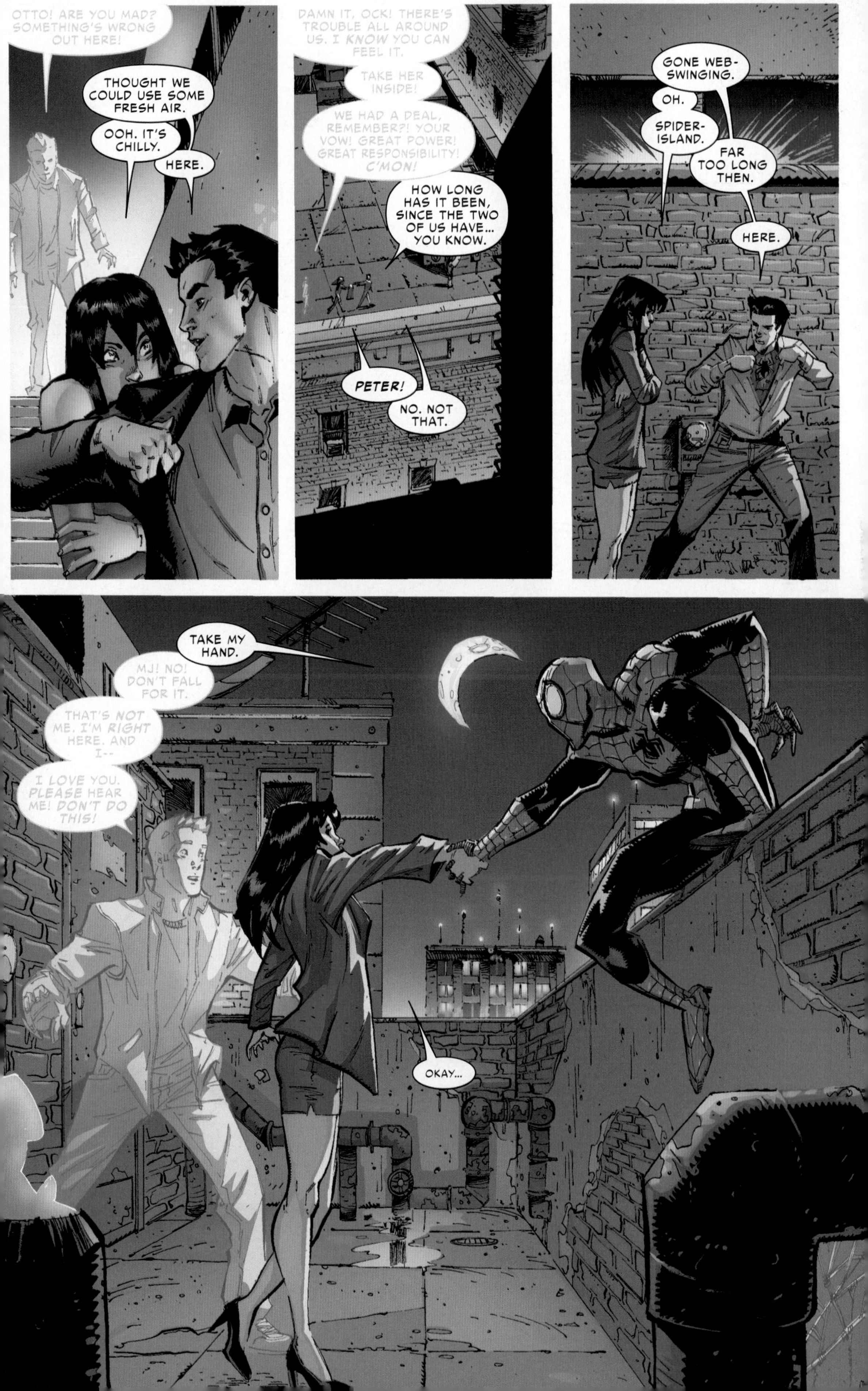
OTTO! ARE YOU MAD? SOMETHING'S WRONG OUT HERE!
THOUGHT WE COULD USE SOME FRESH AIR.
OOH. IT'S CHILLY.
HERE.
DAMN IT, OCK! THERE'S TROUBLE ALL AROUND US. I KNOW YOU CAN FEEL IT.
TAKE HER INSIDE!
WE HAD A DEAL, REMEMBER?! YOUR VOW! GREAT POWER! GREAT RESPONSIBILITY! C'MON!
HOW LONG HAS IT BEEN, SINCE THE TWO OF US HAVE... YOU KNOW.
PETER!
NO. NOT THAT.
GONE WEB-SWINGING.
OH.
SPIDER-ISLAND.
FAR TOO LONG THEN.
HERE.
TAKE MY HAND.
MJ! NO! DON'T FALL FOR IT.
THAT'S NOT ME. I'M RIGHT HERE. AND I--
I LOVE YOU. PLEASE HEAR ME! DON'T DO THIS!
OKAY...

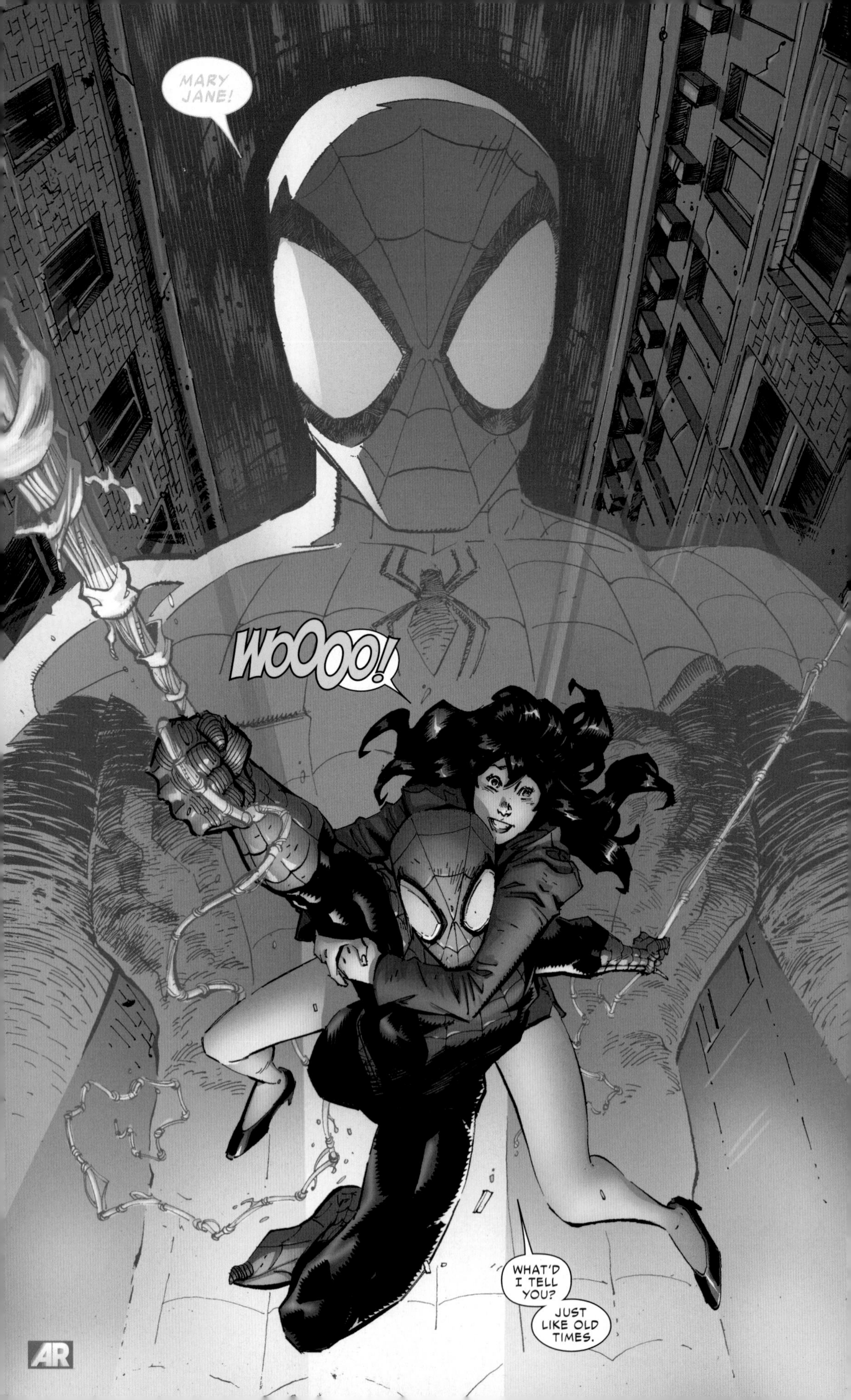

MARY JANE!
WOOOOO!
WHAT'D I TELL YOU?
JUST LIKE OLD TIMES.

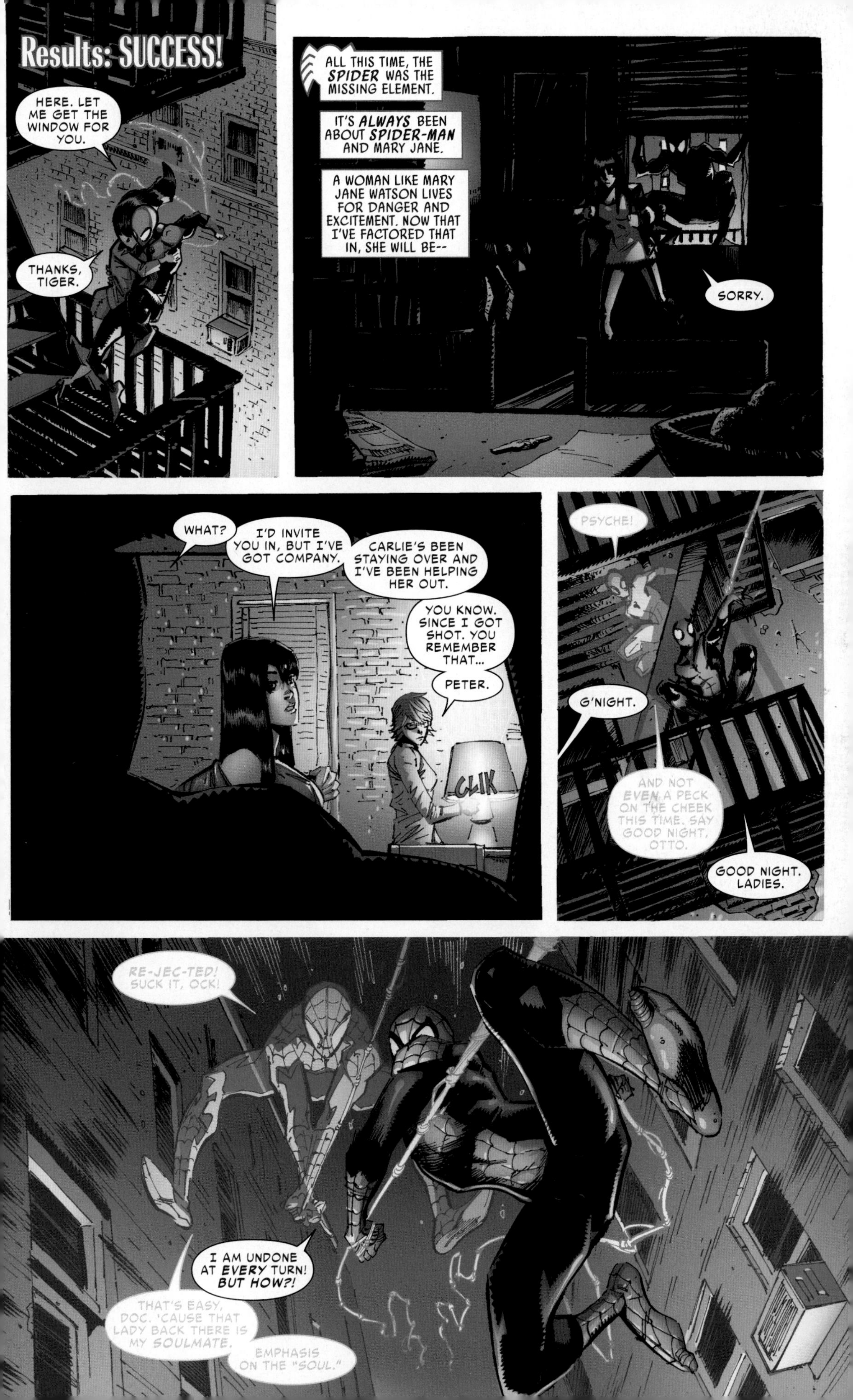
Results: SUCCESS!
HERE. LET ME GET THE WINDOW FOR YOU.
THANKS, TIGER.
ALL THIS TIME, THE SPIDER WAS THE MISSING ELEMENT.
IT'S ALWAYS BEEN ABOUT SPIDER-MAN AND MARY JANE.
A WOMAN LIKE MARY JANE WATSON LIVES FOR DANGER AND EXCITEMENT. NOW THAT I'VE FACTORED THAT IN, SHE WILL BE--
SORRY.
WHAT?
I'D INVITE YOU IN, BUT I'VE GOT COMPANY.
CARLIE'S BEEN STAYING OVER AND I'VE BEEN HELPING HER OUT.
YOU KNOW. SINCE I GOT SHOT. YOU REMEMBER THAT...
PETER.
CLIK
PSYCHE!
G'NIGHT.
AND NOT EVEN A PECK ON THE CHEEK THIS TIME. SAY GOOD NIGHT, OTTO.
GOOD NIGHT. LADIES.
RE-JEC-TED! SUCK IT, OCK!
I AM UNDONE AT EVERY TURN! BUT HOW?!
THAT'S EASY, DOC. 'CAUSE THAT LADY BACK THERE IS MY SOULMATE.
EMPHASIS ON THE "SOUL."

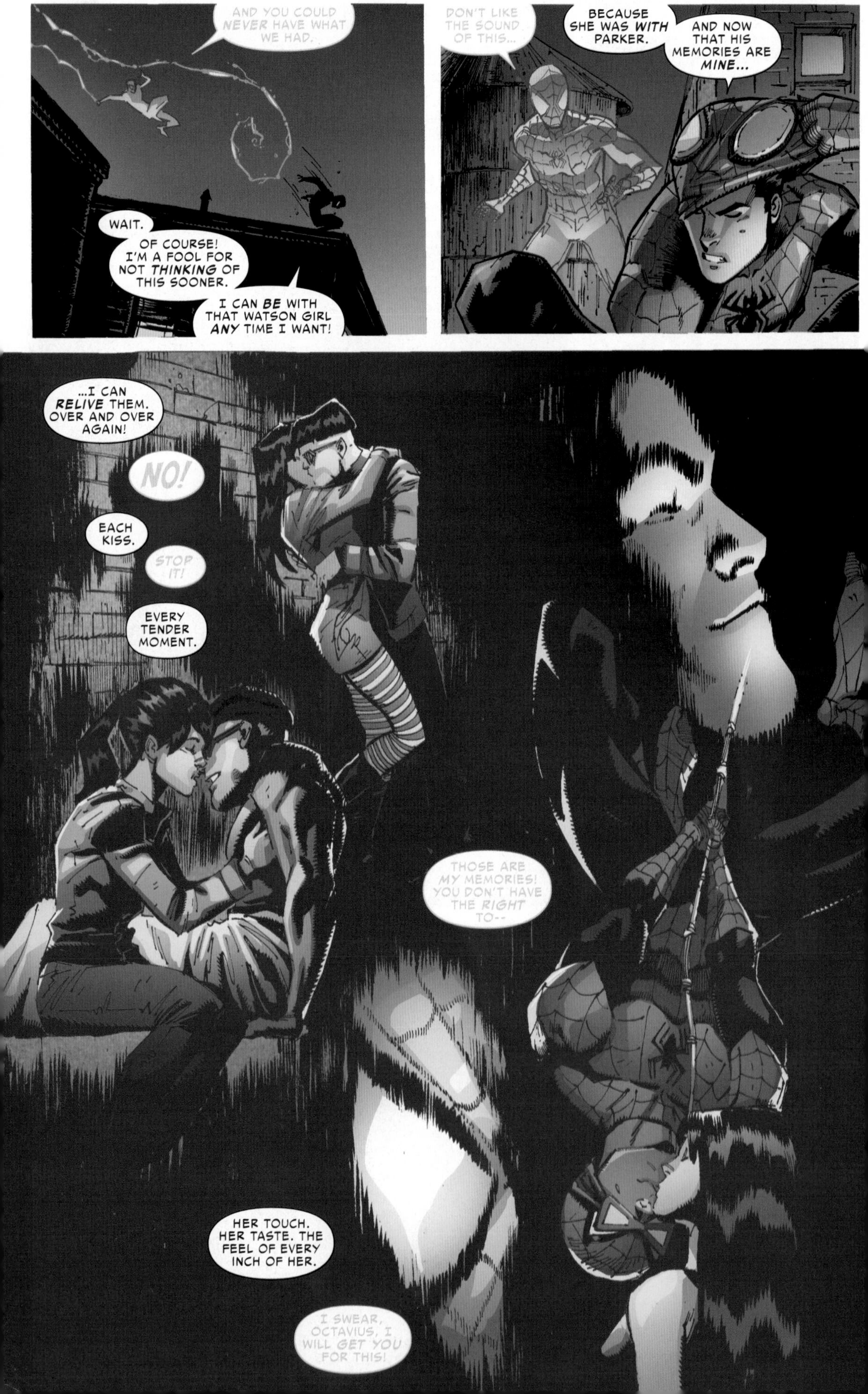
AND YOU COULD NEVER HAVE WHAT WE HAD.
WAIT.
OF COURSE! I'M A FOOL FOR NOT THINKING OF THIS SOONER.
I CAN BE WITH THAT WATSON GIRL ANY TIME I WANT!
DON'T LIKE THE SOUND OF THIS...
BECAUSE SHE WAS WITH PARKER.
AND NOW THAT HIS MEMORIES ARE MINE...
...I CAN RELIVE THEM. OVER AND OVER AGAIN!
NO!
EACH KISS.
STOP IT!
EVERY TENDER MOMENT.
THOSE ARE MY MEMORIES! YOU DON'T HAVE THE RIGHT TO--
HER TOUCH. HER TASTE. THE FEEL OF EVERY INCH OF HER.
I SWEAR, OCTAVIUS, I WILL GET YOU FOR THIS!

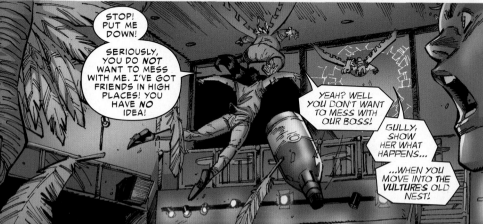

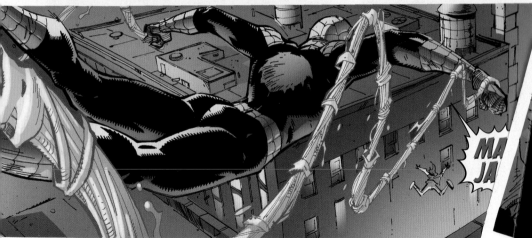

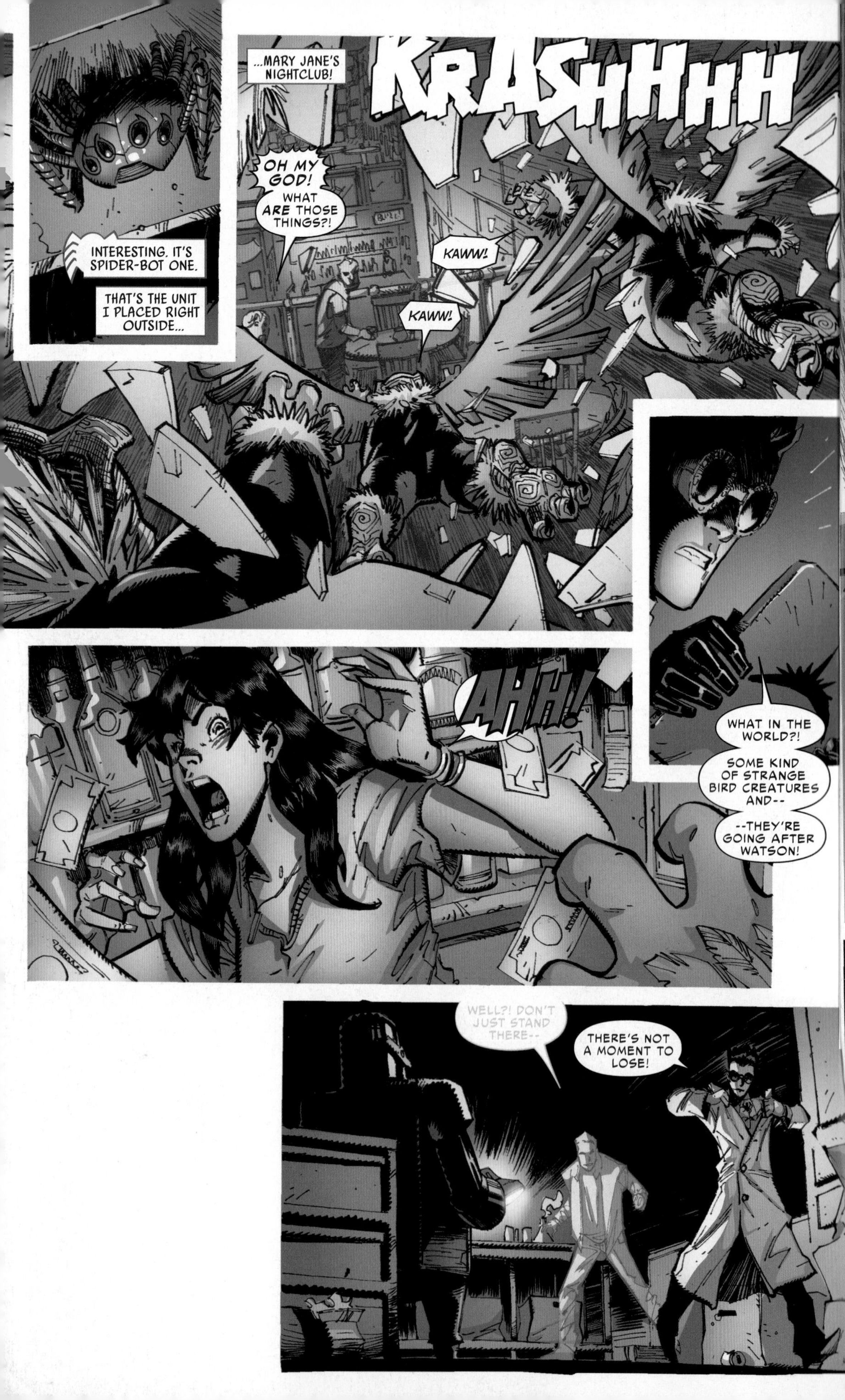
INTERESTING. IT'S SPIDER-BOT ONE.
THAT'S THE UNIT I PLACED RIGHT OUTSIDE...
...MARY JANE'S NIGHTCLUB!
KRASHHHHH
OH MY GOD! WHAT ARE THOSE THINGS?!
KAWW!
KAWW!
WHAT IN THE WORLD?!
SOME KIND OF STRANGE BIRD CREATURES AND--
--THEY'RE GOING AFTER WATSON!
AHH!
WELL?! DON'T JUST STAND THERE--
THERE'S NOT A MOMENT TO LOSE!

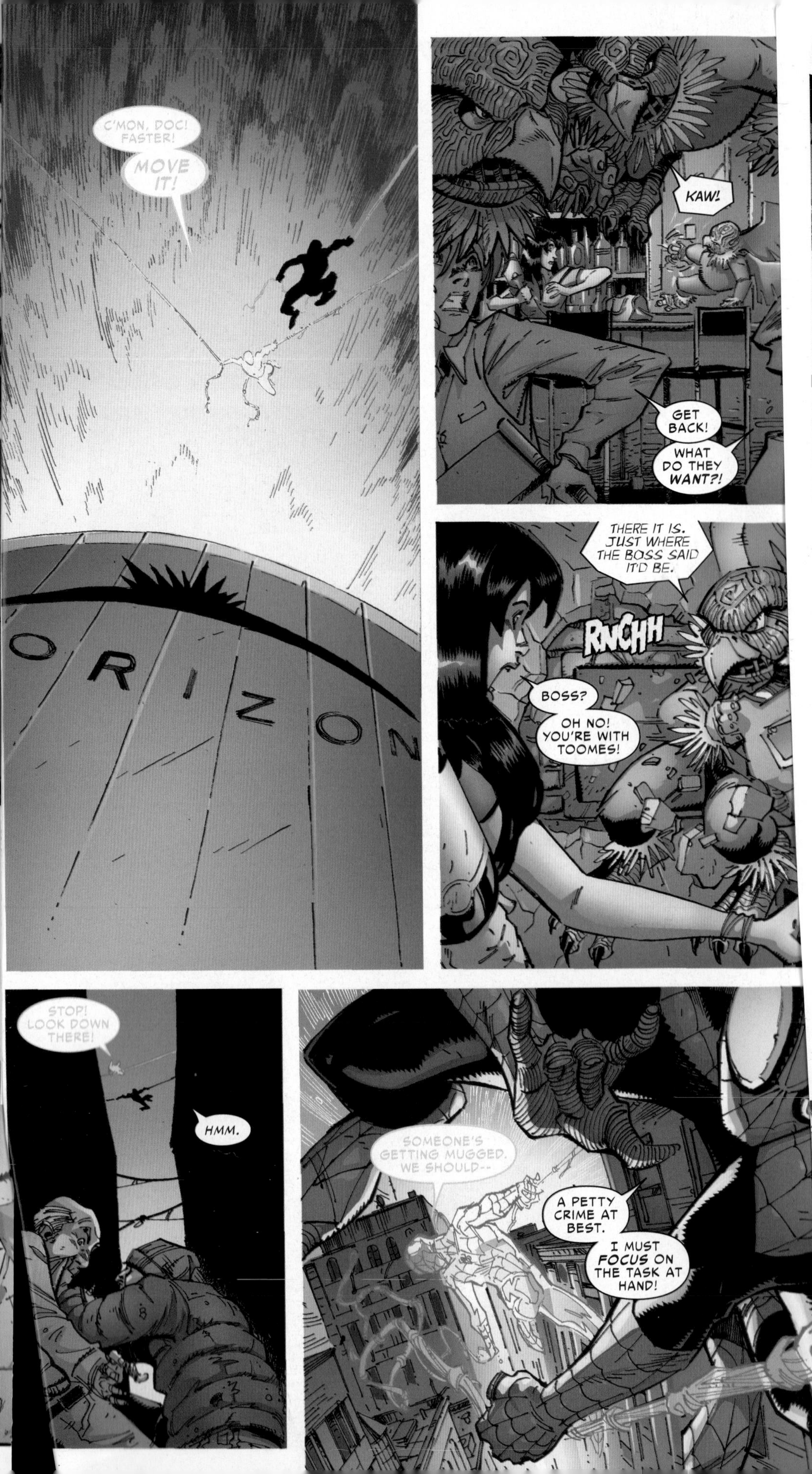
C'MON, DOC! FASTER!
MOVE IT!
ORIZON
KAW!
GET BACK!
WHAT DO THEY WANT?!
THERE IT IS. JUST WHERE THE BOSS SAID IT'D BE.
RNCHH
BOSS?
OH NO! YOU'RE WITH TOOMES!
STOP! LOOK DOWN THERE!
HMM.
SOMEONE'S GETTING MUGGED. WE SHOULD--
A PETTY CRIME AT BEST.
I MUST FOCUS ON THE TASK AT HAND!

OH BOY. SUDDENLY RETHINKING THE WHOLE BUY-A-SUPER-VILLAIN'S-OLD-HANGOUT THING.

YES. IT'S ALL RIGHT HERE. GOT IT!

SORRY, BIRDY, BUT IF THE VULTURE WANTS THAT. I CAN'T LET YOU LEAVE WITH IT.

AND I GOT HER!

OW! WATCH IT!

GOOD!

STOP! PUT ME DOWN!

SERIOUSLY, YOU DO NOT WANT TO MESS WITH ME. I'VE GOT FRIENDS IN HIGH PLACES! YOU HAVE NO IDEA!

YEAH? WELL YOU DON'T WANT TO MESS WITH OUR BOSS!

GULLY, SHOW HER WHAT HAPPENS...

...WHEN YOU MOVE INTO THE VULTURE'S OLD NEST!

GYAHHH!!

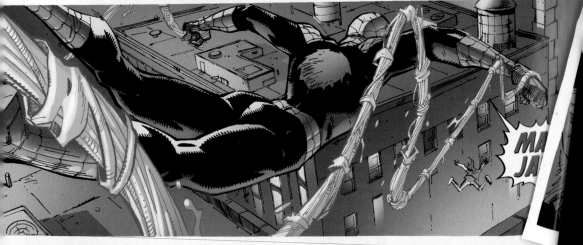

MA
JA

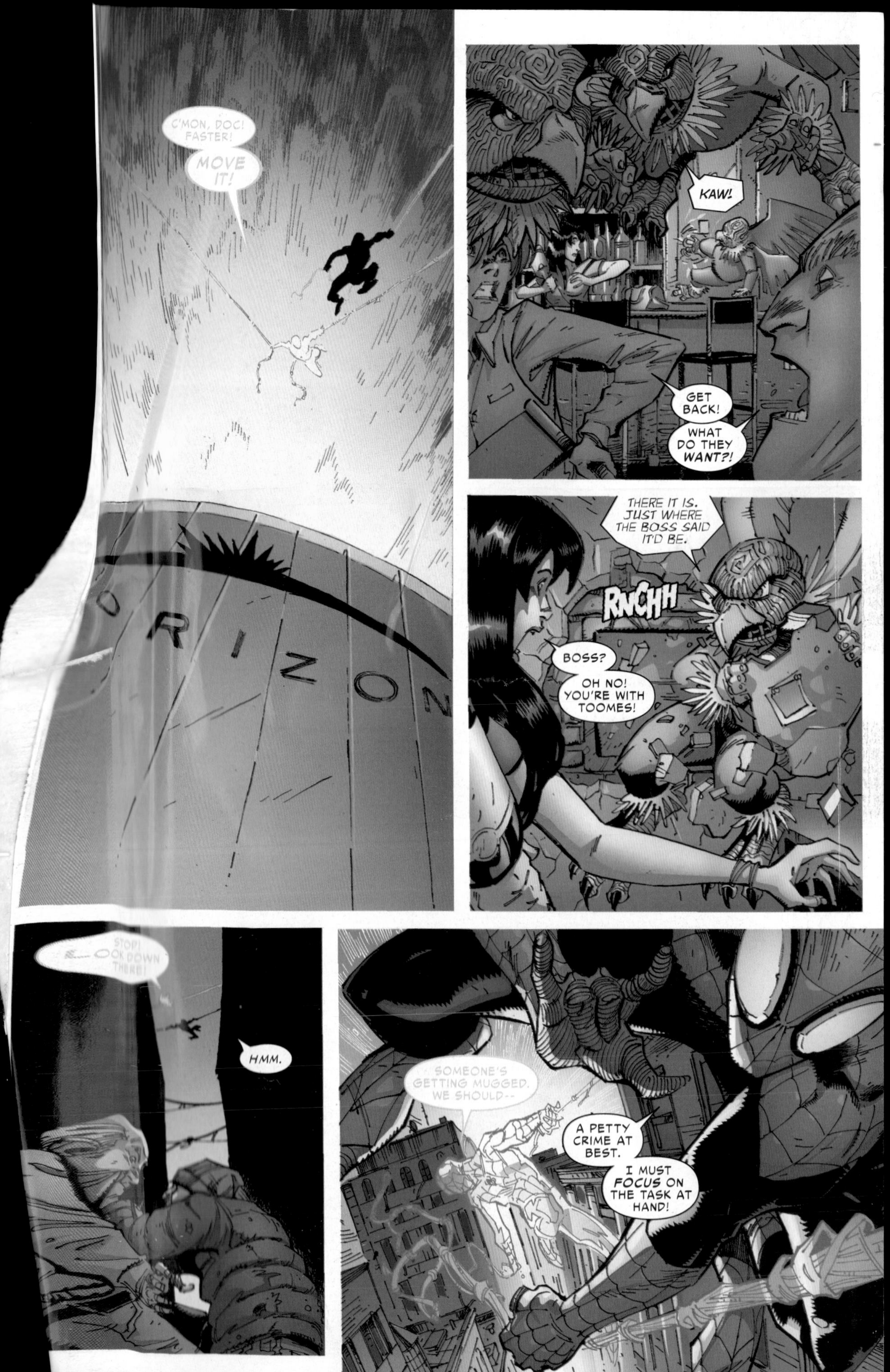
C'MON, DOC! FASTER!
MOVE IT!
ORIZON
KAW!
GET BACK!
WHAT DO THEY WANT?!
THERE IT IS. JUST WHERE THE BOSS SAID IT'D BE.
RNCHH
BOSS?
OH NO! YOU'RE WITH TOOMES!
STOP!
OOK DOWN THERE!
HMM.
SOMEONE'S GETTING MUGGED. WE SHOULD--
A PETTY CRIME AT BEST.
I MUST FOCUS ON THE TASK AT HAND!

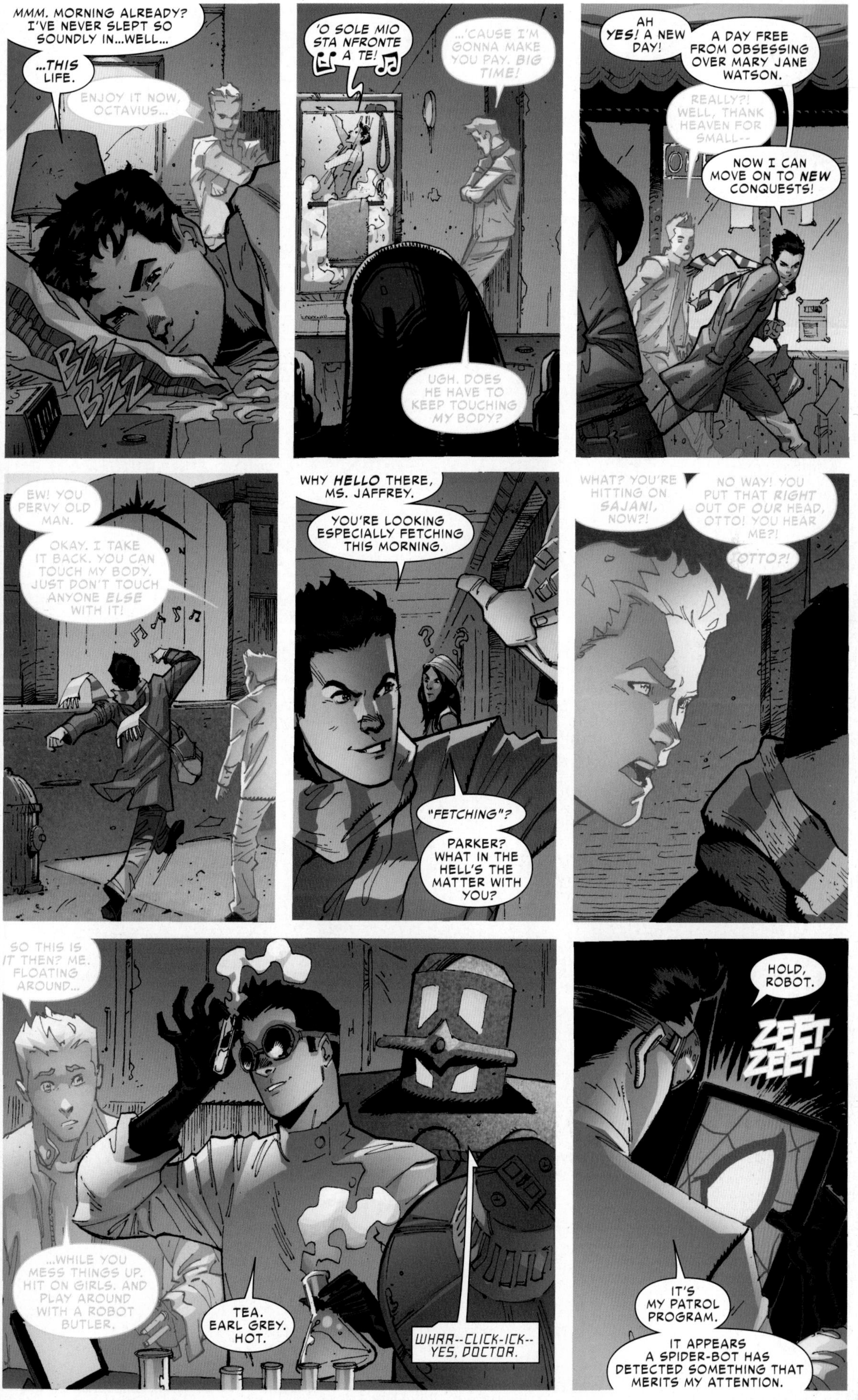
MMM. MORNING ALREADY? I'VE NEVER SLEPT SO SOUNDLY IN...WELL...
...THIS LIFE.
ENJOY IT NOW, OCTAVIUS...
BZZ BZZ
'O SOLE MIO STA NFRONTE A TE!
...'CAUSE I'M GONNA MAKE YOU PAY. BIG TIME!
UGH. DOES HE HAVE TO KEEP TOUCHING MY BODY?
AH YES! A NEW DAY!
A DAY FREE FROM OBSESSING OVER MARY JANE WATSON.
REALLY?! WELL, THANK HEAVEN FOR SMALL--
NOW I CAN MOVE ON TO NEW CONQUESTS!
EW! YOU PERVY OLD MAN.
OKAY. I TAKE IT BACK. YOU CAN TOUCH MY BODY. JUST DON'T TOUCH ANYONE ELSE WITH IT!
WHY HELLO THERE, MS. JAFFREY.
YOU'RE LOOKING ESPECIALLY FETCHING THIS MORNING.
"FETCHING"?
PARKER? WHAT IN THE HELL'S THE MATTER WITH YOU?
WHAT? YOU'RE HITTING ON SAJANI, NOW?!
NO WAY! YOU PUT THAT RIGHT OUT OF OUR HEAD, OTTO! YOU HEAR ME?!
OTTO?!
SO THIS IS IT THEN? ME. FLOATING AROUND...
...WHILE YOU MESS THINGS UP. HIT ON GIRLS. AND PLAY AROUND WITH A ROBOT BUTLER.
TEA. EARL GREY. HOT.
WHRR--CLICK-ICK-- YES, DOCTOR.
HOLD, ROBOT.
ZEET ZEET
IT'S MY PATROL PROGRAM.
IT APPEARS A SPIDER-BOT HAS DETECTED SOMETHING THAT MERITS MY ATTENTION.

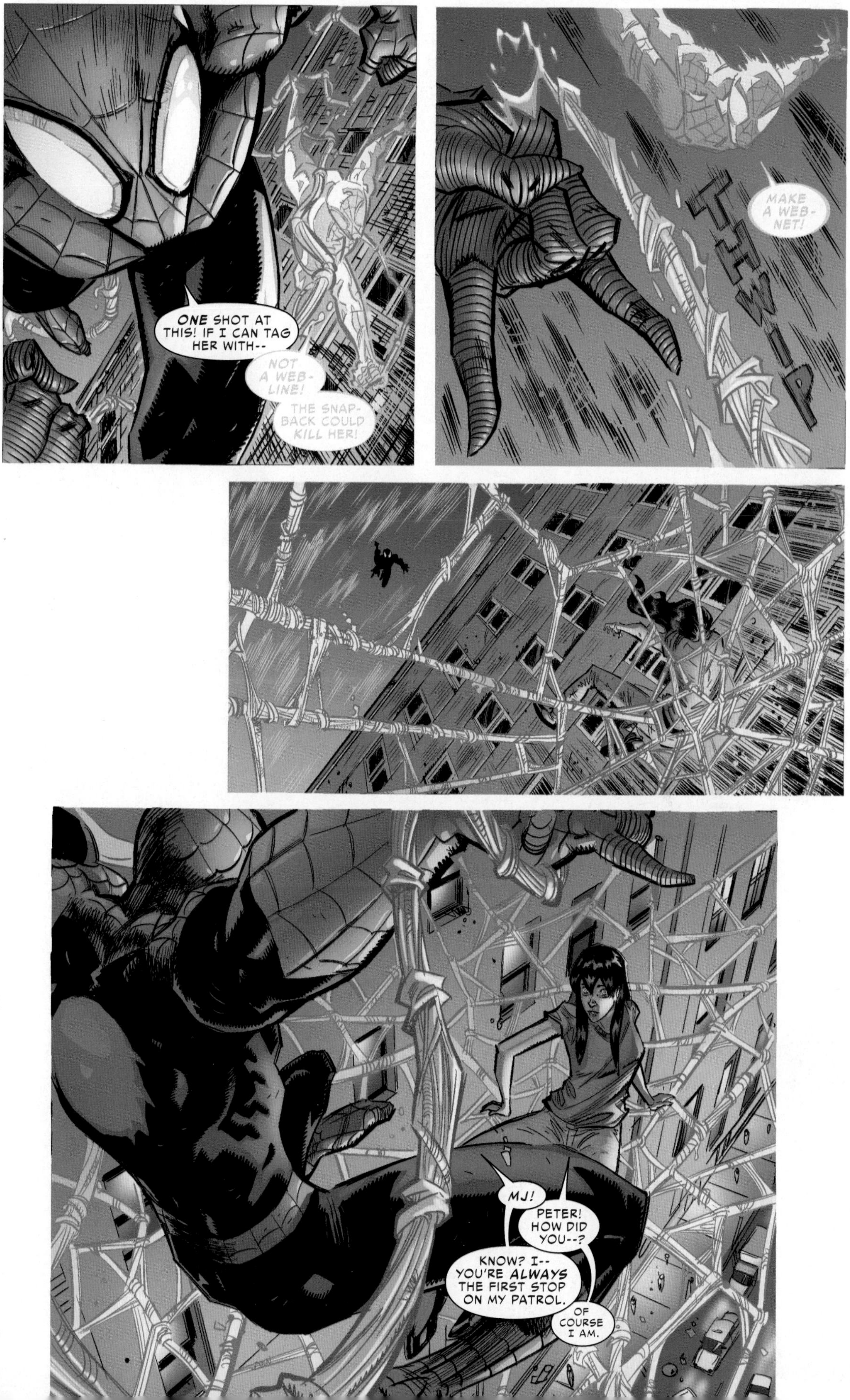
ONE SHOT AT THIS! IF I CAN TAG HER WITH--
NOT A WEB-LINE!
THE SNAP-BACK COULD KILL HER!
THWIP
MAKE A WEB-NET!
MJ!
PETER! HOW DID YOU--?
KNOW? I-- YOU'RE ALWAYS THE FIRST STOP ON MY PATROL.
OF COURSE I AM.

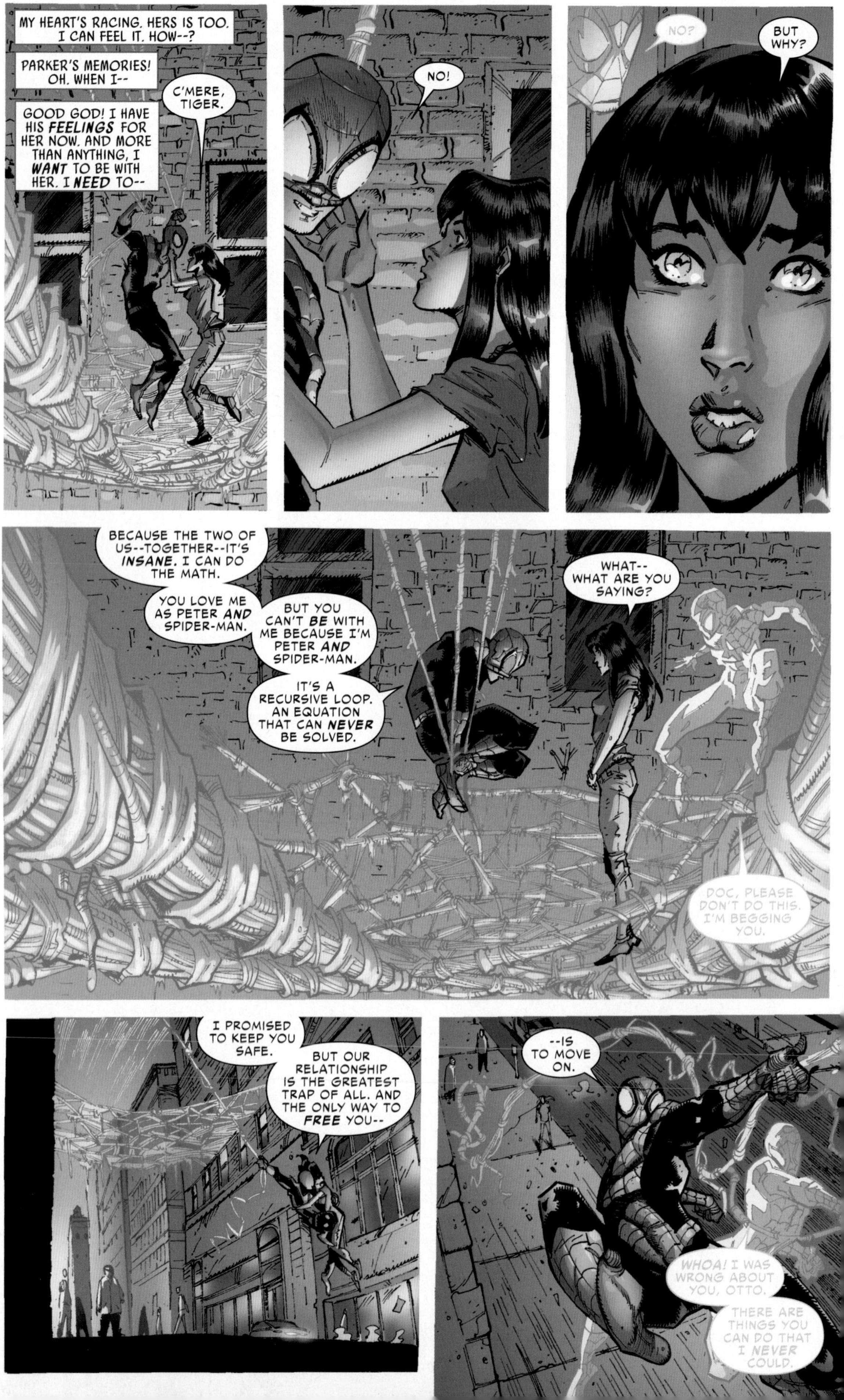
MY HEART'S RACING. HERS IS TOO. I CAN FEEL IT. HOW--?
PARKER'S MEMORIES! OH. WHEN I--
GOOD GOD! I HAVE HIS FEELINGS FOR HER NOW. AND MORE THAN ANYTHING, I WANT TO BE WITH HER. I NEED TO--
C'MERE, TIGER.
NO!
NO?
BUT WHY?
BECAUSE THE TWO OF US--TOGETHER--IT'S INSANE. I CAN DO THE MATH.
YOU LOVE ME AS PETER AND SPIDER-MAN.
BUT YOU CAN'T BE WITH ME BECAUSE I'M PETER AND SPIDER-MAN.
IT'S A RECURSIVE LOOP. AN EQUATION THAT CAN NEVER BE SOLVED.
WHAT-- WHAT ARE YOU SAYING?
DOC, PLEASE DON'T DO THIS. I'M BEGGING YOU.
I PROMISED TO KEEP YOU SAFE.
BUT OUR RELATIONSHIP IS THE GREATEST TRAP OF ALL. AND THE ONLY WAY TO FREE YOU--
--IS TO MOVE ON.
WHOA! I WAS WRONG ABOUT YOU, OTTO.
THERE ARE THINGS YOU CAN DO THAT I NEVER COULD.

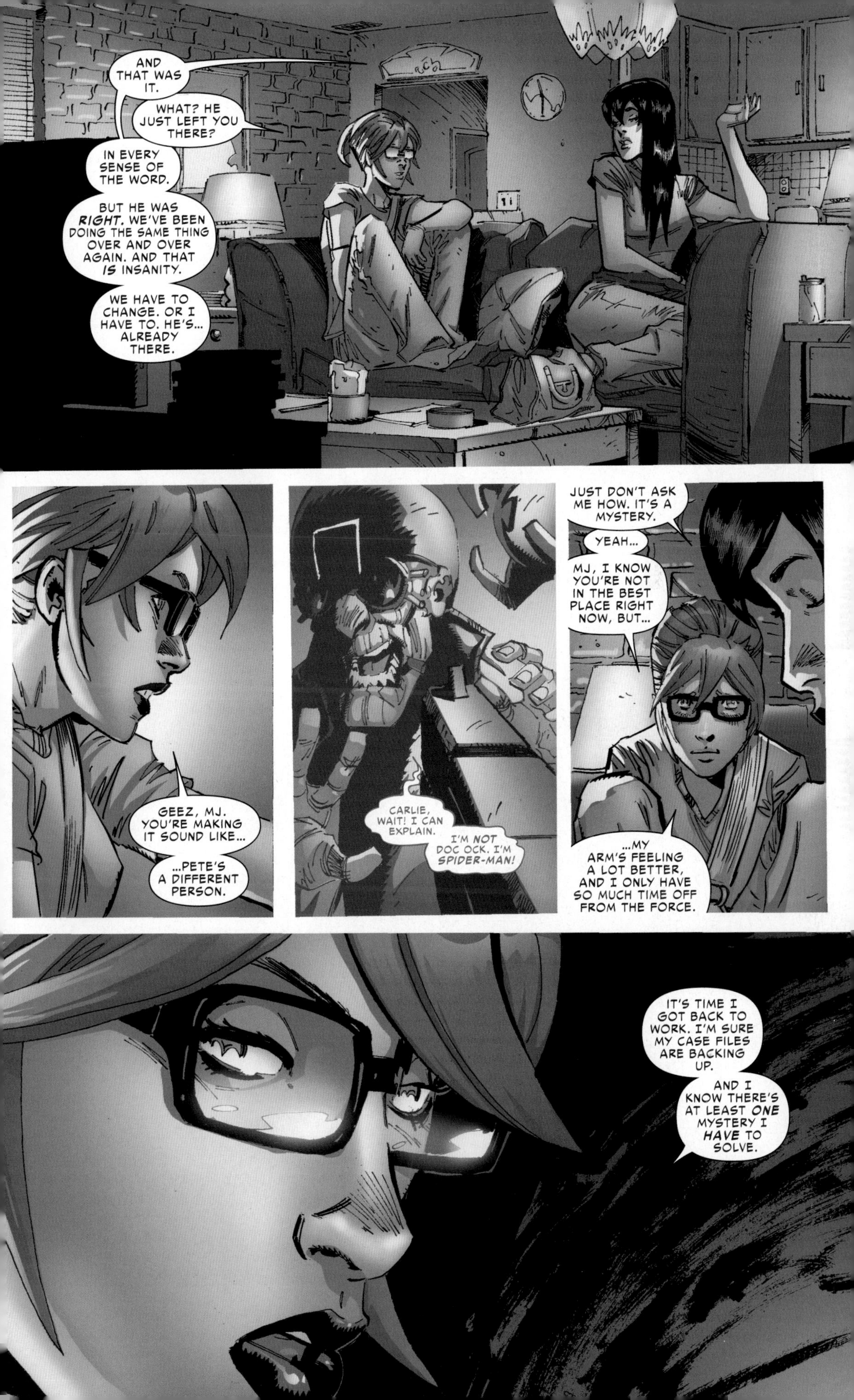
AND THAT WAS IT.
WHAT? HE JUST LEFT YOU THERE?
IN EVERY SENSE OF THE WORD.
BUT HE WAS RIGHT. WE'VE BEEN DOING THE SAME THING OVER AND OVER AGAIN. AND THAT IS INSANITY.
WE HAVE TO CHANGE. OR I HAVE TO. HE'S... ALREADY THERE.
GEEZ, MJ. YOU'RE MAKING IT SOUND LIKE...
...PETE'S A DIFFERENT PERSON.
CARLIE, WAIT! I CAN EXPLAIN.
I'M NOT DOC OCK. I'M SPIDER-MAN!
JUST DON'T ASK ME HOW. IT'S A MYSTERY.
YEAH...
MJ, I KNOW YOU'RE NOT IN THE BEST PLACE RIGHT NOW, BUT...
...MY ARM'S FEELING A LOT BETTER, AND I ONLY HAVE SO MUCH TIME OFF FROM THE FORCE.
IT'S TIME I GOT BACK TO WORK. I'M SURE MY CASE FILES ARE BACKING UP.
AND I KNOW THERE'S AT LEAST ONE MYSTERY I HAVE TO SOLVE.

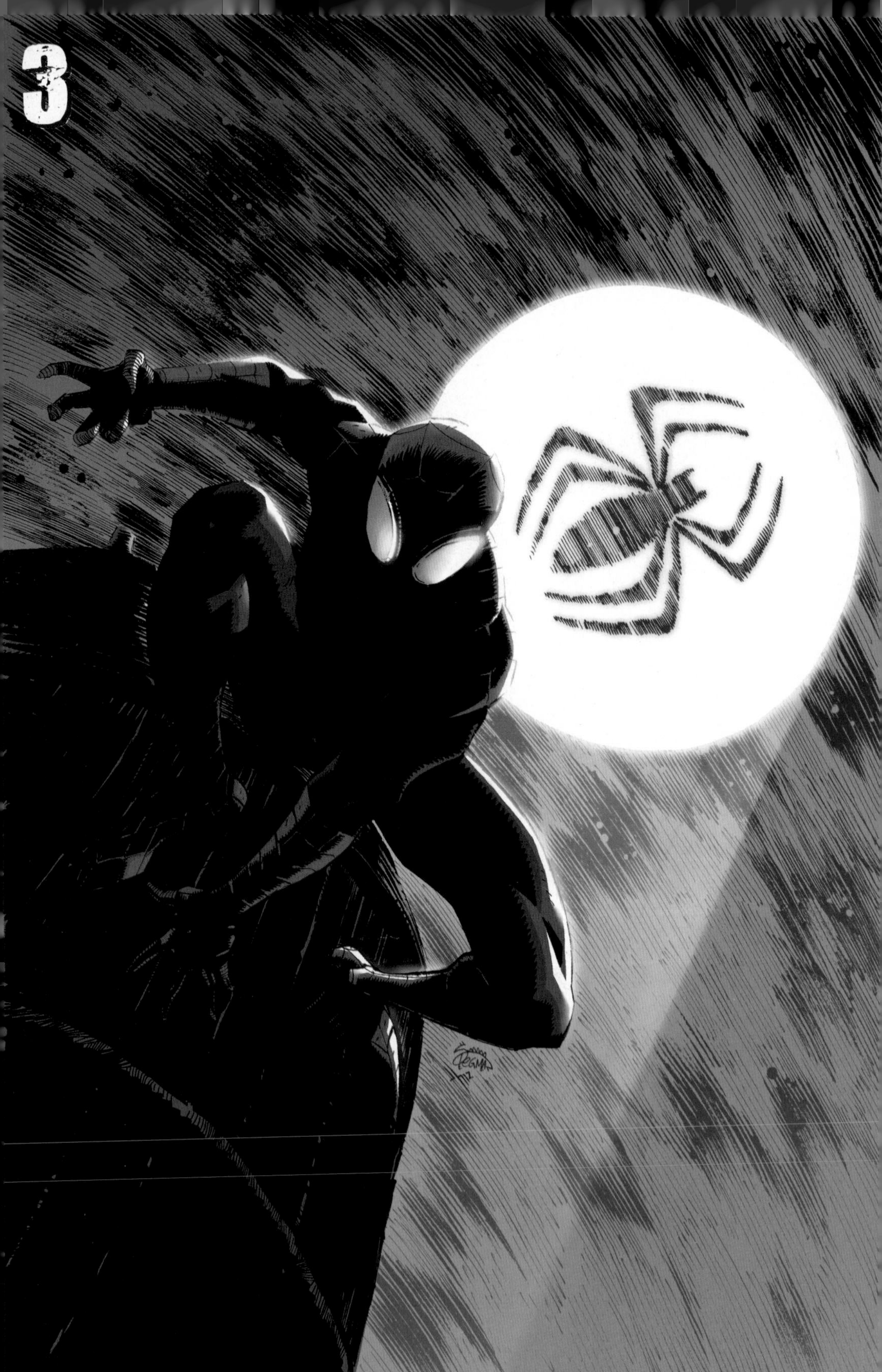
3

EVERYTHING YOU KNOW IS WRONG

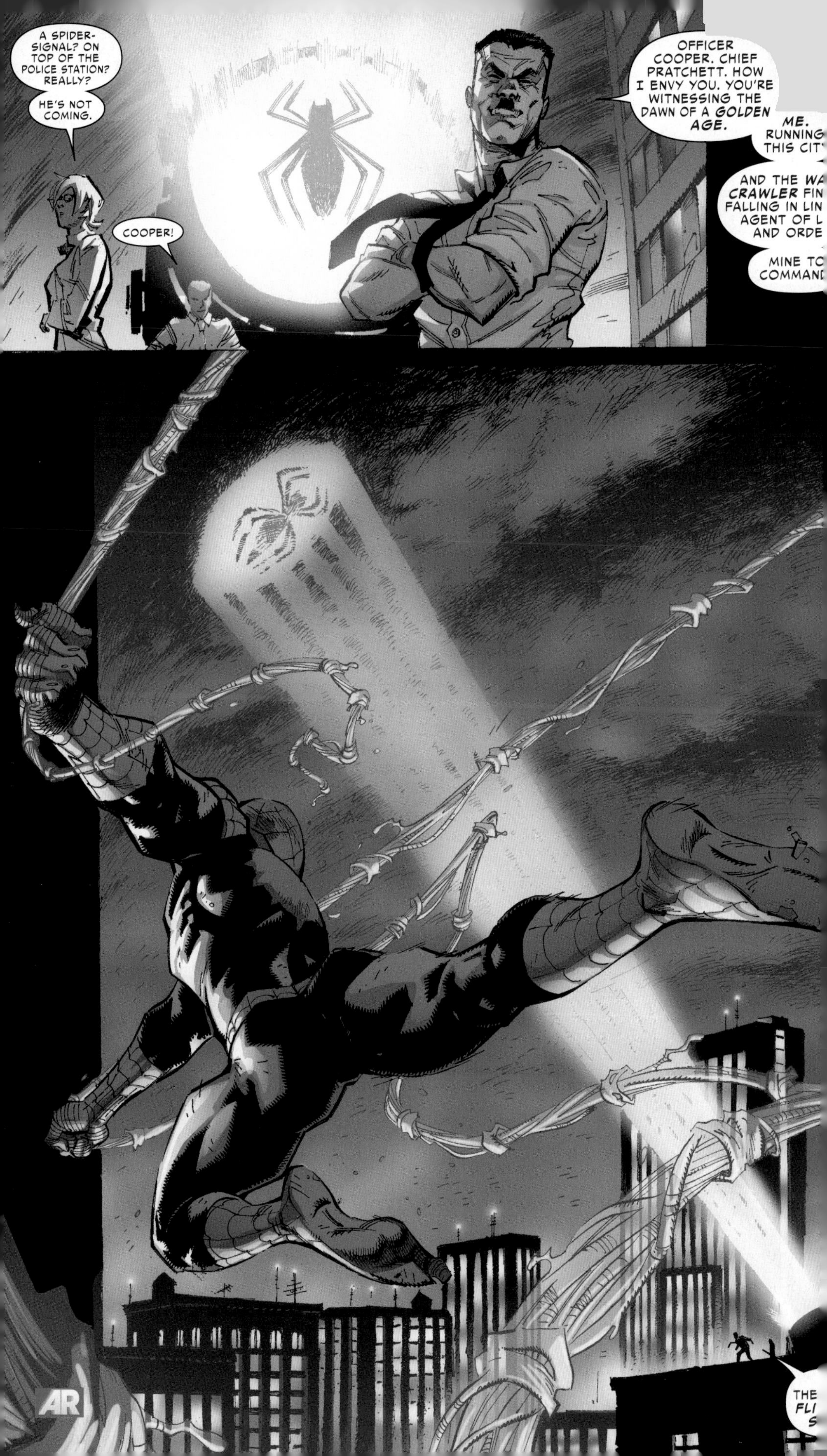

A SPIDER-SIGNAL? ON TOP OF THE POLICE STATION? REALLY?
HE'S NOT COMING.
COOPER!
OFFICER COOPER. CHIEF PRATCHETT. HOW I ENVY YOU. YOU'RE WITNESSING THE DAWN OF A *GOLDEN AGE.*
ME. RUNNING THIS CIT
AND THE *WA* *CRAWLER* FIN FALLING IN LIN AGENT OF L AND ORDE
MINE TO COMMAND
THE *FLI* S

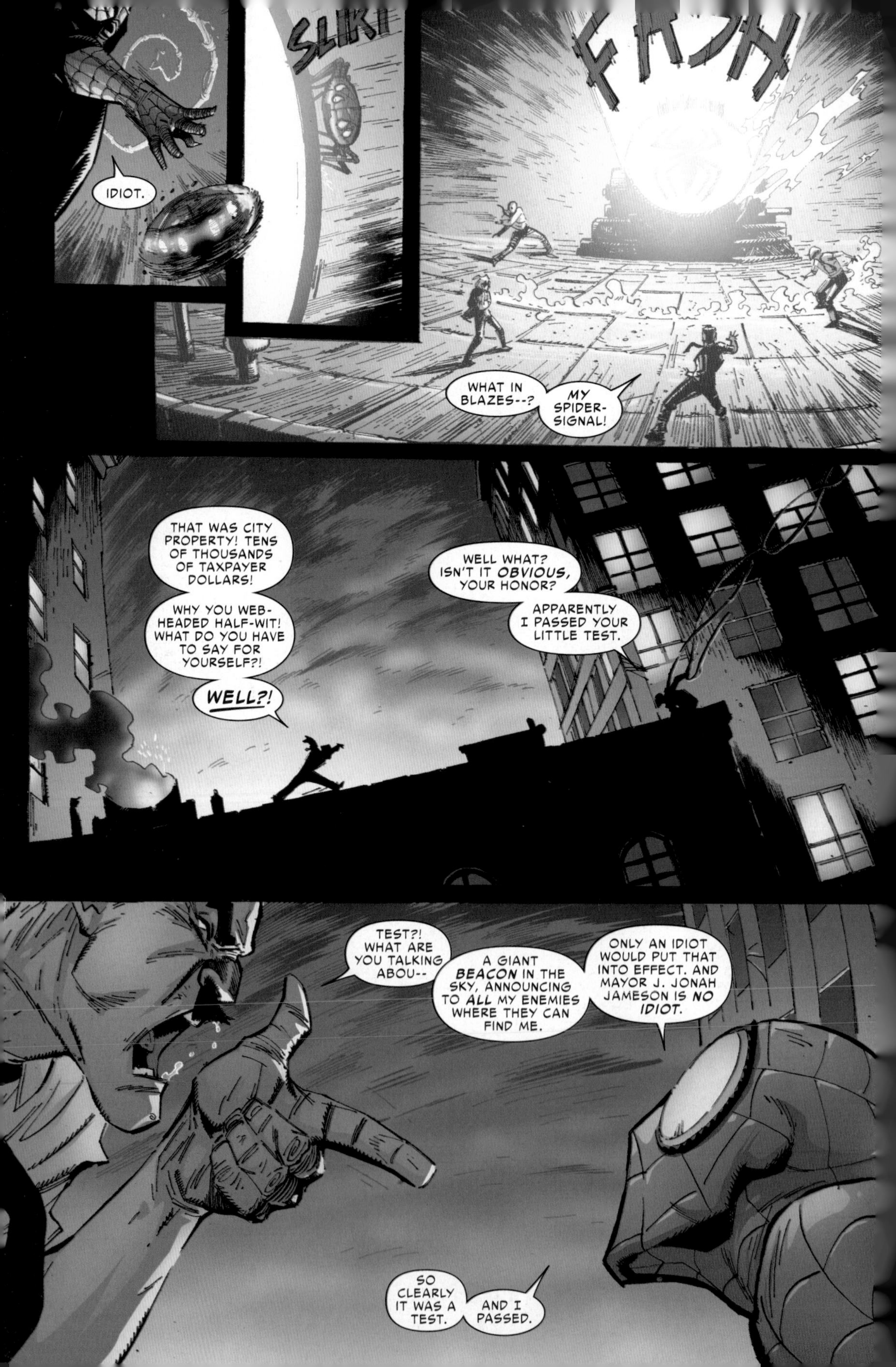
IDIOT.
SLIKT
FRUSH
WHAT IN BLAZES--?
MY SPIDER-SIGNAL!
THAT WAS CITY PROPERTY! TENS OF THOUSANDS OF TAXPAYER DOLLARS!
WHY YOU WEB-HEADED HALF-WIT! WHAT DO YOU HAVE TO SAY FOR YOURSELF?!
WELL?!
WELL WHAT? ISN'T IT OBVIOUS, YOUR HONOR?
APPARENTLY I PASSED YOUR LITTLE TEST.
TEST?! WHAT ARE YOU TALKING ABOU--
A GIANT BEACON IN THE SKY, ANNOUNCING TO ALL MY ENEMIES WHERE THEY CAN FIND ME.
ONLY AN IDIOT WOULD PUT THAT INTO EFFECT. AND MAYOR J. JONAH JAMESON IS NO IDIOT.
SO CLEARLY IT WAS A TEST.
AND I PASSED.

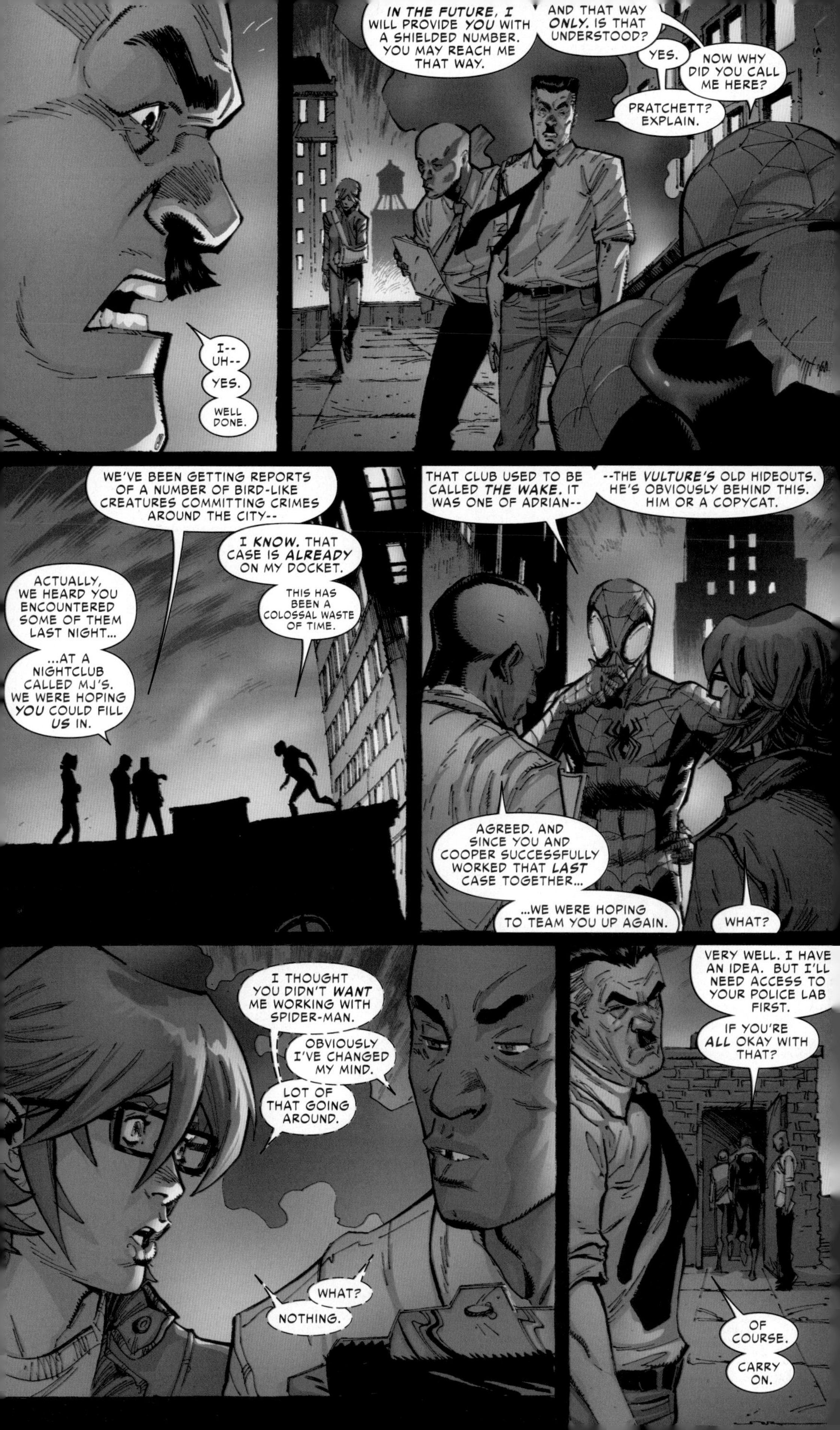
I--
UH--
YES.
WELL DONE.
IN THE FUTURE, I WILL PROVIDE YOU WITH A SHIELDED NUMBER. YOU MAY REACH ME THAT WAY.
AND THAT WAY ONLY. IS THAT UNDERSTOOD?
YES.
NOW WHY DID YOU CALL ME HERE?
PRATCHETT? EXPLAIN.
WE'VE BEEN GETTING REPORTS OF A NUMBER OF BIRD-LIKE CREATURES COMMITTING CRIMES AROUND THE CITY--
I KNOW. THAT CASE IS ALREADY ON MY DOCKET.
THIS HAS BEEN A COLOSSAL WASTE OF TIME.
ACTUALLY, WE HEARD YOU ENCOUNTERED SOME OF THEM LAST NIGHT...
...AT A NIGHTCLUB CALLED MJ'S. WE WERE HOPING YOU COULD FILL US IN.
THAT CLUB USED TO BE CALLED THE WAKE. IT WAS ONE OF ADRIAN--
--THE VULTURE'S OLD HIDEOUTS. HE'S OBVIOUSLY BEHIND THIS. HIM OR A COPYCAT.
AGREED. AND SINCE YOU AND COOPER SUCCESSFULLY WORKED THAT LAST CASE TOGETHER...
...WE WERE HOPING TO TEAM YOU UP AGAIN.
WHAT?
I THOUGHT YOU DIDN'T WANT ME WORKING WITH SPIDER-MAN.
OBVIOUSLY I'VE CHANGED MY MIND.
LOT OF THAT GOING AROUND.
WHAT?
NOTHING.
VERY WELL. I HAVE AN IDEA. BUT I'LL NEED ACCESS TO YOUR POLICE LAB FIRST.
IF YOU'RE ALL OKAY WITH THAT?
OF COURSE.
CARRY ON.

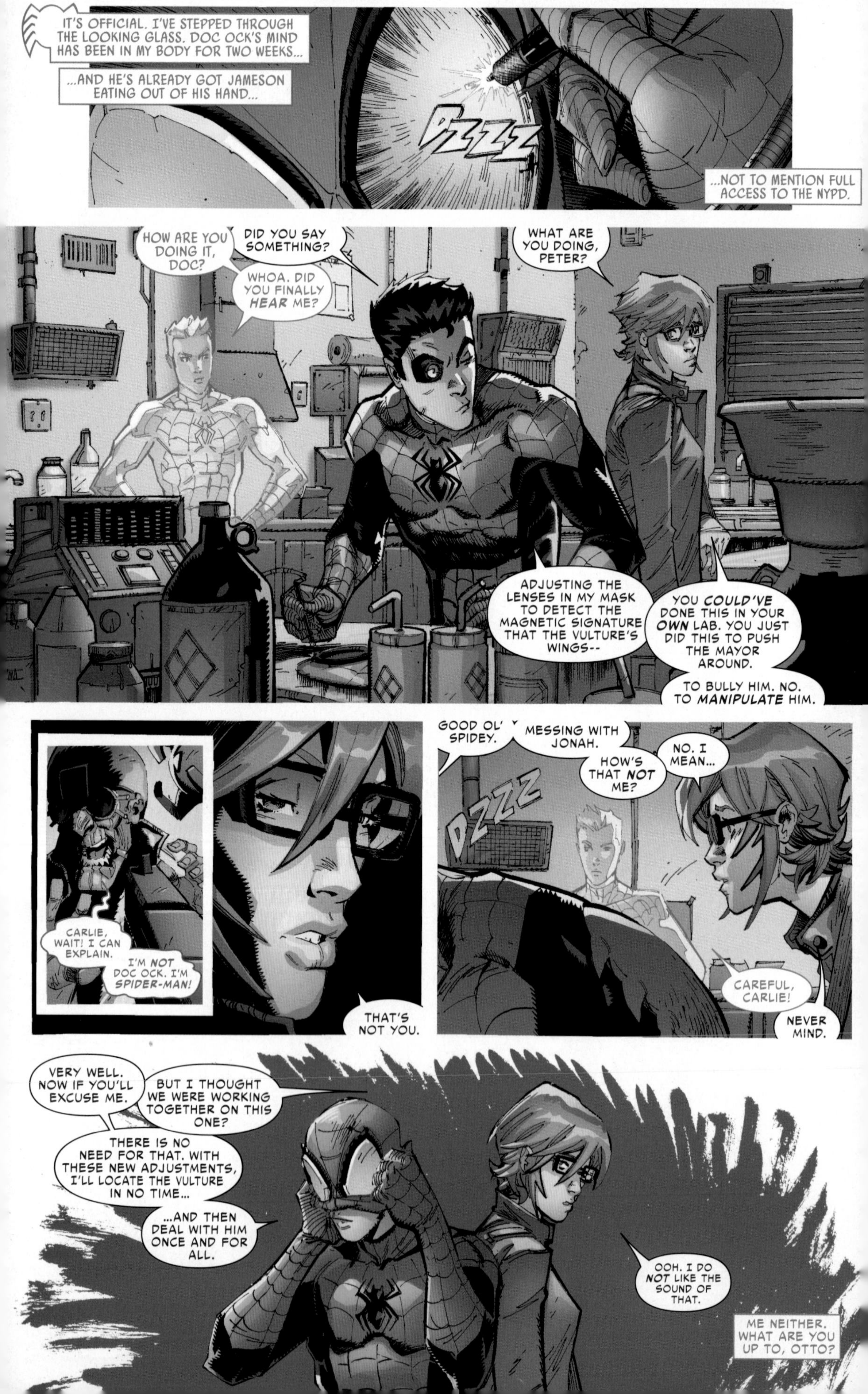

IT'S OFFICIAL. I'VE STEPPED THROUGH THE LOOKING GLASS. DOC OCK'S MIND HAS BEEN IN MY BODY FOR TWO WEEKS...
...AND HE'S ALREADY GOT JAMESON EATING OUT OF HIS HAND...
DZZZ
...NOT TO MENTION FULL ACCESS TO THE NYPD.
HOW ARE YOU DOING IT, DOC?
DID YOU SAY SOMETHING?
WHOA. DID YOU FINALLY HEAR ME?
WHAT ARE YOU DOING, PETER?
ADJUSTING THE LENSES IN MY MASK TO DETECT THE MAGNETIC SIGNATURE THAT THE VULTURE'S WINGS--
YOU COULD'VE DONE THIS IN YOUR OWN LAB. YOU JUST DID THIS TO PUSH THE MAYOR AROUND.
TO BULLY HIM. NO. TO MANIPULATE HIM.
CARLIE, WAIT! I CAN EXPLAIN.
I'M NOT DOC OCK. I'M SPIDER-MAN!
THAT'S NOT YOU.
GOOD OL' SPIDEY.
MESSING WITH JONAH.
HOW'S THAT NOT ME?
NO. I MEAN...
DZZZ
CAREFUL, CARLIE!
NEVER MIND.
VERY WELL. NOW IF YOU'LL EXCUSE ME.
BUT I THOUGHT WE WERE WORKING TOGETHER ON THIS ONE?
THERE IS NO NEED FOR THAT. WITH THESE NEW ADJUSTMENTS, I'LL LOCATE THE VULTURE IN NO TIME...
...AND THEN DEAL WITH HIM ONCE AND FOR ALL.
OOH. I DO NOT LIKE THE SOUND OF THAT.
ME NEITHER. WHAT ARE YOU UP TO, OTTO?

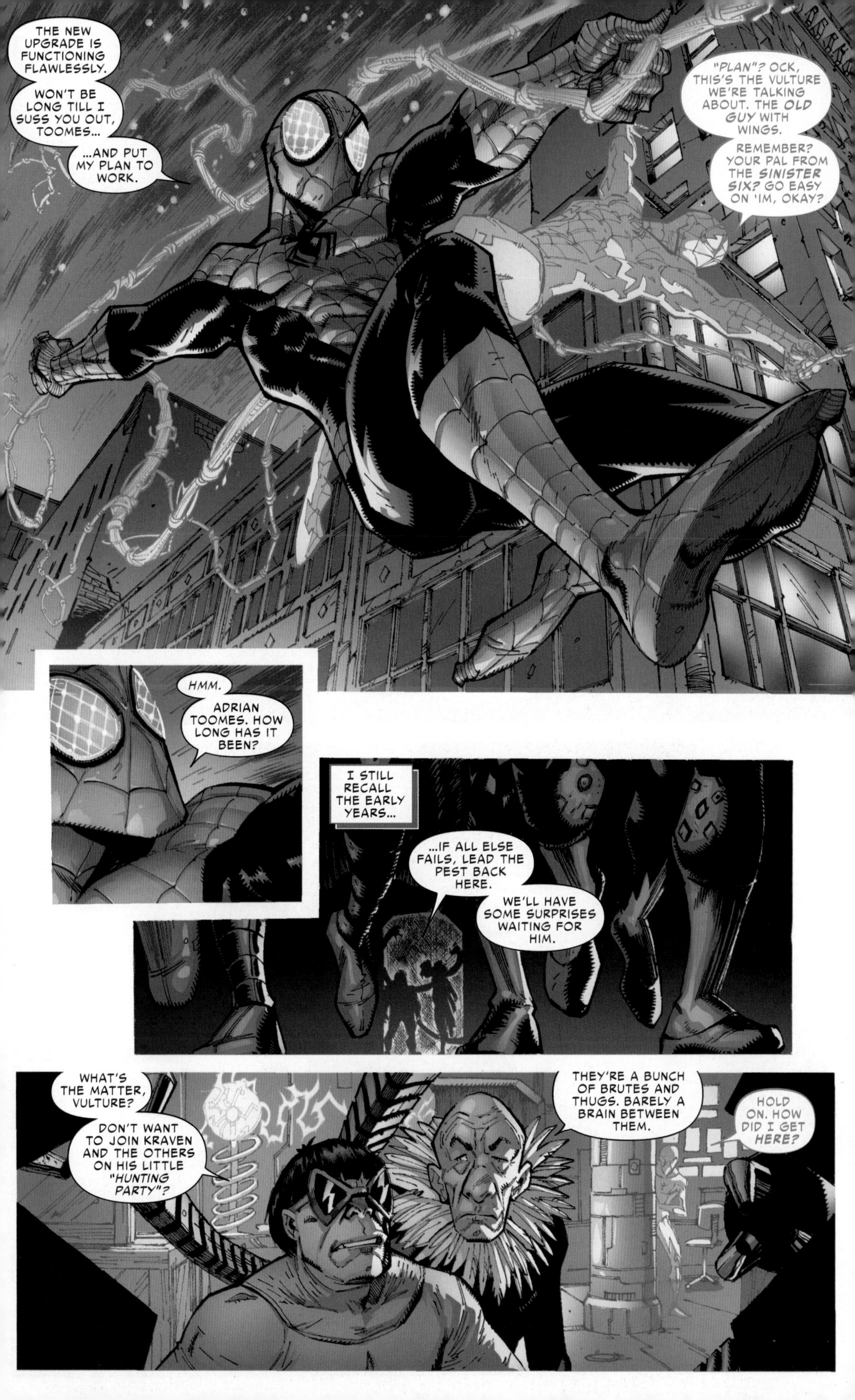
THE NEW UPGRADE IS FUNCTIONING FLAWLESSLY.
WON'T BE LONG TILL I SUSS YOU OUT, TOOMES...
...AND PUT MY PLAN TO WORK.
"PLAN"? OCK, THIS'S THE VULTURE WE'RE TALKING ABOUT. THE OLD GUY WITH WINGS.
REMEMBER? YOUR PAL FROM THE SINISTER SIX? GO EASY ON 'IM, OKAY?
HMM.
ADRIAN TOOMES. HOW LONG HAS IT BEEN?
I STILL RECALL THE EARLY YEARS...
...IF ALL ELSE FAILS, LEAD THE PEST BACK HERE.
WE'LL HAVE SOME SURPRISES WAITING FOR HIM.
WHAT'S THE MATTER, VULTURE?
DON'T WANT TO JOIN KRAVEN AND THE OTHERS ON HIS LITTLE "HUNTING PARTY"?
THEY'RE A BUNCH OF BRUTES AND THUGS. BARELY A BRAIN BETWEEN THEM.
HOLD ON. HOW DID I GET HERE?

ONE SEC I'M SWINGING ALONGSIDE OTTO AND THE NEXT I'M...

HEY! I KNOW THIS PLACE! IT'S ONE OF THE FIRST SINISTER SIX BASES.

I'M INSIDE ONE OF *DOC'S* MEMORIES! WELL *THAT'S* NEW.

YOU'RE DIFFERENT, THOUGH. THIS BASE. YOUR INVENTIONS... VERY IMPRESSIVE.

THANK YOU. AS IS YOUR FLYING HARNESS. CLEVER DESIGN, VULTURE.

PLEASE, CALL ME ADRIAN.

NOW WHAT DO YOU SAY WE WORK ON SOME OF THESE DEATH TRAPS OF YOURS?

AGREED... ADRIAN.

SO? WHAT WILL *YOU* DO, ONCE WE'VE KILLED THE BUG?

HOPEFULLY I'LL PULL OFF THAT *ONE* BIG SCORE. THAT'S ALL I'VE EVER WANTED.

BUT THAT ANNOYING BRAT KEEPS GETTING IN THE WAY.

AND YOU, OTTO? WHAT ARE YOU AFTER?

OH MY AMBITIONS GO FAR BEYOND SIMPLE LARCEN--

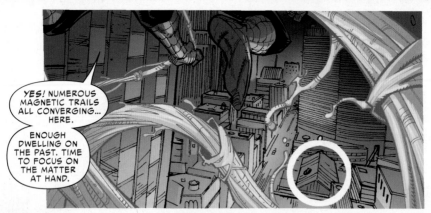

YES! NUMEROUS MAGNETIC TRAILS ALL CONVERGING... HERE.

ENOUGH DWELLING ON THE PAST. TIME TO FOCUS ON THE MATTER AT HAND.

WHAT? THIS IS *SO* WEIRD. LIKE SOMEONE HIT THE PAUSE BUTTON.

HMM. YOU'RE ON YOUR OWN FOR A WHILE, DOC.

GONNA SNOOP AROUND DOWN HERE IN YOUR HEAD. SEE IF THERE'S ANYTHING I CAN PUT TO GOOD USE.

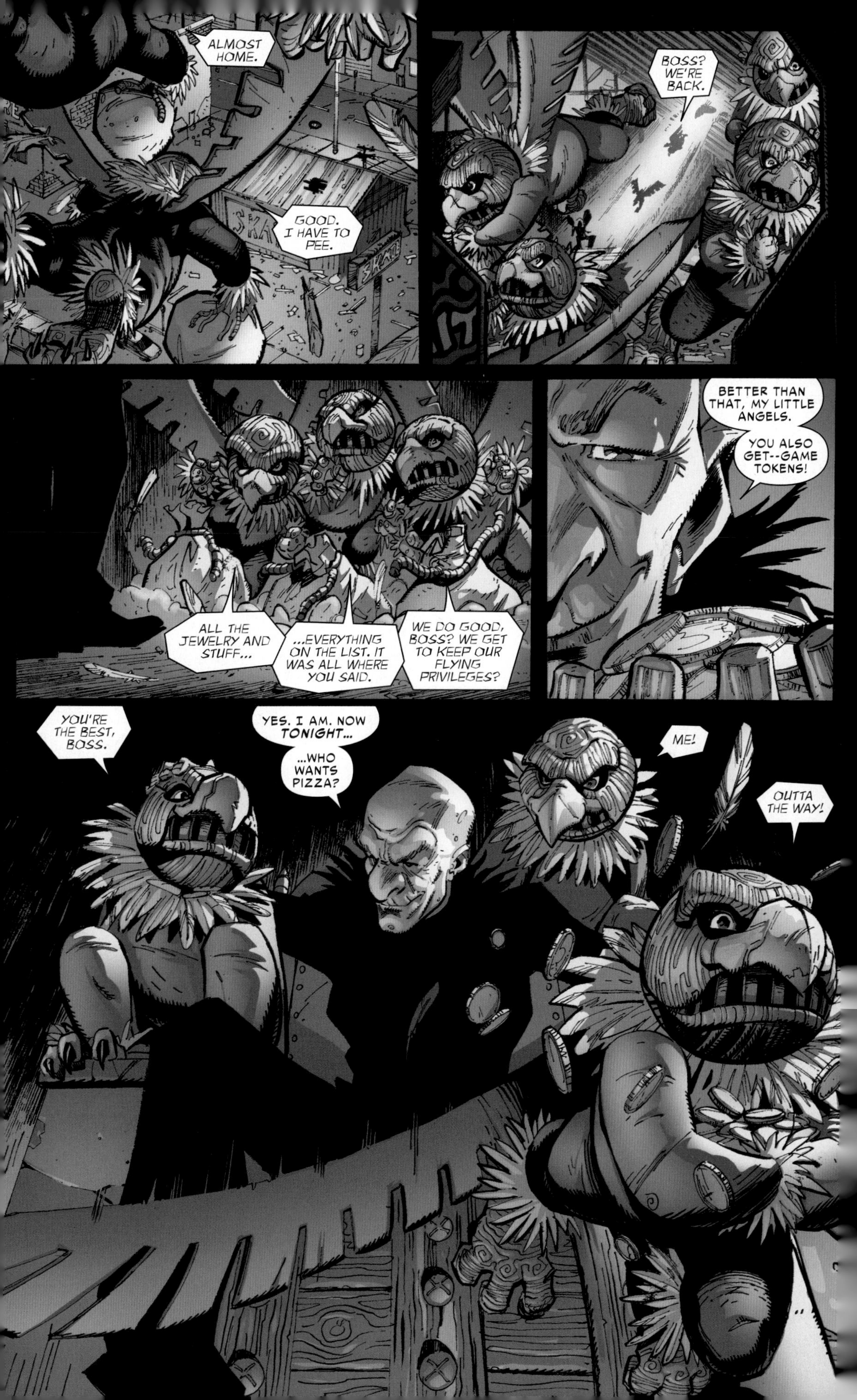
ALMOST HOME.
GOOD. I HAVE TO PEE.
BOSS? WE'RE BACK.
ALL THE JEWELRY AND STUFF...
...EVERYTHING ON THE LIST. IT WAS ALL WHERE YOU SAID.
WE DO GOOD, BOSS? WE GET TO KEEP OUR FLYING PRIVILEGES?
BETTER THAN THAT, MY LITTLE ANGELS.
YOU ALSO GET--GAME TOKENS!
YOU'RE THE BEST, BOSS.
YES. I AM. NOW TONIGHT...
...WHO WANTS PIZZA?
ME!
OUTTA THE WAY!

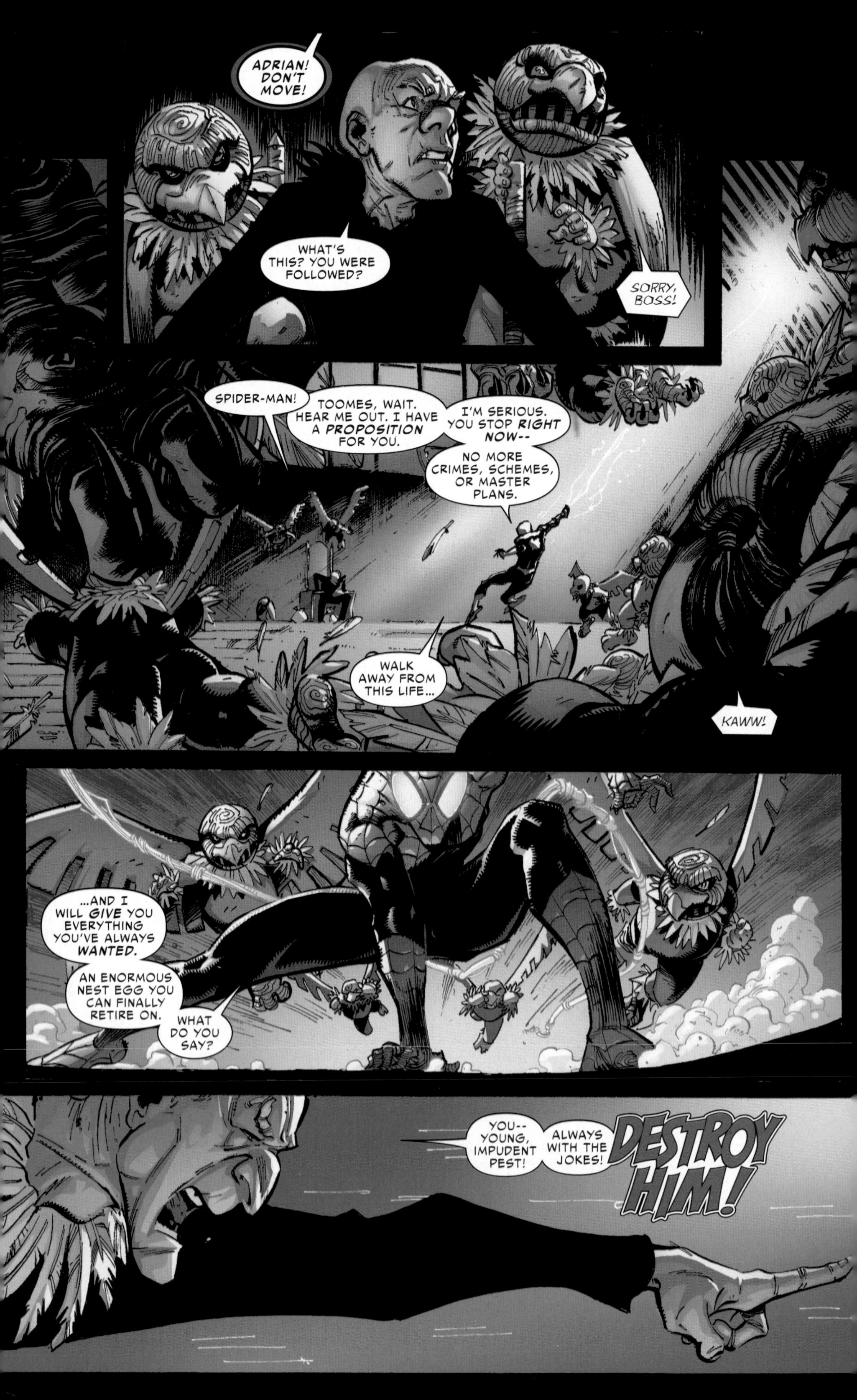
ADRIAN! DON'T MOVE!
WHAT'S THIS? YOU WERE FOLLOWED?
SORRY, BOSS!
SPIDER-MAN!
TOOMES, WAIT. HEAR ME OUT. I HAVE A PROPOSITION FOR YOU.
I'M SERIOUS. YOU STOP RIGHT NOW--
NO MORE CRIMES, SCHEMES, OR MASTER PLANS.
WALK AWAY FROM THIS LIFE...
KAWW!
...AND I WILL GIVE YOU EVERYTHING YOU'VE ALWAYS WANTED.
AN ENORMOUS NEST EGG YOU CAN FINALLY RETIRE ON.
WHAT DO YOU SAY?
YOU-- YOUNG, IMPUDENT PEST!
ALWAYS WITH THE JOKES!
DESTROY HIM!

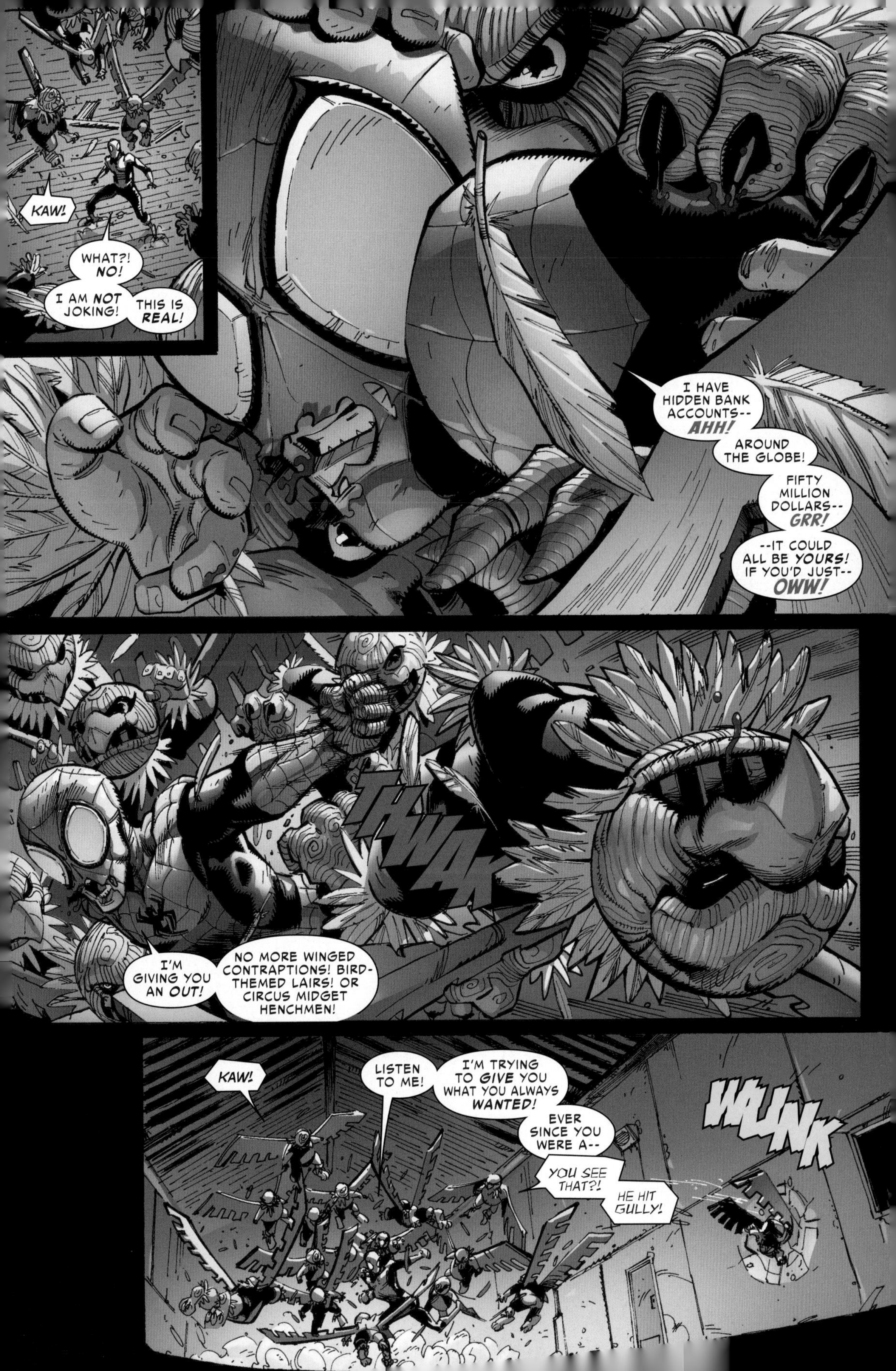
KAW!
WHAT?! NO!
I AM NOT JOKING!
THIS IS REAL!
I HAVE HIDDEN BANK ACCOUNTS-- AHH!
AROUND THE GLOBE!
FIFTY MILLION DOLLARS-- GRR!
--IT COULD ALL BE YOURS! IF YOU'D JUST-- OWW!
THWAK
I'M GIVING YOU AN OUT!
NO MORE WINGED CONTRAPTIONS! BIRD-THEMED LAIRS! OR CIRCUS MIDGET HENCHMEN!
KAW!
LISTEN TO ME!
I'M TRYING TO GIVE YOU WHAT YOU ALWAYS WANTED!
EVER SINCE YOU WERE A--
WUNK
YOU SEE THAT?!
HE HIT GULLY!

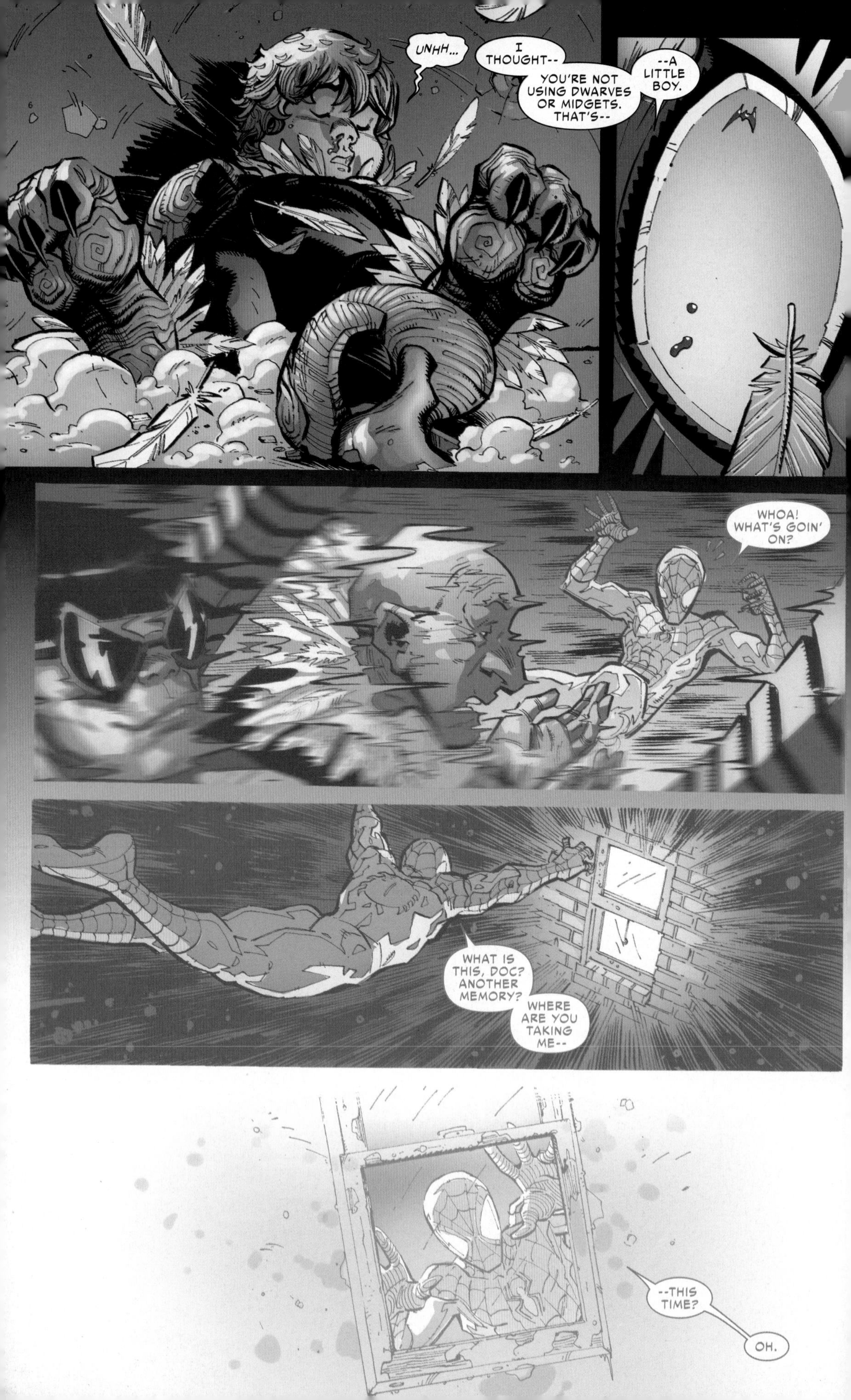
UNHH...
I THOUGHT--
YOU'RE NOT USING DWARVES OR MIDGETS. THAT'S--
--A LITTLE BOY.
WHOA! WHAT'S GOIN' ON?
WHAT IS THIS, DOC? ANOTHER MEMORY?
WHERE ARE YOU TAKING ME--
--THIS TIME?
OH.

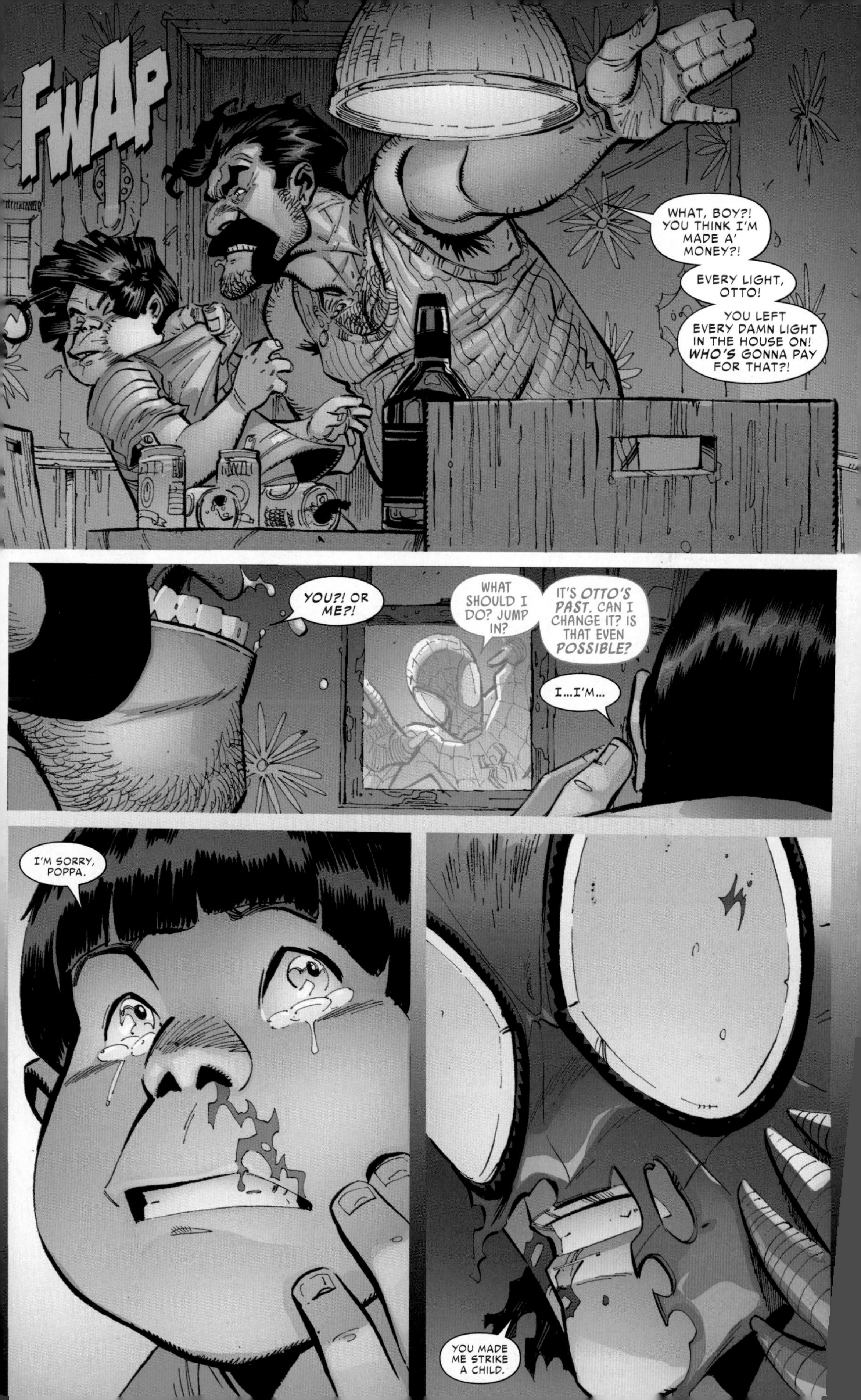
FWAP
WHAT, BOY?! YOU THINK I'M MADE A' MONEY?!
EVERY LIGHT, OTTO!
YOU LEFT EVERY DAMN LIGHT IN THE HOUSE ON! WHO'S GONNA PAY FOR THAT?!
YOU?! OR ME?!
WHAT SHOULD I DO? JUMP IN?
IT'S OTTO'S PAST. CAN I CHANGE IT? IS THAT EVEN POSSIBLE?
I...I'M...
I'M SORRY, POPPA.
YOU MADE ME STRIKE A CHILD.

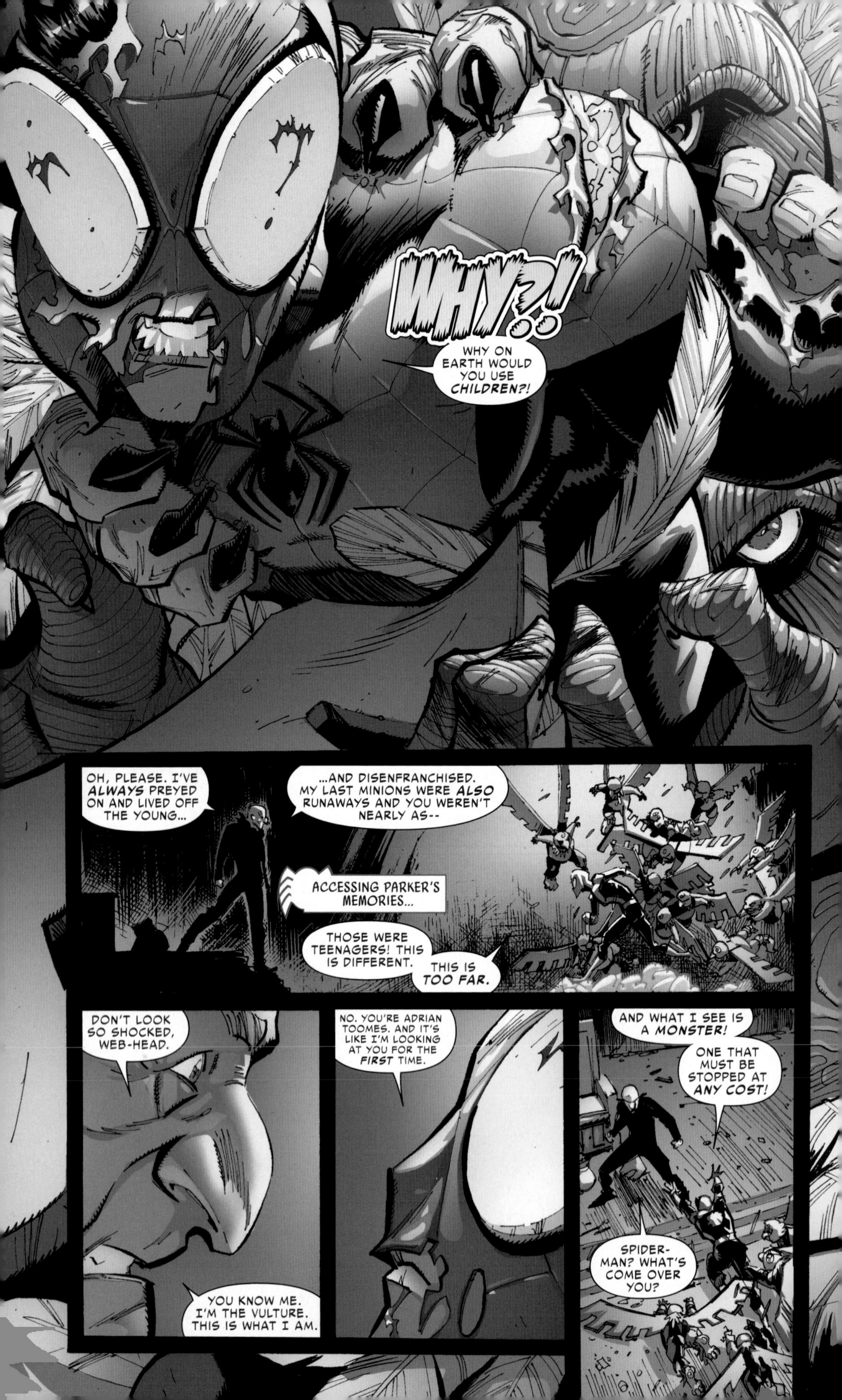
WHY?!
WHY ON EARTH WOULD YOU USE CHILDREN?!
OH, PLEASE. I'VE ALWAYS PREYED ON AND LIVED OFF THE YOUNG...
...AND DISENFRANCHISED. MY LAST MINIONS WERE ALSO RUNAWAYS AND YOU WEREN'T NEARLY AS--
ACCESSING PARKER'S MEMORIES...
THOSE WERE TEENAGERS! THIS IS DIFFERENT.
THIS IS TOO FAR.
DON'T LOOK SO SHOCKED, WEB-HEAD.
YOU KNOW ME. I'M THE VULTURE. THIS IS WHAT I AM.
NO. YOU'RE ADRIAN TOOMES. AND IT'S LIKE I'M LOOKING AT YOU FOR THE FIRST TIME.
AND WHAT I SEE IS A MONSTER!
ONE THAT MUST BE STOPPED AT ANY COST!
SPIDER-MAN? WHAT'S COME OVER YOU?

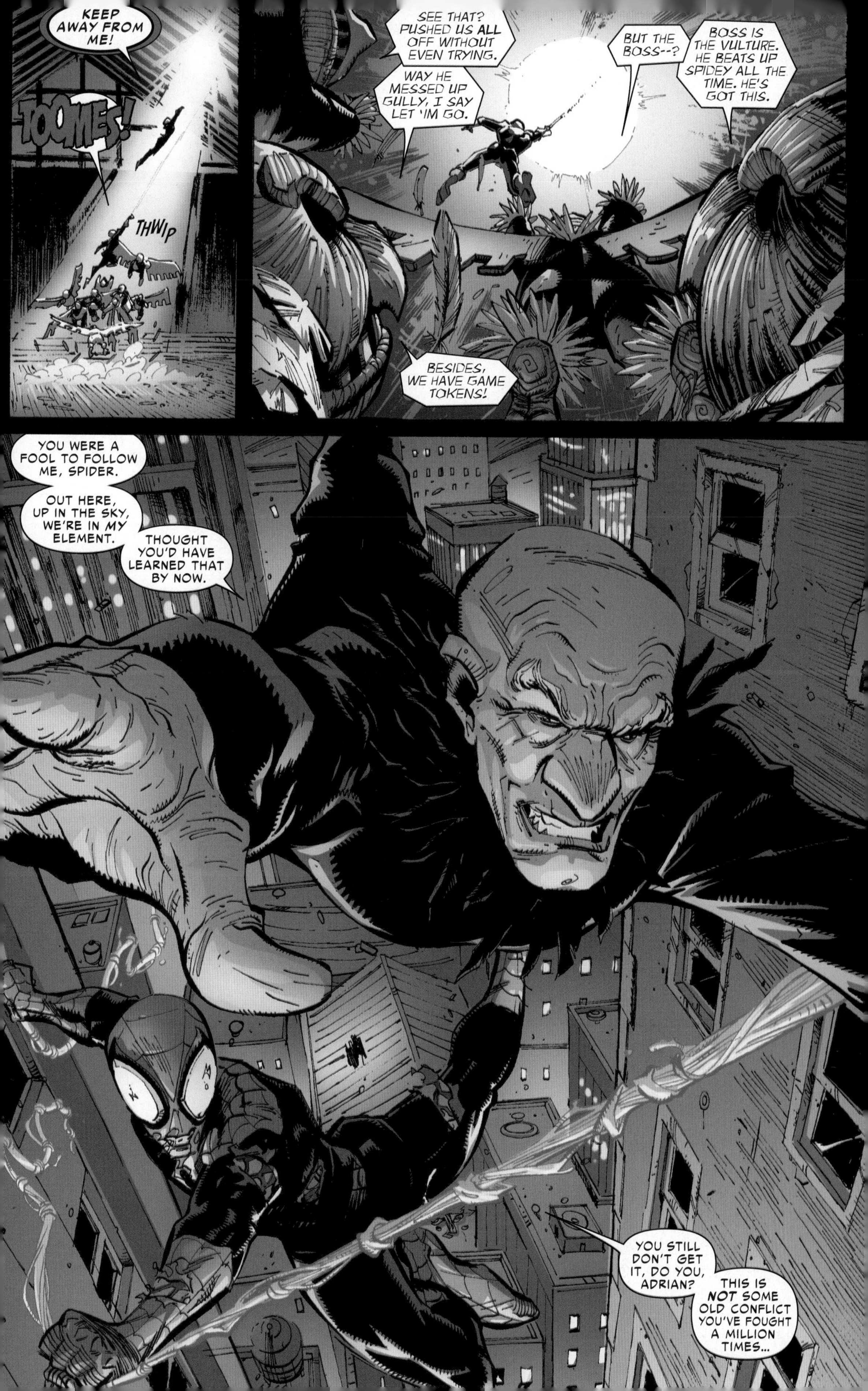
KEEP AWAY FROM ME!
TOOMES!
THWIP
SEE THAT? PUSHED US ALL OFF WITHOUT EVEN TRYING.
WAY HE MESSED UP GULLY, I SAY LET 'IM GO.
BUT THE BOSS--?
BOSS IS THE VULTURE. HE BEATS UP SPIDEY ALL THE TIME. HE'S GOT THIS.
BESIDES, WE HAVE GAME TOKENS!
YOU WERE A FOOL TO FOLLOW ME, SPIDER.
OUT HERE, UP IN THE SKY, WE'RE IN MY ELEMENT.
THOUGHT YOU'D HAVE LEARNED THAT BY NOW.
YOU STILL DON'T GET IT, DO YOU, ADRIAN?
THIS IS NOT SOME OLD CONFLICT YOU'VE FOUGHT A MILLION TIMES...

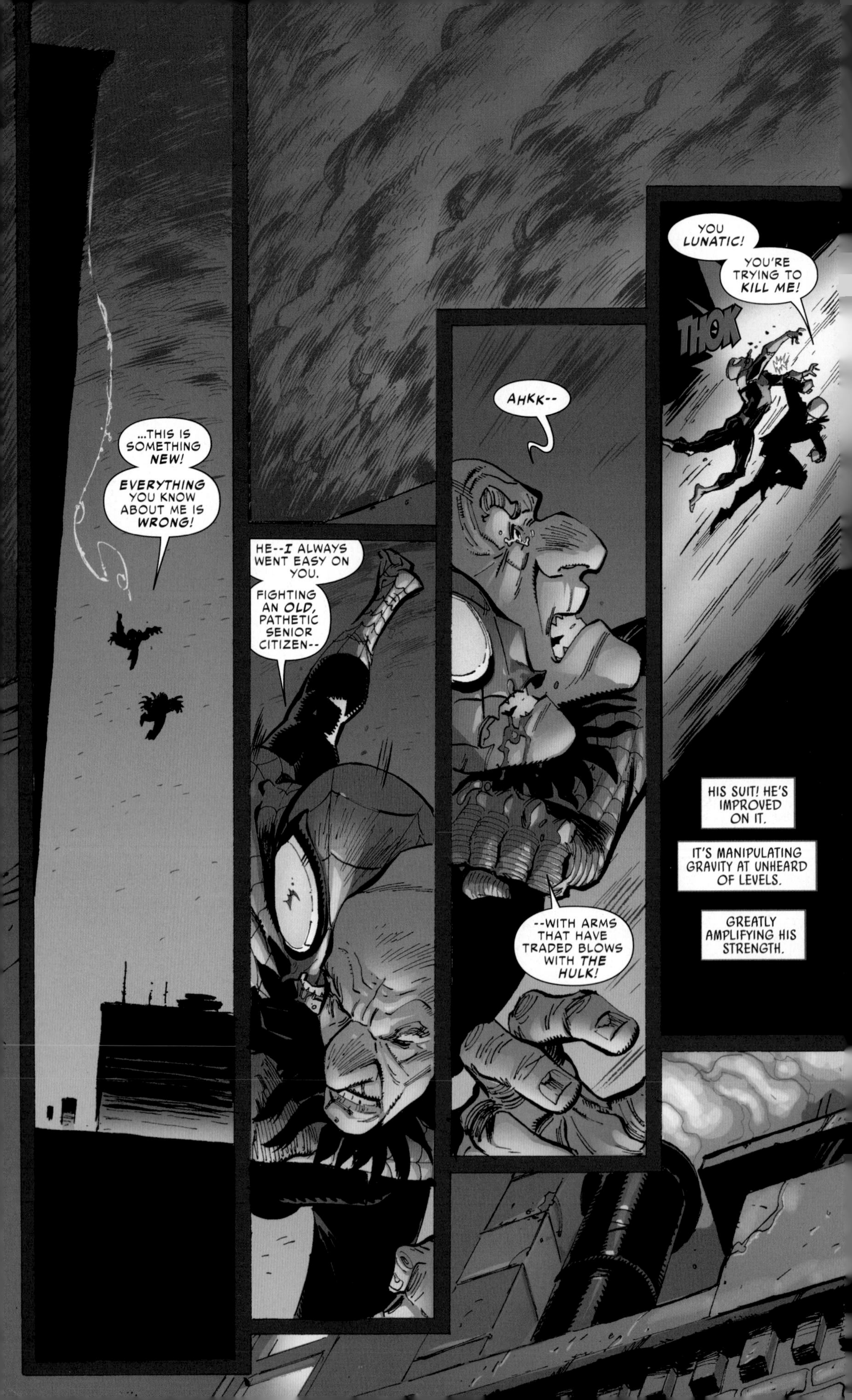

...THIS IS SOMETHING NEW!
EVERYTHING YOU KNOW ABOUT ME IS WRONG!
HE--I ALWAYS WENT EASY ON YOU.
FIGHTING AN OLD, PATHETIC SENIOR CITIZEN--
AHKK--
--WITH ARMS THAT HAVE TRADED BLOWS WITH THE HULK!
YOU LUNATIC!
YOU'RE TRYING TO KILL ME!
THOK
HIS SUIT! HE'S IMPROVED ON IT.
IT'S MANIPULATING GRAVITY AT UNHEARD OF LEVELS.
GREATLY AMPLIFYING HIS STRENGTH.

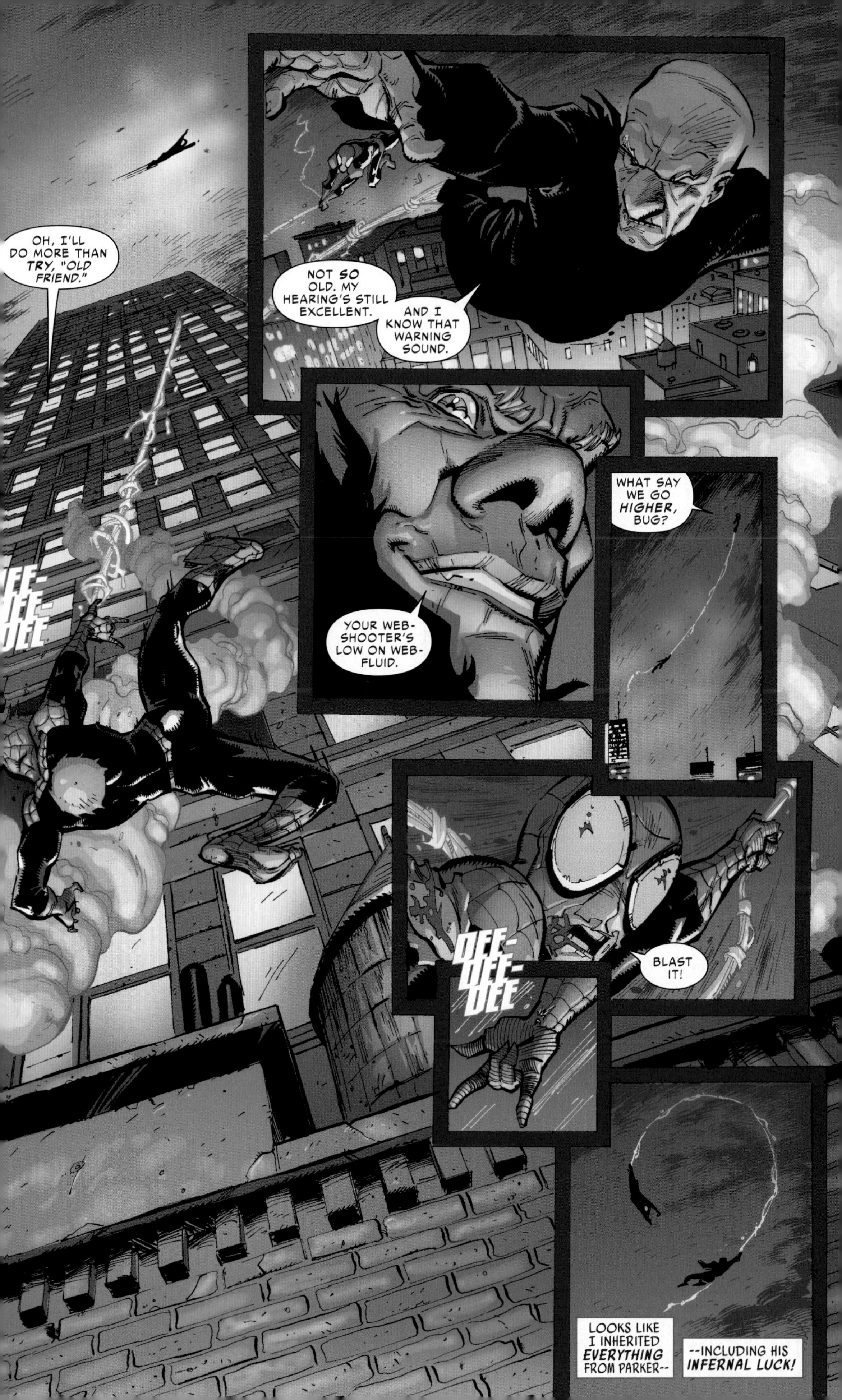

OH, I'LL DO MORE THAN TRY, "OLD FRIEND."
DEE-DEE-DEE
NOT SO OLD. MY HEARING'S STILL EXCELLENT.
AND I KNOW THAT WARNING SOUND.
YOUR WEB-SHOOTER'S LOW ON WEB-FLUID.
WHAT SAY WE GO HIGHER, BUG?
DEE-DEE-DEE
BLAST IT!
LOOKS LIKE I INHERITED EVERYTHING FROM PARKER--
--INCLUDING HIS INFERNAL LUCK!

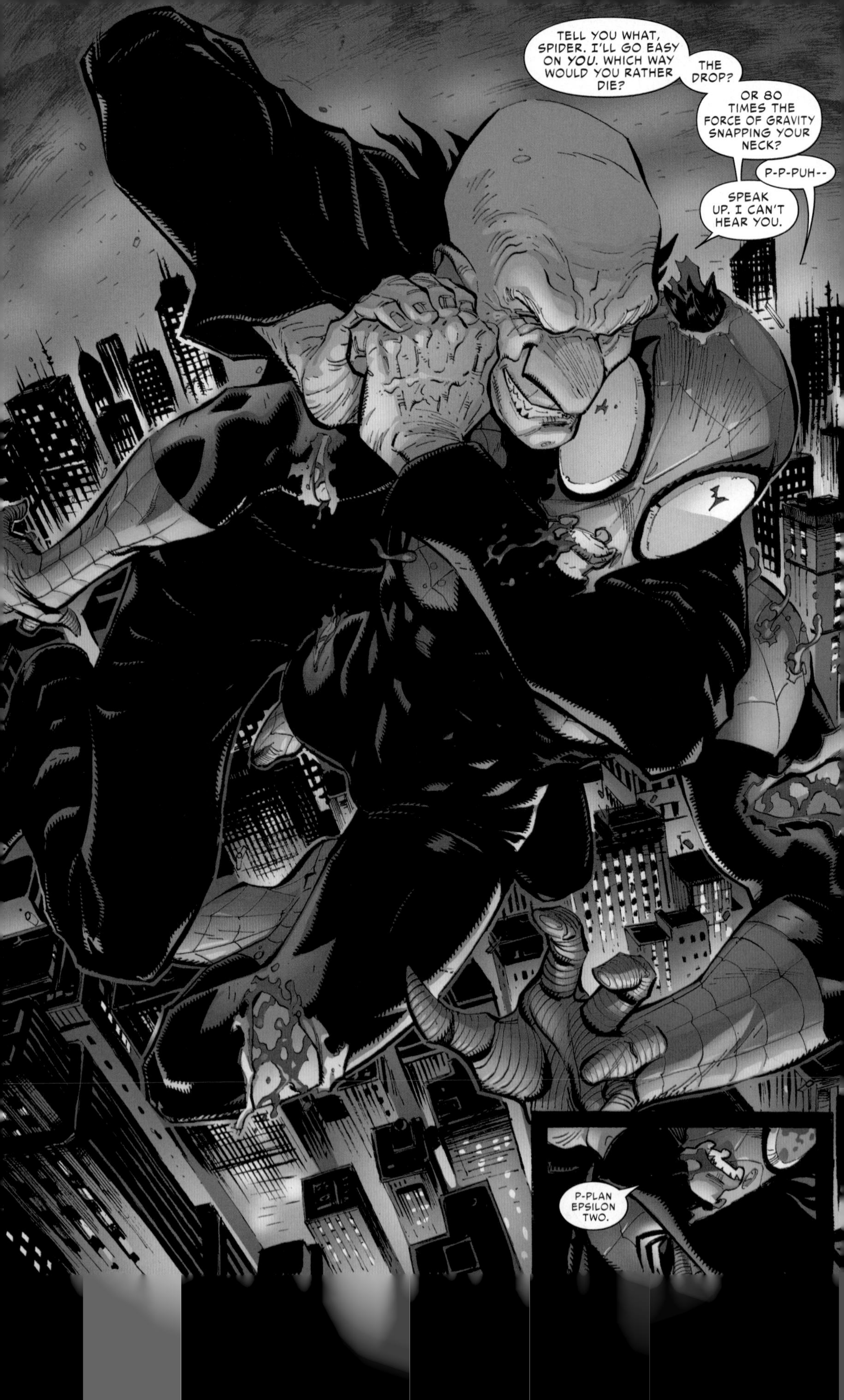
TELL YOU WHAT, SPIDER. I'LL GO EASY ON YOU. WHICH WAY WOULD YOU RATHER DIE?
THE DROP?
OR 80 TIMES THE FORCE OF GRAVITY SNAPPING YOUR NECK?
P-P-PUH--
SPEAK UP. I CAN'T HEAR YOU.
P-PLAN EPSILON TWO.

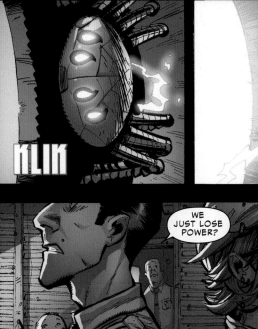

KLIK

HM

K-K-RKZZ

WE JUST LOSE POWER?

HEY, YOU HEAR THAT?

THE ROOF!

KRZZ-ZK-KK

OH MY...

HEH. ADORABLE. YOUR BUG EYES ARE BLACKING OUT.

N-NO, YOU DOLT. P-POLARIZING LENSES.

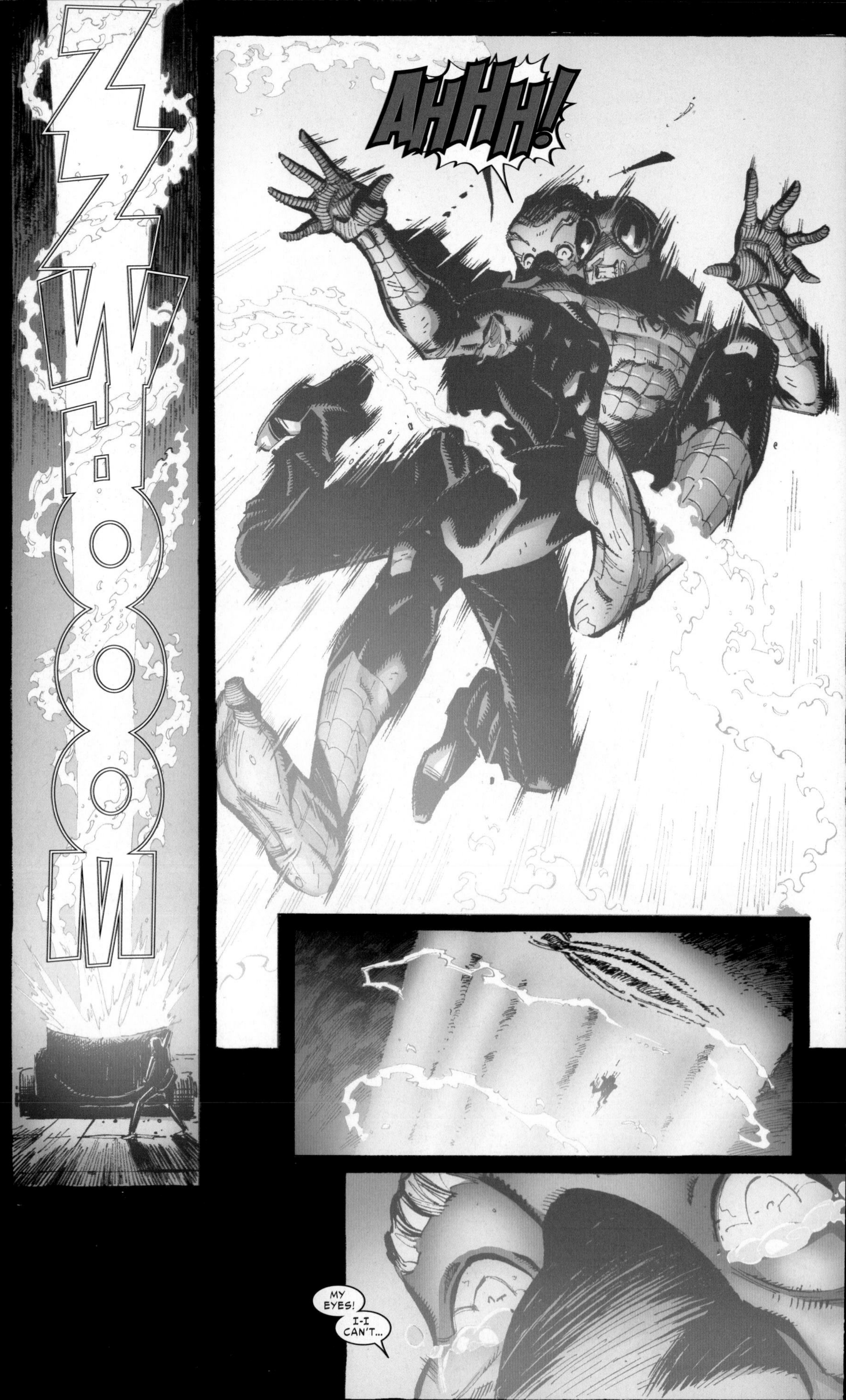

ZWHOOOM
AHHH!
MY EYES! I-I CAN'T...

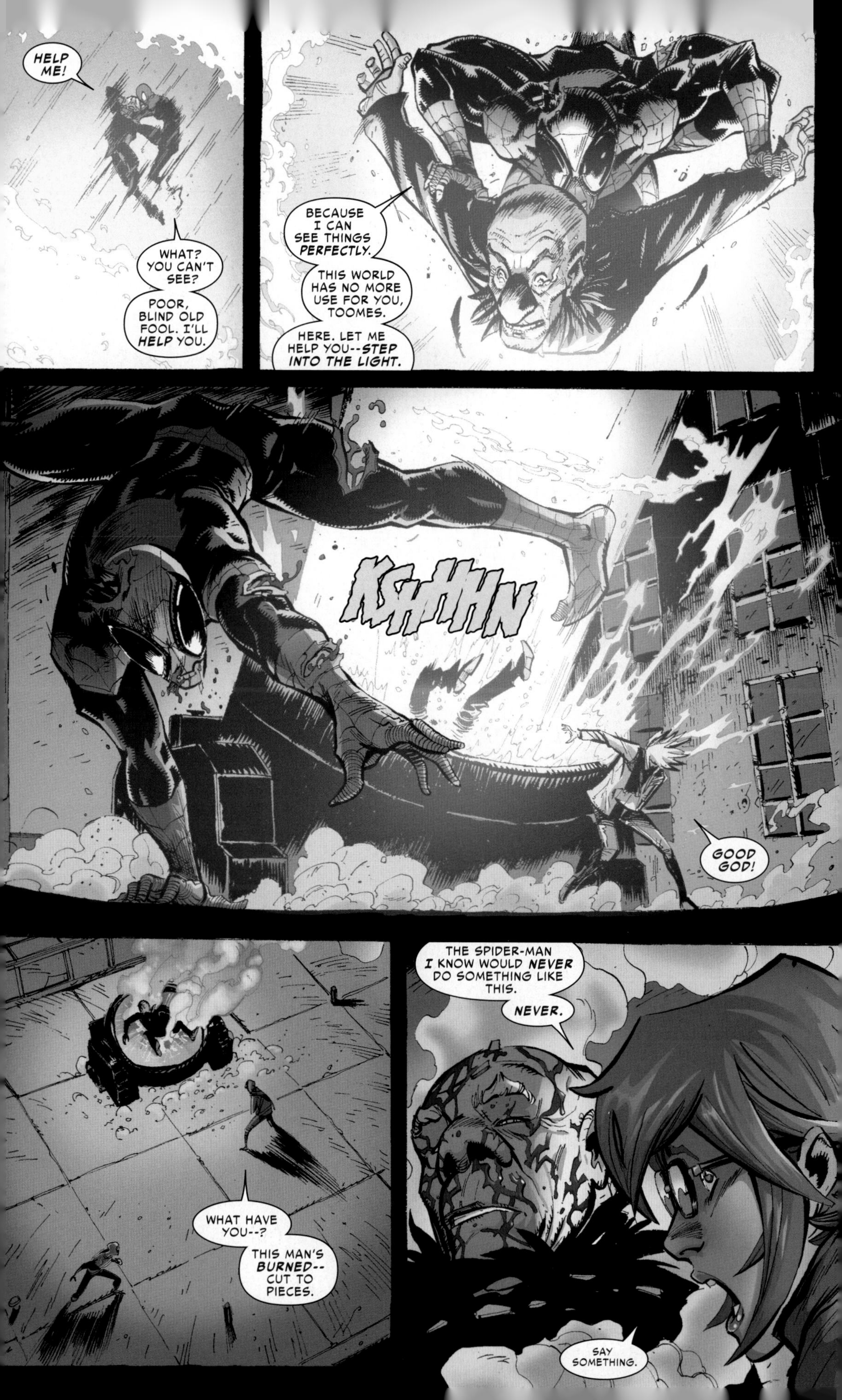

HELP ME!
WHAT? YOU CAN'T SEE?
POOR, BLIND OLD FOOL. I'LL HELP YOU.
BECAUSE I CAN SEE THINGS PERFECTLY.
THIS WORLD HAS NO MORE USE FOR YOU, TOOMES.
HERE. LET ME HELP YOU--STEP INTO THE LIGHT.
KSHHHN
GOOD GOD!
WHAT HAVE YOU--?
THIS MAN'S BURNED-- CUT TO PIECES.
THE SPIDER-MAN I KNOW WOULD NEVER DO SOMETHING LIKE THIS.
NEVER.
SAY SOMETHING.

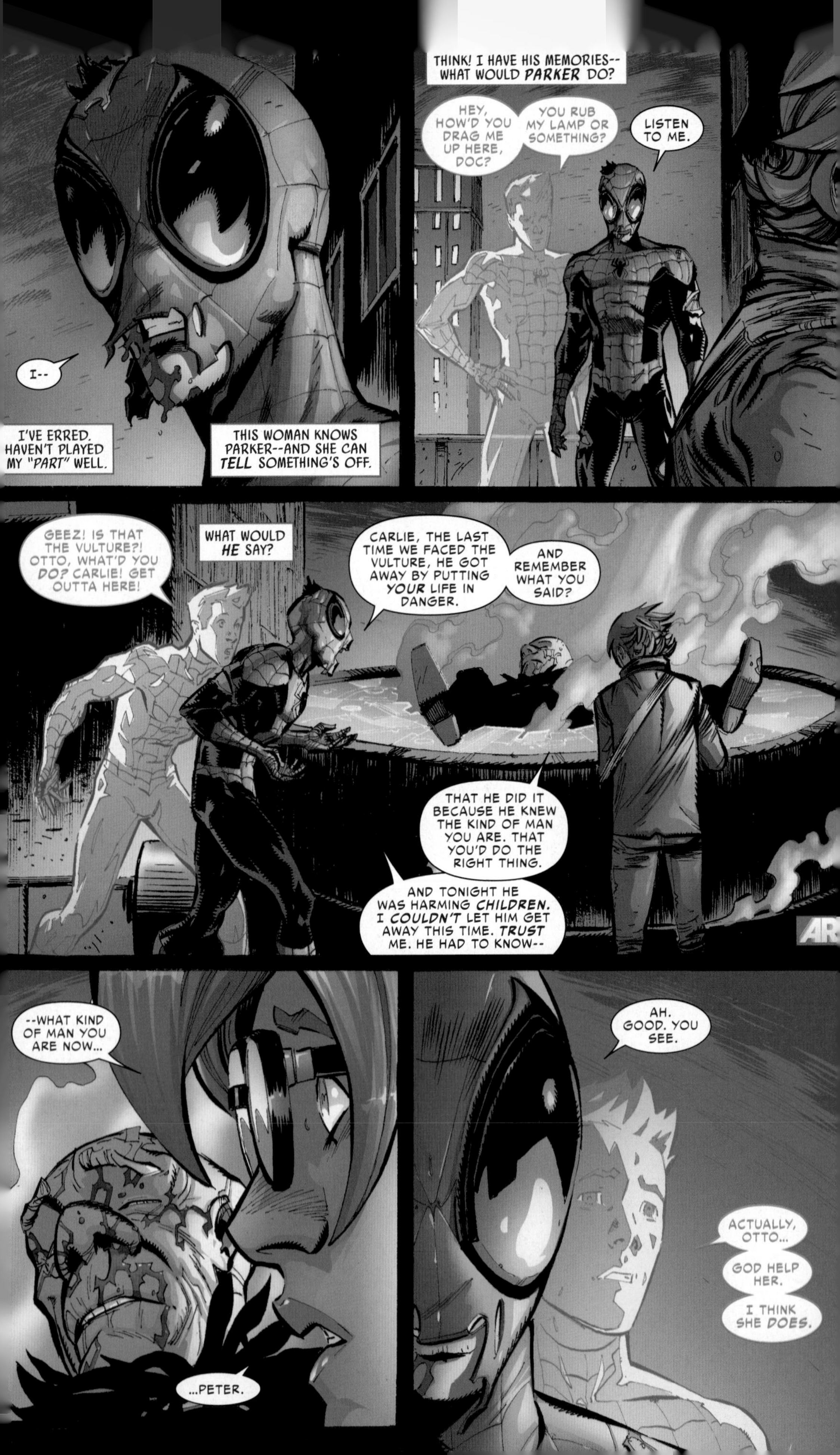
I--
I'VE ERRED. HAVEN'T PLAYED MY "PART" WELL.
THIS WOMAN KNOWS PARKER--AND SHE CAN TELL SOMETHING'S OFF.
THINK! I HAVE HIS MEMORIES-- WHAT WOULD PARKER DO?
HEY, HOW'D YOU DRAG ME UP HERE, DOC?
YOU RUB MY LAMP OR SOMETHING?
LISTEN TO ME.
GEEZ! IS THAT THE VULTURE?! OTTO, WHAT'D YOU DO? CARLIE! GET OUTTA HERE!
WHAT WOULD HE SAY?
CARLIE, THE LAST TIME WE FACED THE VULTURE, HE GOT AWAY BY PUTTING YOUR LIFE IN DANGER.
AND REMEMBER WHAT YOU SAID?
THAT HE DID IT BECAUSE HE KNEW THE KIND OF MAN YOU ARE. THAT YOU'D DO THE RIGHT THING.
AND TONIGHT HE WAS HARMING CHILDREN. I COULDN'T LET HIM GET AWAY THIS TIME. TRUST ME. HE HAD TO KNOW--
--WHAT KIND OF MAN YOU ARE NOW...
...PETER.
AH. GOOD. YOU SEE.
ACTUALLY, OTTO...
GOD HELP HER.
I THINK SHE DOES.

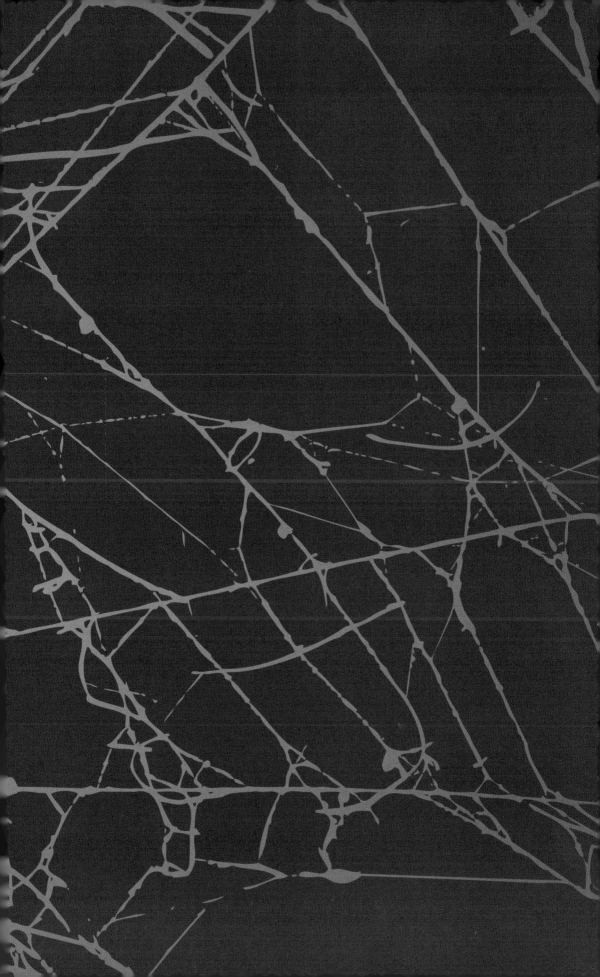

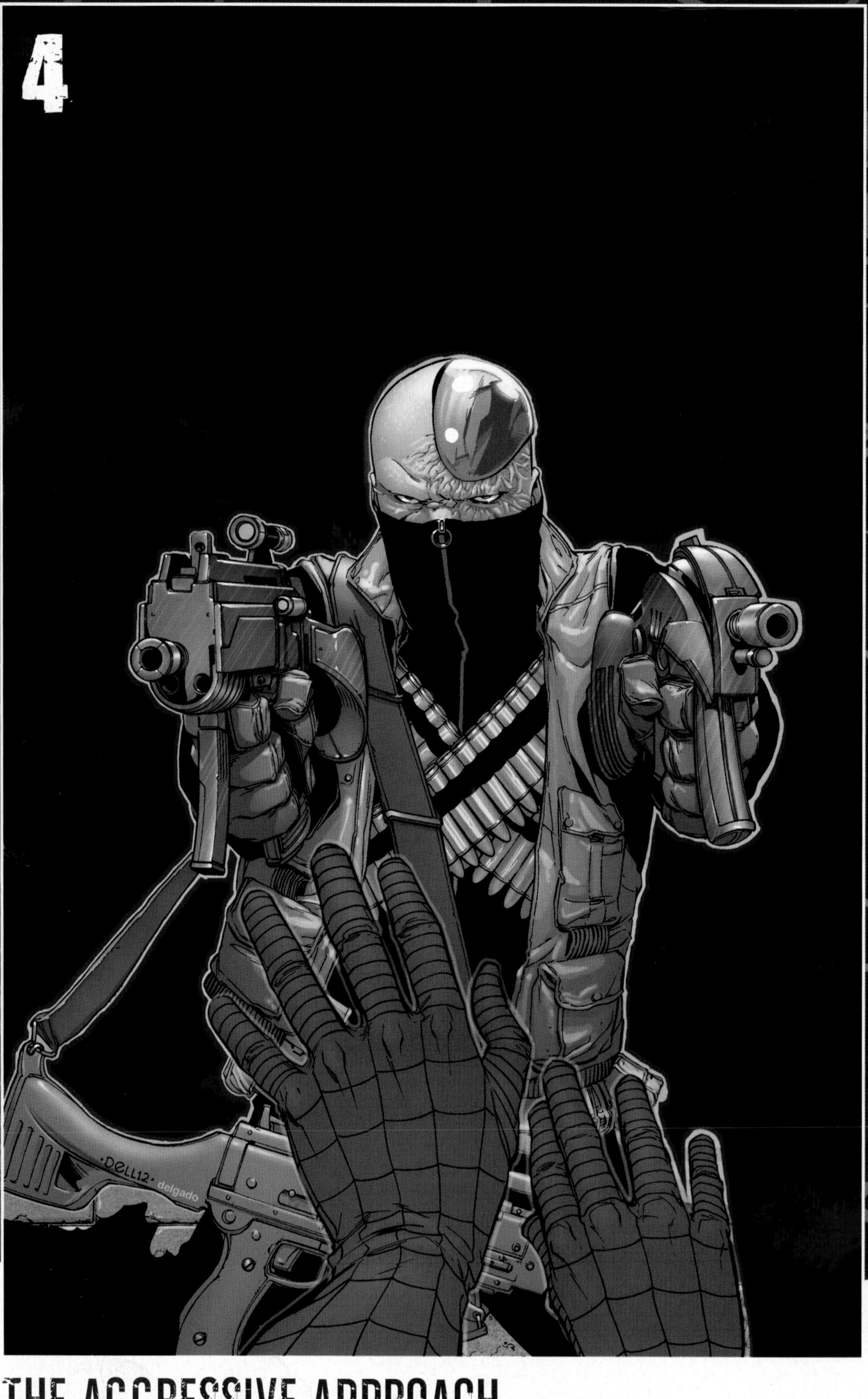

4

THE AGGRESSIVE APPROACH

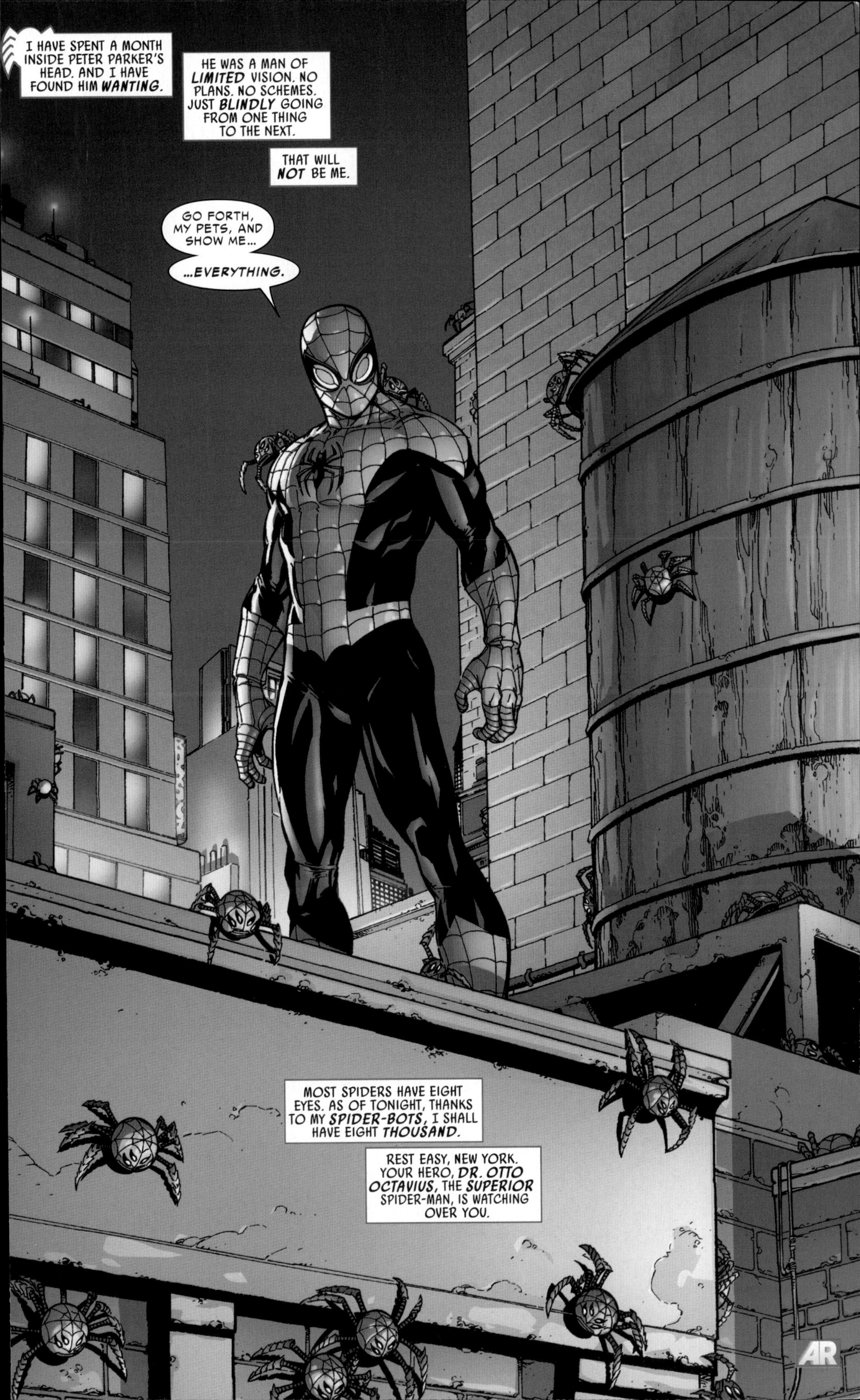
I HAVE SPENT A MONTH INSIDE PETER PARKER'S HEAD. AND I HAVE FOUND HIM WANTING.
HE WAS A MAN OF LIMITED VISION. NO PLANS. NO SCHEMES. JUST BLINDLY GOING FROM ONE THING TO THE NEXT.
THAT WILL NOT BE ME.
GO FORTH, MY PETS, AND SHOW ME...
...EVERYTHING.
MOST SPIDERS HAVE EIGHT EYES. AS OF TONIGHT, THANKS TO MY SPIDER-BOTS, I SHALL HAVE EIGHT THOUSAND.
REST EASY, NEW YORK. YOUR HERO, DR. OTTO OCTAVIUS, THE SUPERIOR SPIDER-MAN, IS WATCHING OVER YOU.

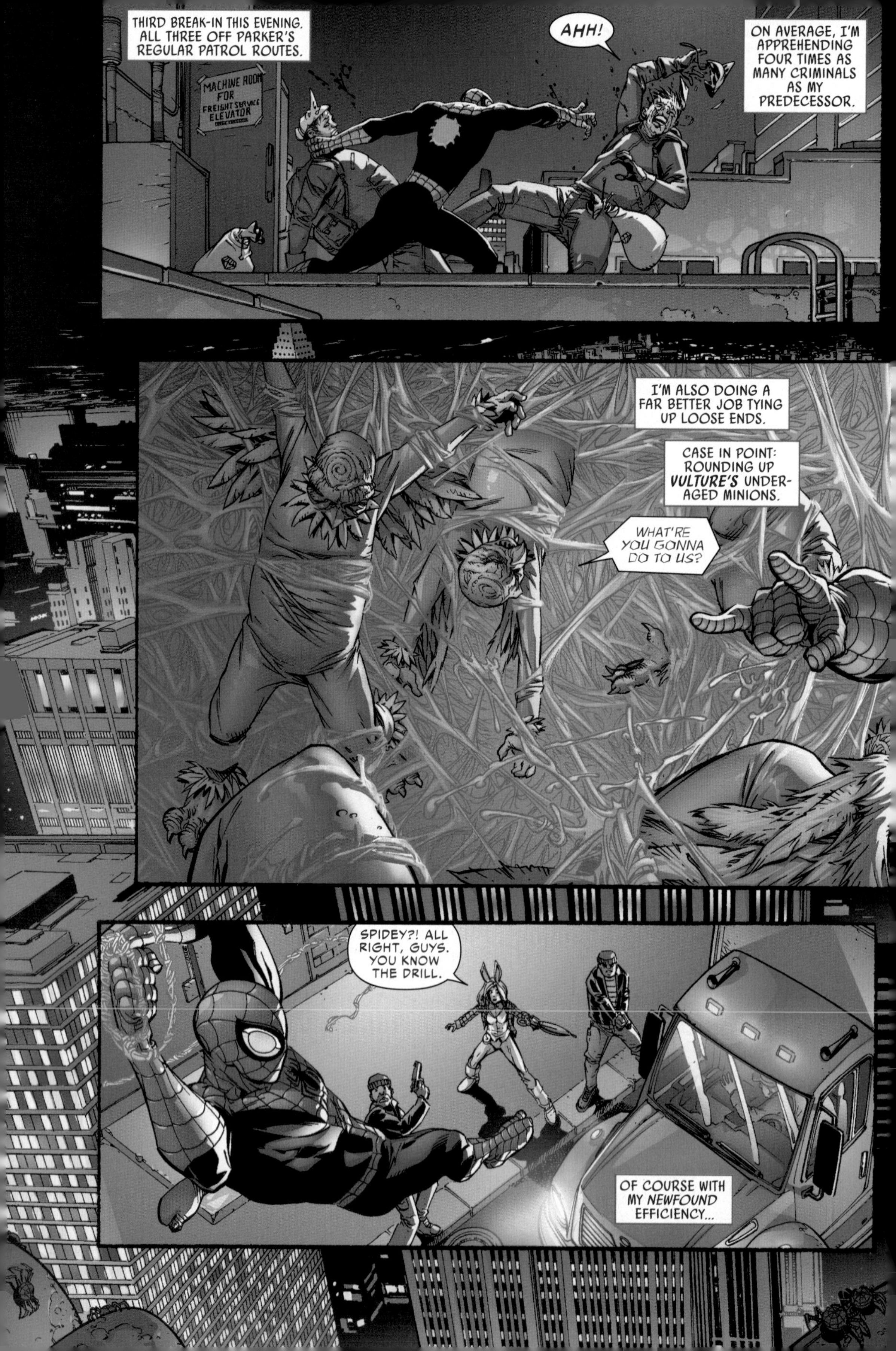
THIRD BREAK-IN THIS EVENING. ALL THREE OFF PARKER'S REGULAR PATROL ROUTES.
AHH!
ON AVERAGE, I'M APPREHENDING FOUR TIMES AS MANY CRIMINALS AS MY PREDECESSOR.
MACHINE ROOM FOR FREIGHT SERVICE ELEVATOR
I'M ALSO DOING A FAR BETTER JOB TYING UP LOOSE ENDS.
CASE IN POINT: ROUNDING UP VULTURE'S UNDER-AGED MINIONS.
WHAT'RE YOU GONNA DO TO US?
SPIDEY?! ALL RIGHT, GUYS. YOU KNOW THE DRILL.
OF COURSE WITH MY NEWFOUND EFFICIENCY...

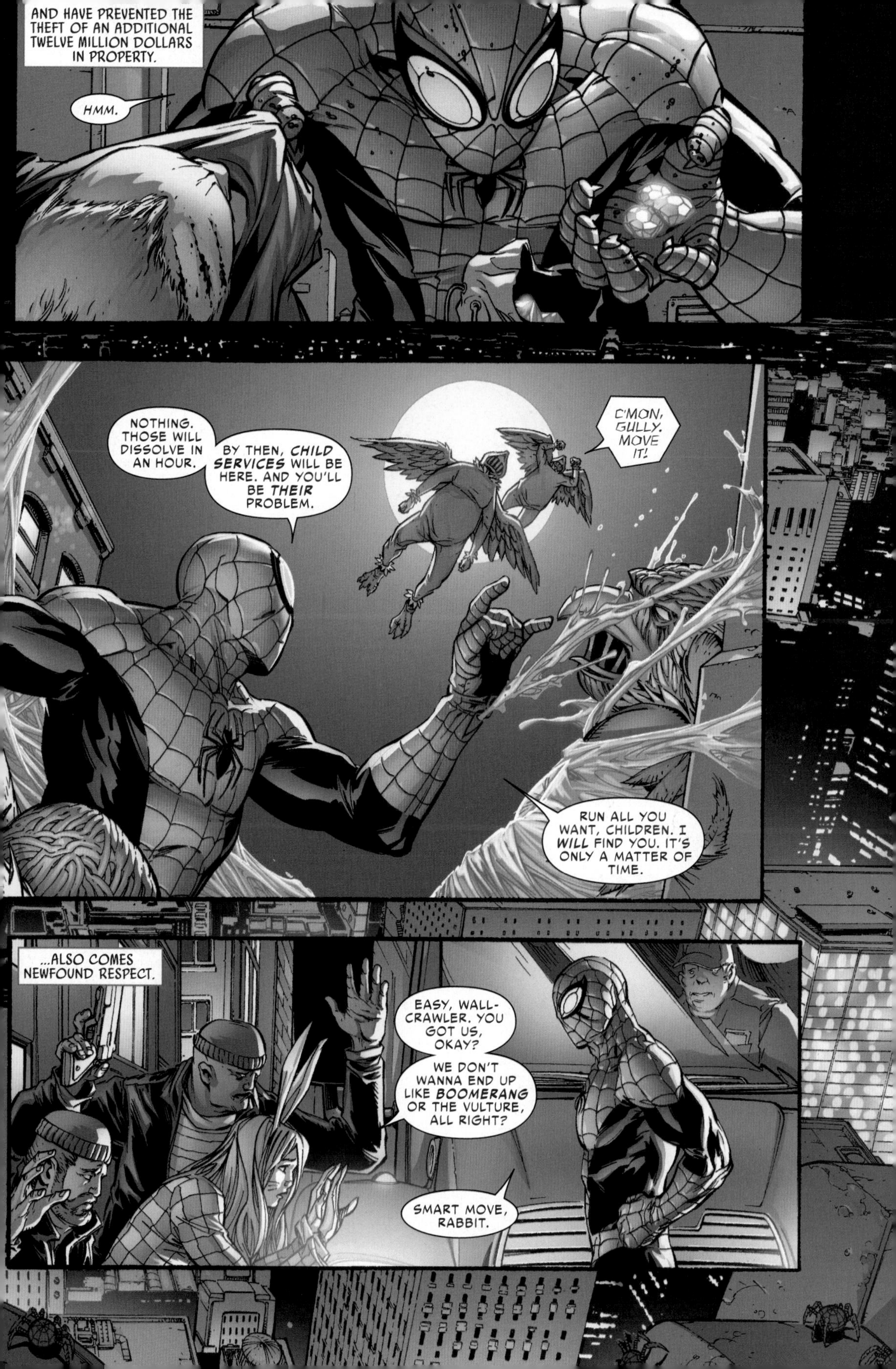
AND HAVE PREVENTED THE THEFT OF AN ADDITIONAL TWELVE MILLION DOLLARS IN PROPERTY.
HMM.
NOTHING. THOSE WILL DISSOLVE IN AN HOUR.
BY THEN, CHILD SERVICES WILL BE HERE. AND YOU'LL BE THEIR PROBLEM.
C'MON, GULLY. MOVE IT!
RUN ALL YOU WANT, CHILDREN. I WILL FIND YOU. IT'S ONLY A MATTER OF TIME.
...ALSO COMES NEWFOUND RESPECT.
EASY, WALL-CRAWLER. YOU GOT US, OKAY?
WE DON'T WANNA END UP LIKE BOOMERANG OR THE VULTURE, ALL RIGHT?
SMART MOVE, RABBIT.

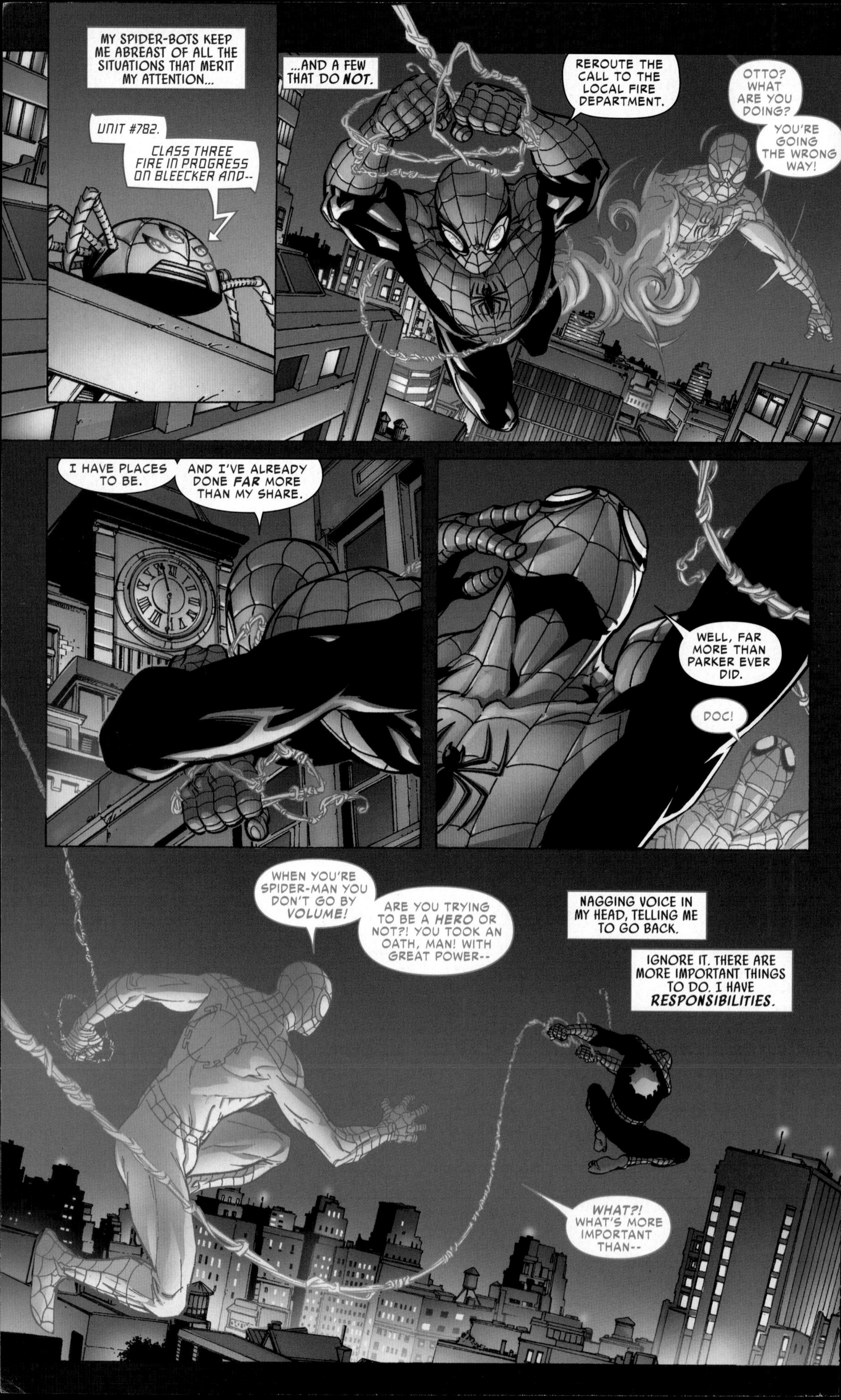

MY SPIDER-BOTS KEEP ME ABREAST OF ALL THE SITUATIONS THAT MERIT MY ATTENTION...
UNIT #782.
CLASS THREE FIRE IN PROGRESS ON BLEECKER AND--
...AND A FEW THAT DO NOT.
REROUTE THE CALL TO THE LOCAL FIRE DEPARTMENT.
OTTO? WHAT ARE YOU DOING?
YOU'RE GOING THE WRONG WAY!
I HAVE PLACES TO BE.
AND I'VE ALREADY DONE FAR MORE THAN MY SHARE.
WELL, FAR MORE THAN PARKER EVER DID.
DOC!
WHEN YOU'RE SPIDER-MAN YOU DON'T GO BY VOLUME!
ARE YOU TRYING TO BE A HERO OR NOT?! YOU TOOK AN OATH, MAN! WITH GREAT POWER--
NAGGING VOICE IN MY HEAD, TELLING ME TO GO BACK.
IGNORE IT. THERE ARE MORE IMPORTANT THINGS TO DO. I HAVE RESPONSIBILITIES.
WHAT?! WHAT'S MORE IMPORTANT THAN--

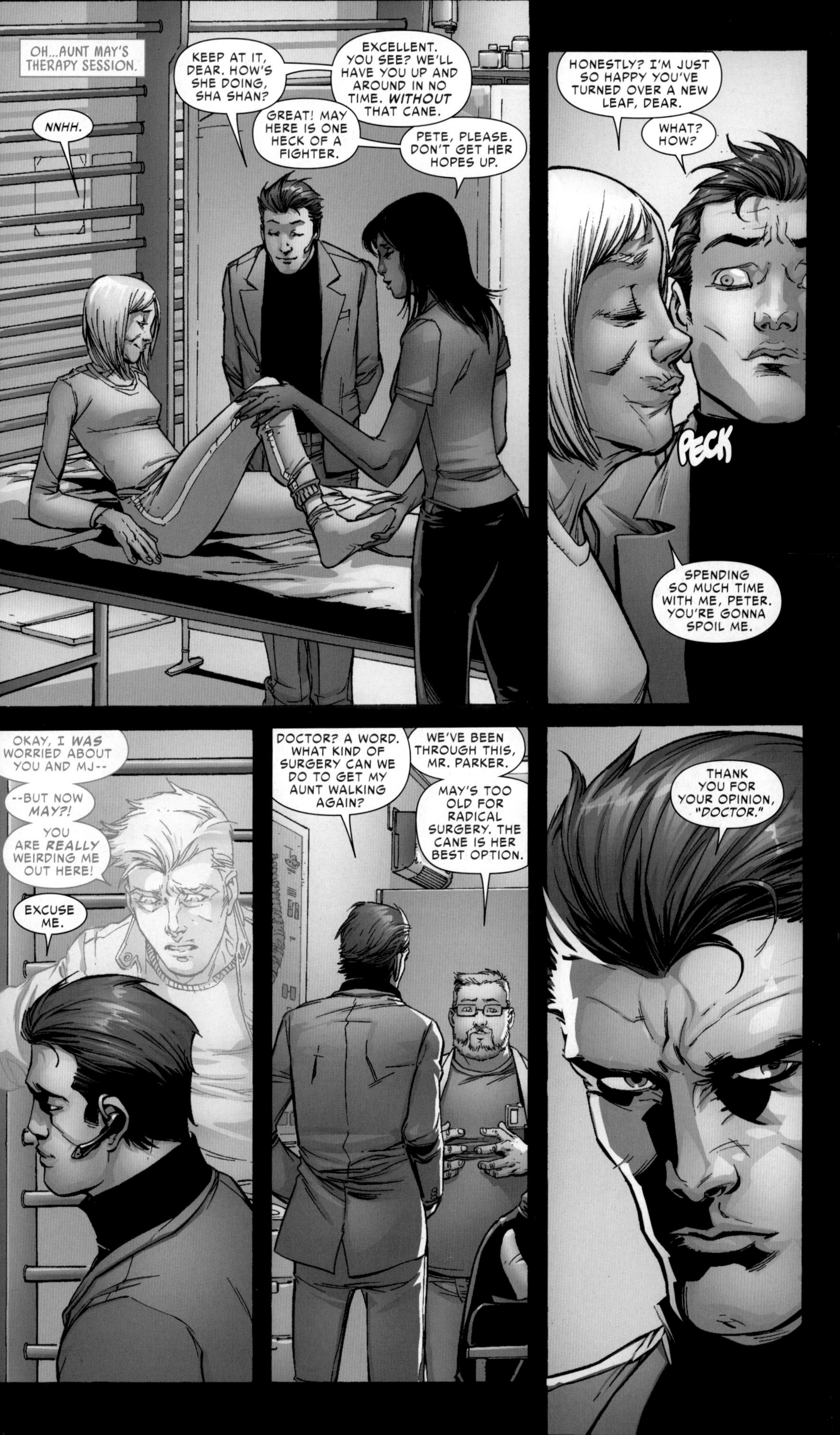

OH...AUNT MAY'S THERAPY SESSION.
NNHH.
KEEP AT IT, DEAR. HOW'S SHE DOING, SHA SHAN?
EXCELLENT. YOU SEE? WE'LL HAVE YOU UP AND AROUND IN NO TIME. WITHOUT THAT CANE.
GREAT! MAY HERE IS ONE HECK OF A FIGHTER.
PETE, PLEASE. DON'T GET HER HOPES UP.
HONESTLY? I'M JUST SO HAPPY YOU'VE TURNED OVER A NEW LEAF, DEAR.
WHAT? HOW?
PECK
SPENDING SO MUCH TIME WITH ME, PETER. YOU'RE GONNA SPOIL ME.
OKAY, I WAS WORRIED ABOUT YOU AND MJ--
--BUT NOW MAY?!
YOU ARE REALLY WEIRDING ME OUT HERE!
EXCUSE ME.
DOCTOR? A WORD. WHAT KIND OF SURGERY CAN WE DO TO GET MY AUNT WALKING AGAIN?
WE'VE BEEN THROUGH THIS, MR. PARKER.
MAY'S TOO OLD FOR RADICAL SURGERY. THE CANE IS HER BEST OPTION.
THANK YOU FOR YOUR OPINION, "DOCTOR."

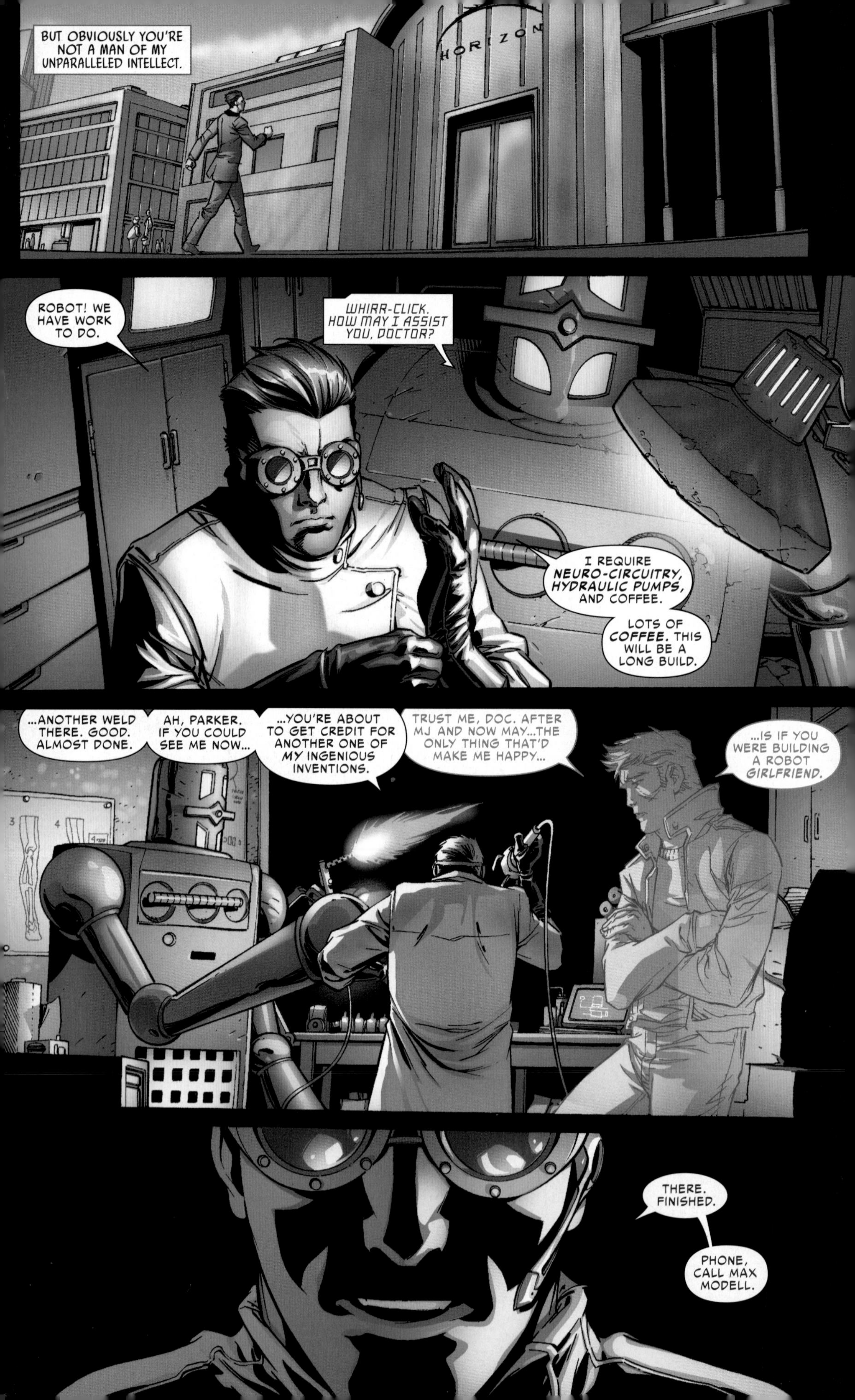

BUT OBVIOUSLY YOU'RE NOT A MAN OF MY UNPARALLELED INTELLECT.
HORIZON
ROBOT! WE HAVE WORK TO DO.
WHIRR-CLICK. HOW MAY I ASSIST YOU, DOCTOR?
I REQUIRE NEURO-CIRCUITRY, HYDRAULIC PUMPS, AND COFFEE.
LOTS OF COFFEE. THIS WILL BE A LONG BUILD.
...ANOTHER WELD THERE. GOOD. ALMOST DONE.
AH, PARKER. IF YOU COULD SEE ME NOW...
...YOU'RE ABOUT TO GET CREDIT FOR ANOTHER ONE OF MY INGENIOUS INVENTIONS.
TRUST ME, DOC. AFTER MJ AND NOW MAY...THE ONLY THING THAT'D MAKE ME HAPPY...
...IS IF YOU WERE BUILDING A ROBOT GIRLFRIEND.
THERE. FINISHED.
PHONE, CALL MAX MODELL.

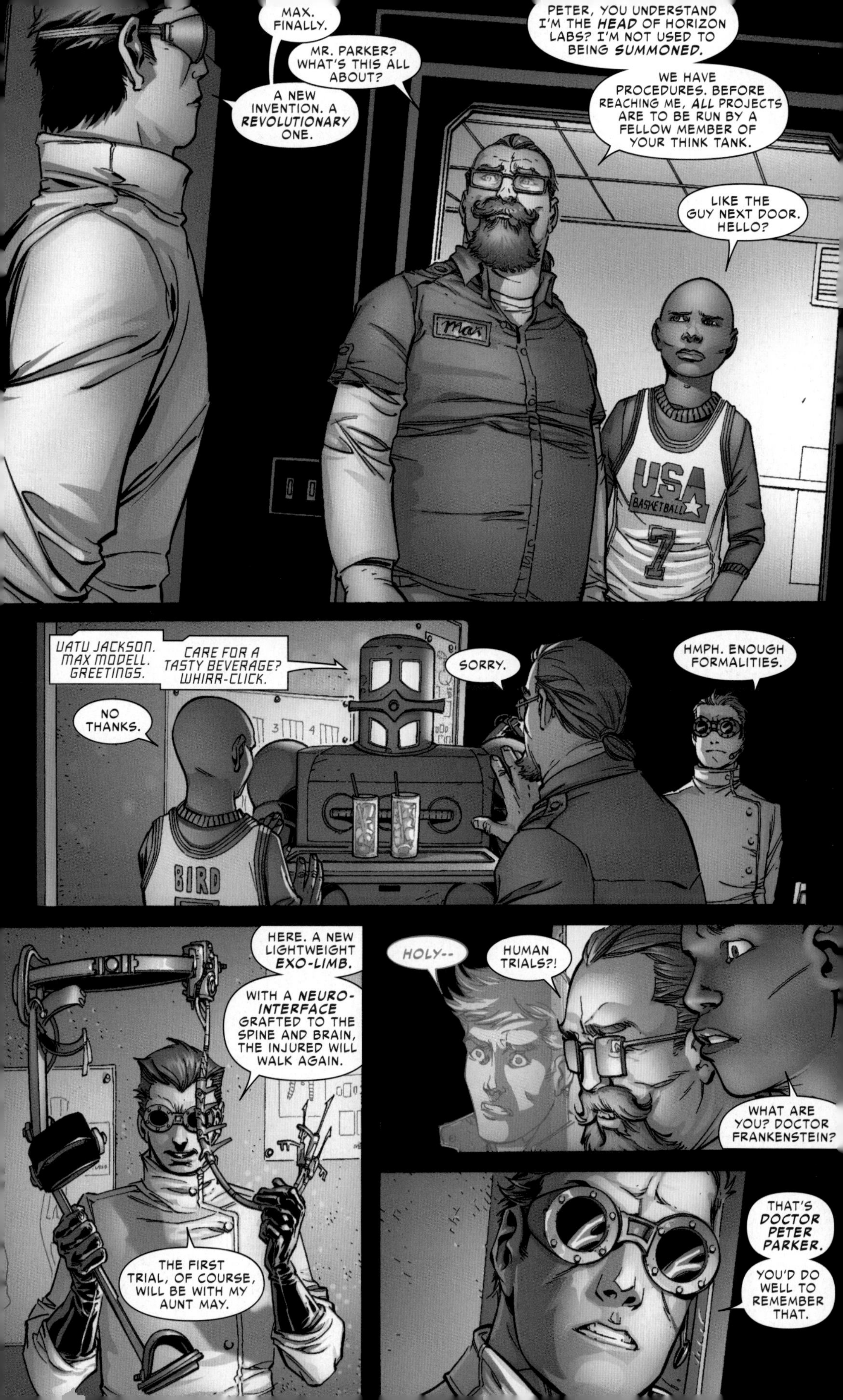

MAX. FINALLY.
MR. PARKER? WHAT'S THIS ALL ABOUT?
A NEW INVENTION. A REVOLUTIONARY ONE.
PETER, YOU UNDERSTAND I'M THE HEAD OF HORIZON LABS? I'M NOT USED TO BEING SUMMONED.
WE HAVE PROCEDURES. BEFORE REACHING ME, ALL PROJECTS ARE TO BE RUN BY A FELLOW MEMBER OF YOUR THINK TANK.
LIKE THE GUY NEXT DOOR. HELLO?
MAX
USA BASKETBALL 7
UATU JACKSON. MAX MODELL. GREETINGS.
CARE FOR A TASTY BEVERAGE? WHIRR-CLICK.
NO THANKS.
SORRY.
HMPH. ENOUGH FORMALITIES.
BIRD
HERE. A NEW LIGHTWEIGHT EXO-LIMB.
WITH A NEURO-INTERFACE GRAFTED TO THE SPINE AND BRAIN, THE INJURED WILL WALK AGAIN.
THE FIRST TRIAL, OF COURSE, WILL BE WITH MY AUNT MAY.
HOLY--
HUMAN TRIALS?!
WHAT ARE YOU? DOCTOR FRANKENSTEIN?
THAT'S DOCTOR PETER PARKER.
YOU'D DO WELL TO REMEMBER THAT.

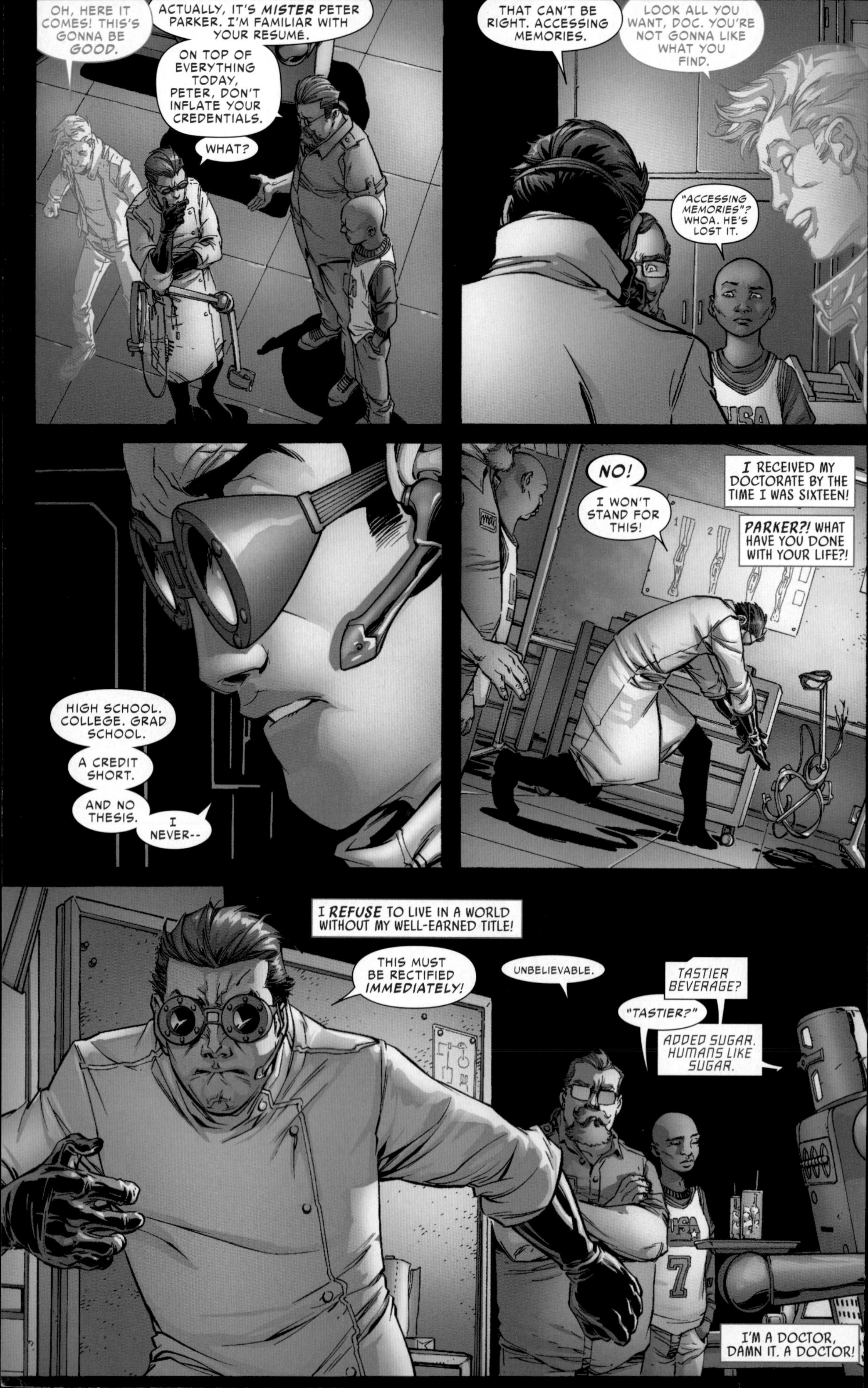
OH, HERE IT COMES! THIS'S GONNA BE GOOD.
ACTUALLY, IT'S MISTER PETER PARKER. I'M FAMILIAR WITH YOUR RESUMÉ.
ON TOP OF EVERYTHING TODAY, PETER, DON'T INFLATE YOUR CREDENTIALS.
WHAT?
THAT CAN'T BE RIGHT. ACCESSING MEMORIES.
LOOK ALL YOU WANT, DOC. YOU'RE NOT GONNA LIKE WHAT YOU FIND.
"ACCESSING MEMORIES"? WHOA. HE'S LOST IT.
HIGH SCHOOL. COLLEGE. GRAD SCHOOL.
A CREDIT SHORT.
AND NO THESIS.
I NEVER--
NO!
I WON'T STAND FOR THIS!
I RECEIVED MY DOCTORATE BY THE TIME I WAS SIXTEEN!
PARKER?! WHAT HAVE YOU DONE WITH YOUR LIFE?!
I REFUSE TO LIVE IN A WORLD WITHOUT MY WELL-EARNED TITLE!
THIS MUST BE RECTIFIED IMMEDIATELY!
UNBELIEVABLE.
TASTIER BEVERAGE?
"TASTIER?"
ADDED SUGAR. HUMANS LIKE SUGAR.
I'M A DOCTOR, DAMN IT. A DOCTOR!

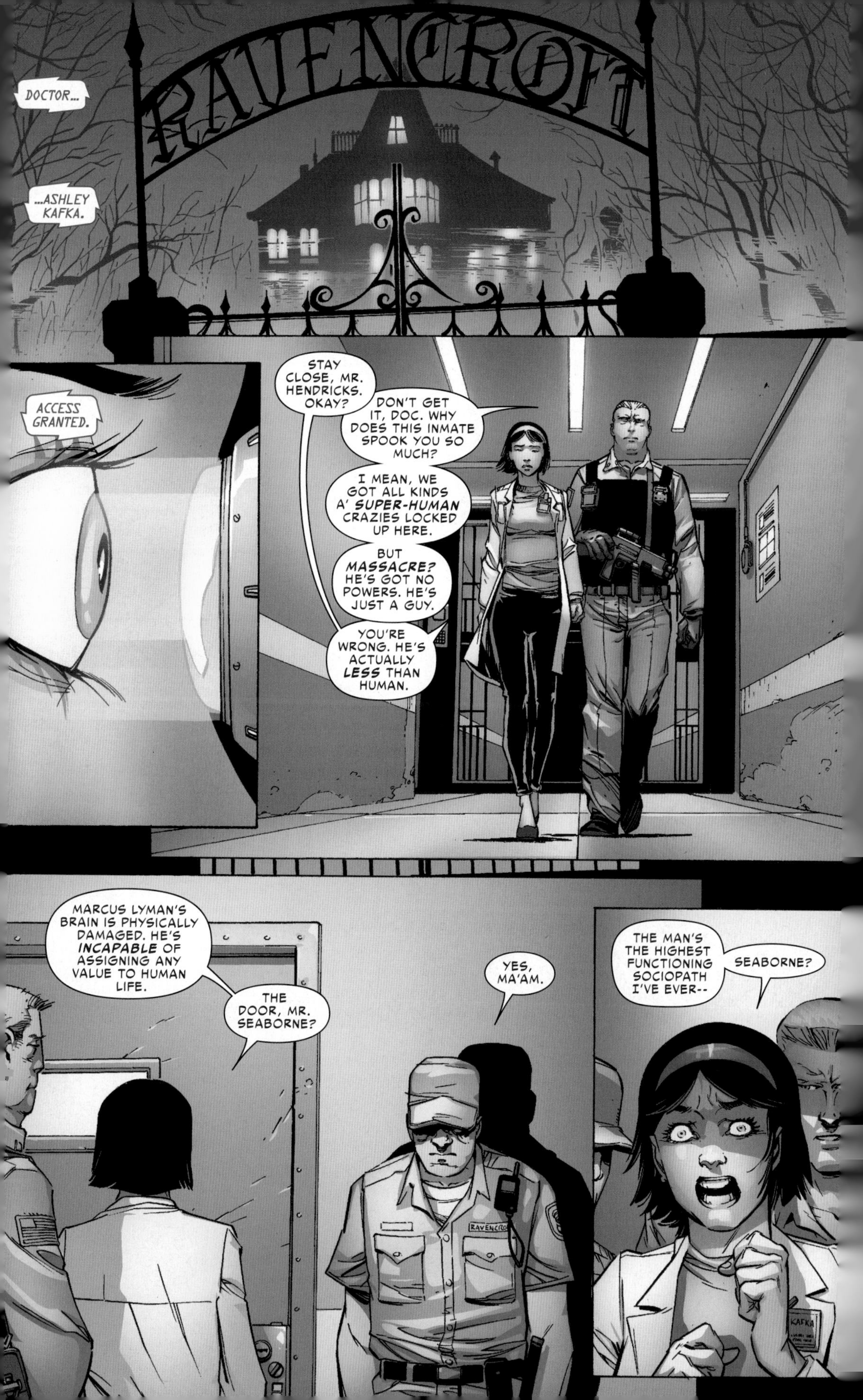
RAVENCROFT
DOCTOR...
...ASHLEY KAFKA.
ACCESS GRANTED.
STAY CLOSE, MR. HENDRICKS. OKAY?
DON'T GET IT, DOC. WHY DOES THIS INMATE SPOOK YOU SO MUCH?
I MEAN, WE GOT ALL KINDS A' SUPER-HUMAN CRAZIES LOCKED UP HERE.
BUT MASSACRE? HE'S GOT NO POWERS. HE'S JUST A GUY.
YOU'RE WRONG. HE'S ACTUALLY LESS THAN HUMAN.
MARCUS LYMAN'S BRAIN IS PHYSICALLY DAMAGED. HE'S INCAPABLE OF ASSIGNING ANY VALUE TO HUMAN LIFE.
THE DOOR, MR. SEABORNE?
YES, MA'AM.
THE MAN'S THE HIGHEST FUNCTIONING SOCIOPATH I'VE EVER--
SEABORNE?
KAFKA

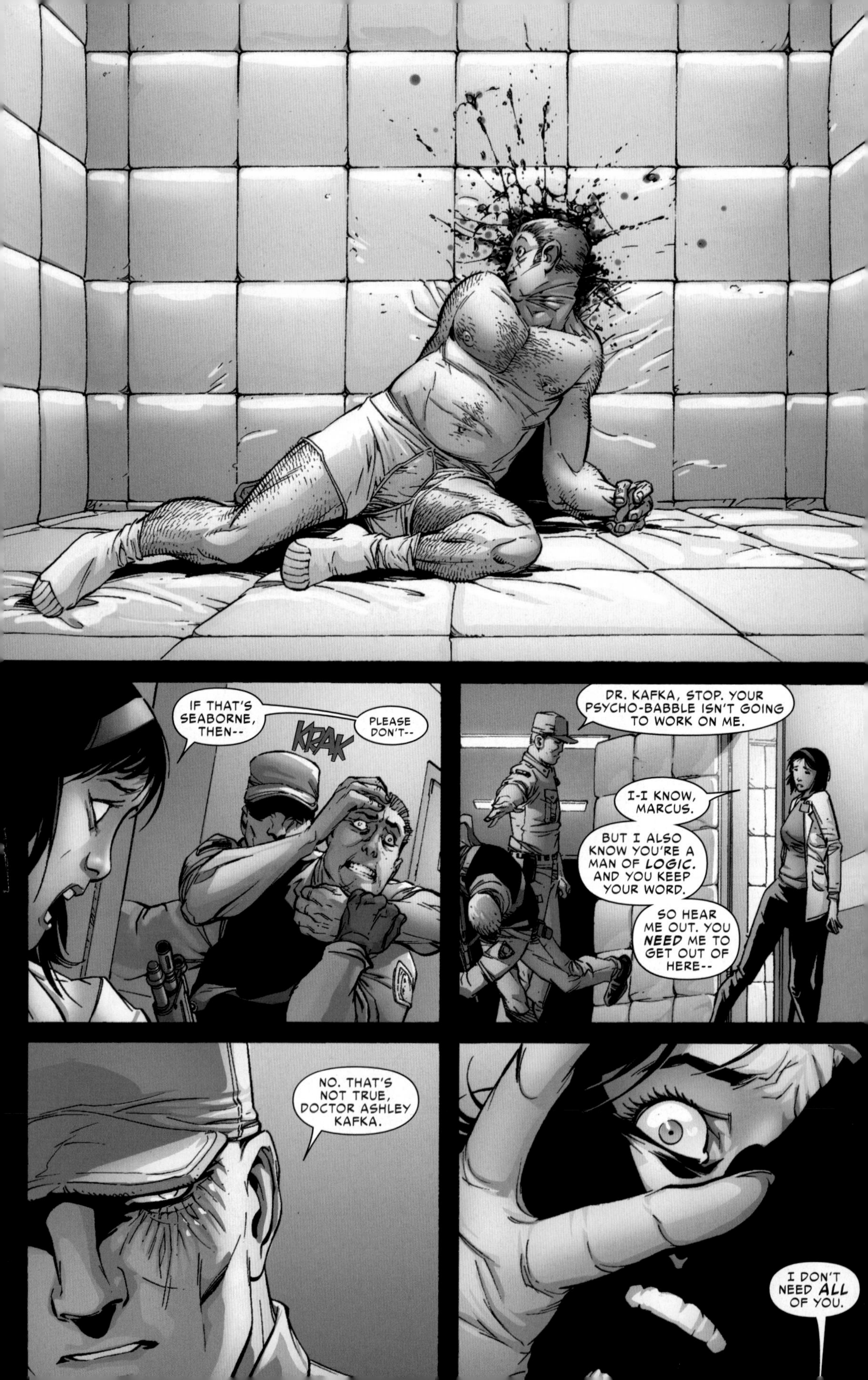
IF THAT'S SEABORNE, THEN--
PLEASE DON'T--
KRAK
DR. KAFKA, STOP. YOUR PSYCHO-BABBLE ISN'T GOING TO WORK ON ME.
I-I KNOW, MARCUS.
BUT I ALSO KNOW YOU'RE A MAN OF *LOGIC.* AND YOU KEEP YOUR WORD.
SO HEAR ME OUT. YOU *NEED* ME TO GET OUT OF HERE--
NO. THAT'S NOT TRUE, DOCTOR ASHLEY KAFKA.
I DON'T NEED *ALL* OF YOU.

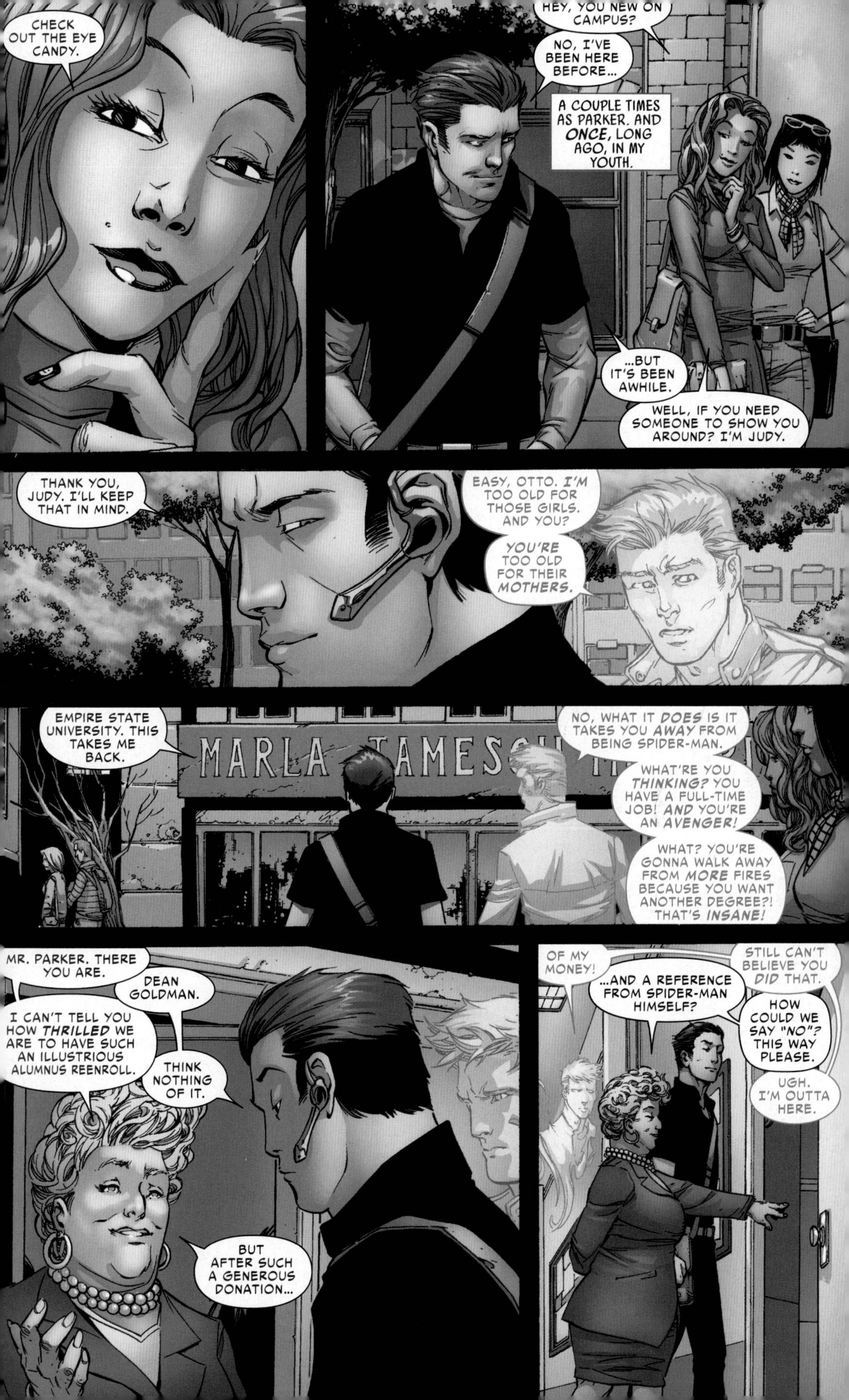

CHECK OUT THE EYE CANDY.
HEY, YOU NEW ON CAMPUS?
NO, I'VE BEEN HERE BEFORE...
A COUPLE TIMES AS PARKER. AND ONCE, LONG AGO, IN MY YOUTH.
...BUT IT'S BEEN AWHILE.
WELL, IF YOU NEED SOMEONE TO SHOW YOU AROUND? I'M JUDY.
THANK YOU, JUDY. I'LL KEEP THAT IN MIND.
EASY, OTTO. I'M TOO OLD FOR THOSE GIRLS. AND YOU?
YOU'RE TOO OLD FOR THEIR MOTHERS.
EMPIRE STATE UNIVERSITY. THIS TAKES ME BACK.
MARLA JAMESO
NO, WHAT IT DOES IS IT TAKES YOU AWAY FROM BEING SPIDER-MAN.
WHAT'RE YOU THINKING? YOU HAVE A FULL-TIME JOB! AND YOU'RE AN AVENGER!
WHAT? YOU'RE GONNA WALK AWAY FROM MORE FIRES BECAUSE YOU WANT ANOTHER DEGREE?! THAT'S INSANE!
MR. PARKER. THERE YOU ARE.
DEAN GOLDMAN.
I CAN'T TELL YOU HOW THRILLED WE ARE TO HAVE SUCH AN ILLUSTRIOUS ALUMNUS REENROLL.
THINK NOTHING OF IT.
BUT AFTER SUCH A GENEROUS DONATION...
OF MY MONEY!
...AND A REFERENCE FROM SPIDER-MAN HIMSELF?
STILL CAN'T BELIEVE YOU DID THAT.
HOW COULD WE SAY "NO"? THIS WAY PLEASE.
UGH. I'M OUTTA HERE.

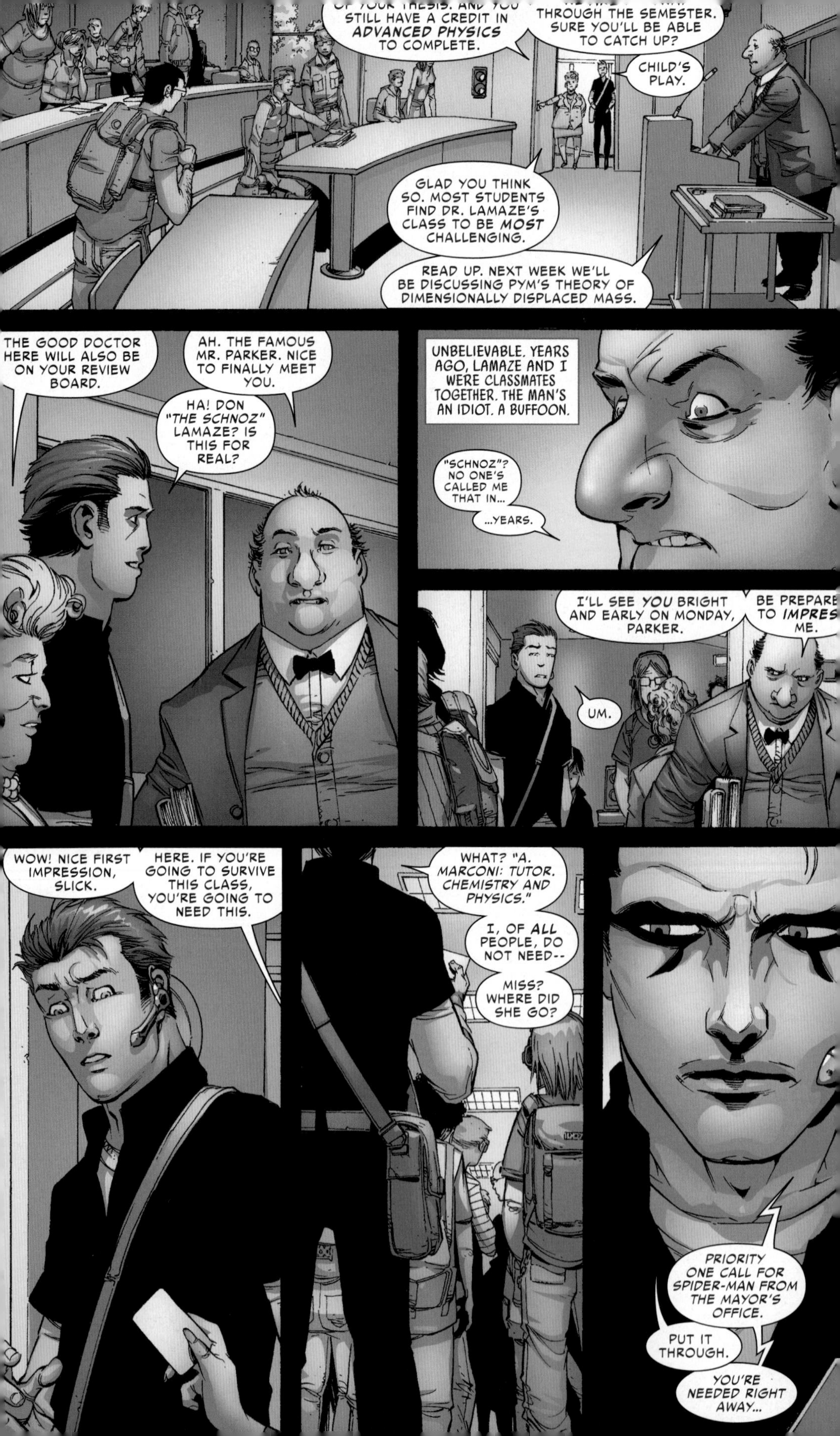
STILL HAVE A CREDIT IN ADVANCED PHYSICS TO COMPLETE.
THROUGH THE SEMESTER. SURE YOU'LL BE ABLE TO CATCH UP?
CHILD'S PLAY.
GLAD YOU THINK SO. MOST STUDENTS FIND DR. LAMAZE'S CLASS TO BE MOST CHALLENGING.
READ UP. NEXT WEEK WE'LL BE DISCUSSING PYM'S THEORY OF DIMENSIONALLY DISPLACED MASS.
THE GOOD DOCTOR HERE WILL ALSO BE ON YOUR REVIEW BOARD.
AH. THE FAMOUS MR. PARKER. NICE TO FINALLY MEET YOU.
HA! DON "THE SCHNOZ" LAMAZE? IS THIS FOR REAL?
UNBELIEVABLE. YEARS AGO, LAMAZE AND I WERE CLASSMATES TOGETHER. THE MAN'S AN IDIOT. A BUFFOON.
"SCHNOZ"? NO ONE'S CALLED ME THAT IN...
...YEARS.
I'LL SEE YOU BRIGHT AND EARLY ON MONDAY, PARKER.
UM.
WOW! NICE FIRST IMPRESSION, SLICK.
HERE. IF YOU'RE GOING TO SURVIVE THIS CLASS, YOU'RE GOING TO NEED THIS.
WHAT? "A. MARCONI: TUTOR. CHEMISTRY AND PHYSICS."
I, OF ALL PEOPLE, DO NOT NEED--
MISS? WHERE DID SHE GO?
PRIORITY ONE CALL FOR SPIDER-MAN FROM THE MAYOR'S OFFICE.
PUT IT THROUGH.
YOU'RE NEEDED RIGHT AWAY...

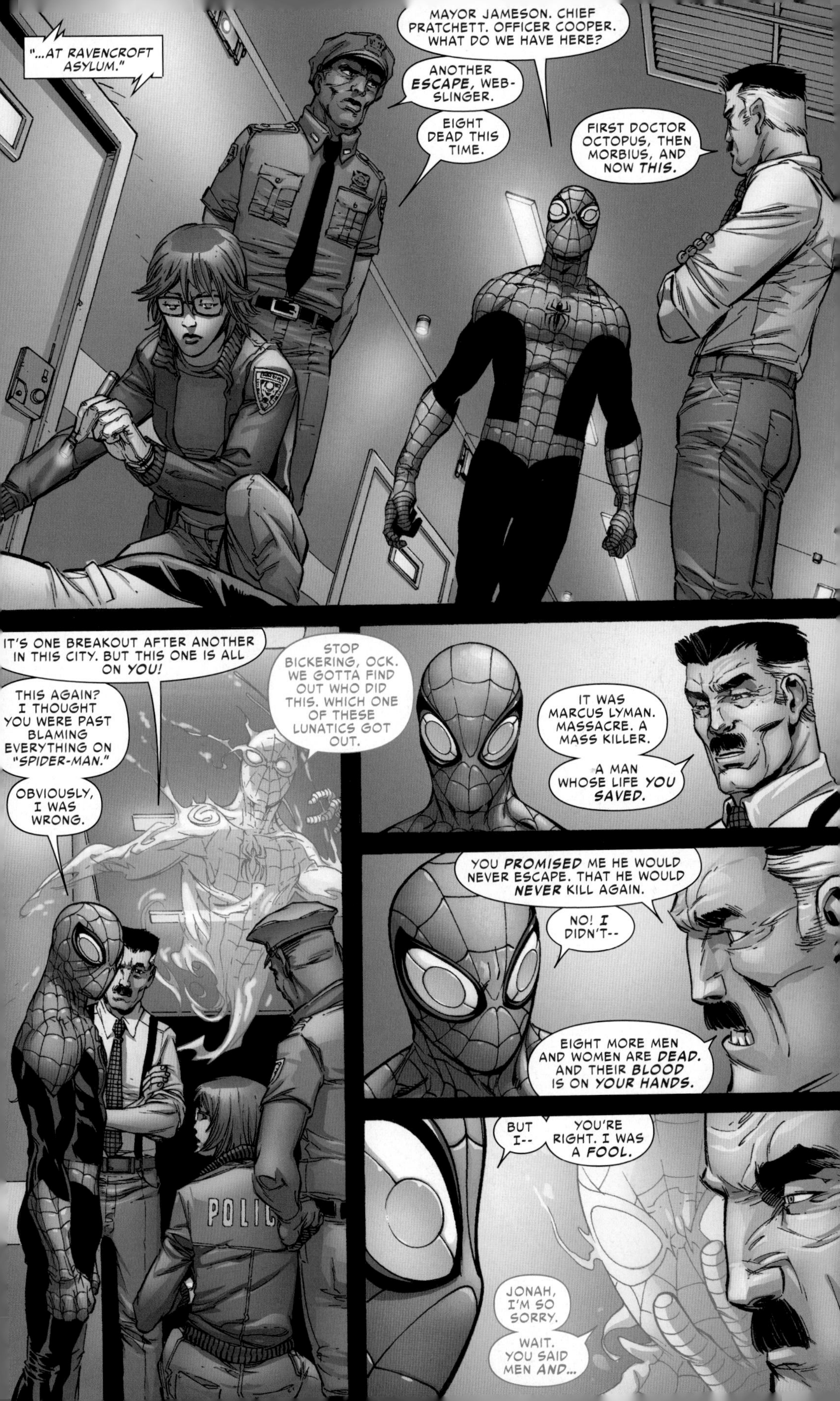

"...AT RAVENCROFT ASYLUM."
MAYOR JAMESON. CHIEF PRATCHETT. OFFICER COOPER. WHAT DO WE HAVE HERE?
ANOTHER ESCAPE, WEB-SLINGER.
EIGHT DEAD THIS TIME.
FIRST DOCTOR OCTOPUS, THEN MORBIUS, AND NOW THIS.
IT'S ONE BREAKOUT AFTER ANOTHER IN THIS CITY. BUT THIS ONE IS ALL ON YOU!
THIS AGAIN? I THOUGHT YOU WERE PAST BLAMING EVERYTHING ON "SPIDER-MAN."
OBVIOUSLY, I WAS WRONG.
STOP BICKERING, OCK. WE GOTTA FIND OUT WHO DID THIS. WHICH ONE OF THESE LUNATICS GOT OUT.
POLIC
IT WAS MARCUS LYMAN. MASSACRE. A MASS KILLER.
A MAN WHOSE LIFE YOU SAVED.
YOU PROMISED ME HE WOULD NEVER ESCAPE. THAT HE WOULD NEVER KILL AGAIN.
NO! I DIDN'T--
EIGHT MORE MEN AND WOMEN ARE DEAD. AND THEIR BLOOD IS ON YOUR HANDS.
BUT I--
YOU'RE RIGHT. I WAS A FOOL.
JONAH, I'M SO SORRY.
WAIT. YOU SAID MEN AND...

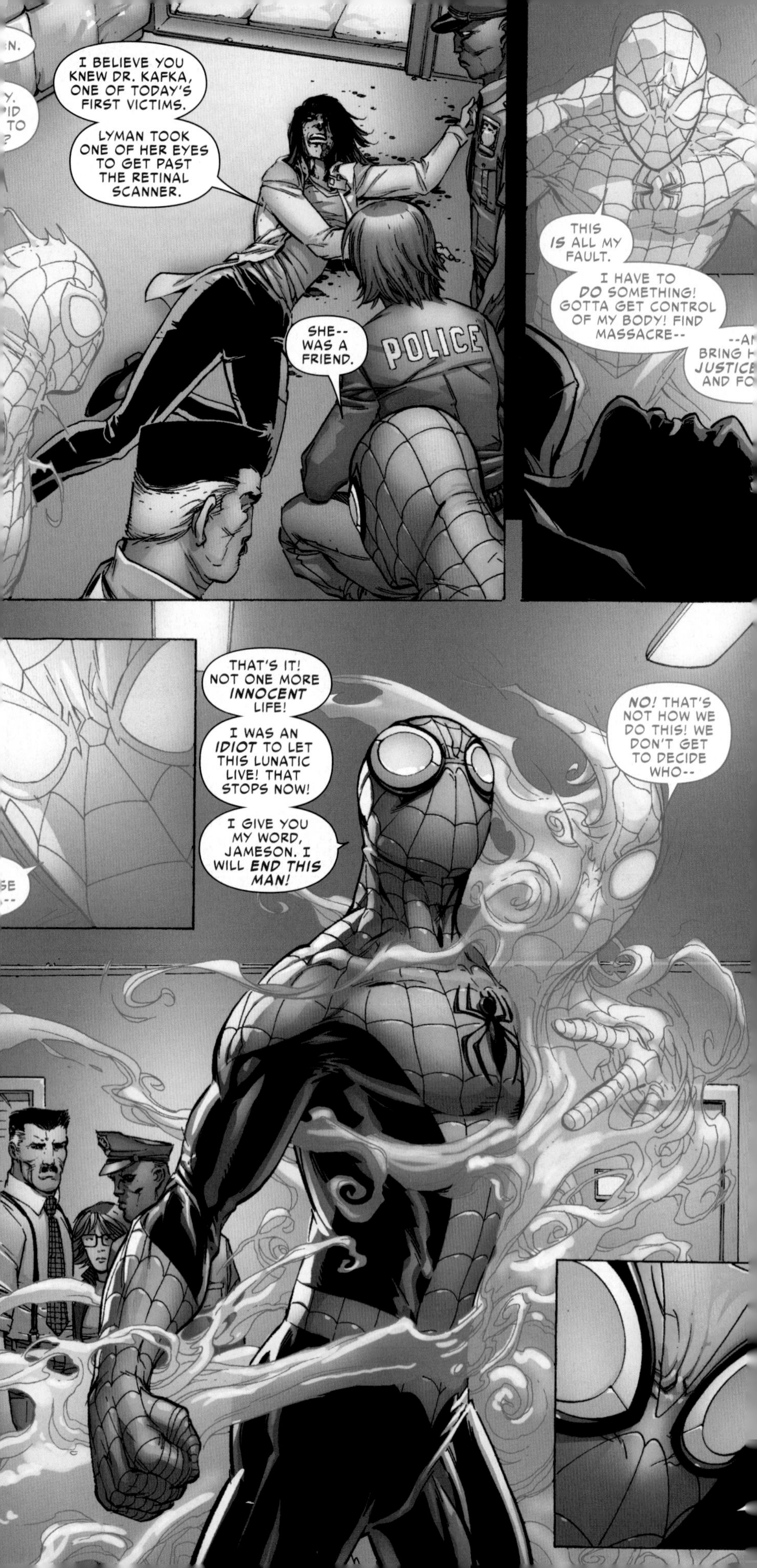

I BELIEVE YOU KNEW DR. KAFKA, ONE OF TODAY'S FIRST VICTIMS.
LYMAN TOOK ONE OF HER EYES TO GET PAST THE RETINAL SCANNER.
POLICE
SHE-- WAS A FRIEND.
THIS *IS* ALL MY FAULT.
I HAVE TO *DO* SOMETHING! GOTTA GET CONTROL OF MY BODY! FIND MASSACRE--
THAT'S IT! NOT ONE MORE ***INNOCENT*** LIFE!
I WAS AN ***IDIOT*** TO LET THIS LUNATIC LIVE! THAT STOPS NOW!
I GIVE YOU MY WORD, JAMESON. I WILL ***END THIS MAN!***
NO! THAT'S NOT HOW WE DO THIS! WE DON'T GET TO DECIDE WHO--

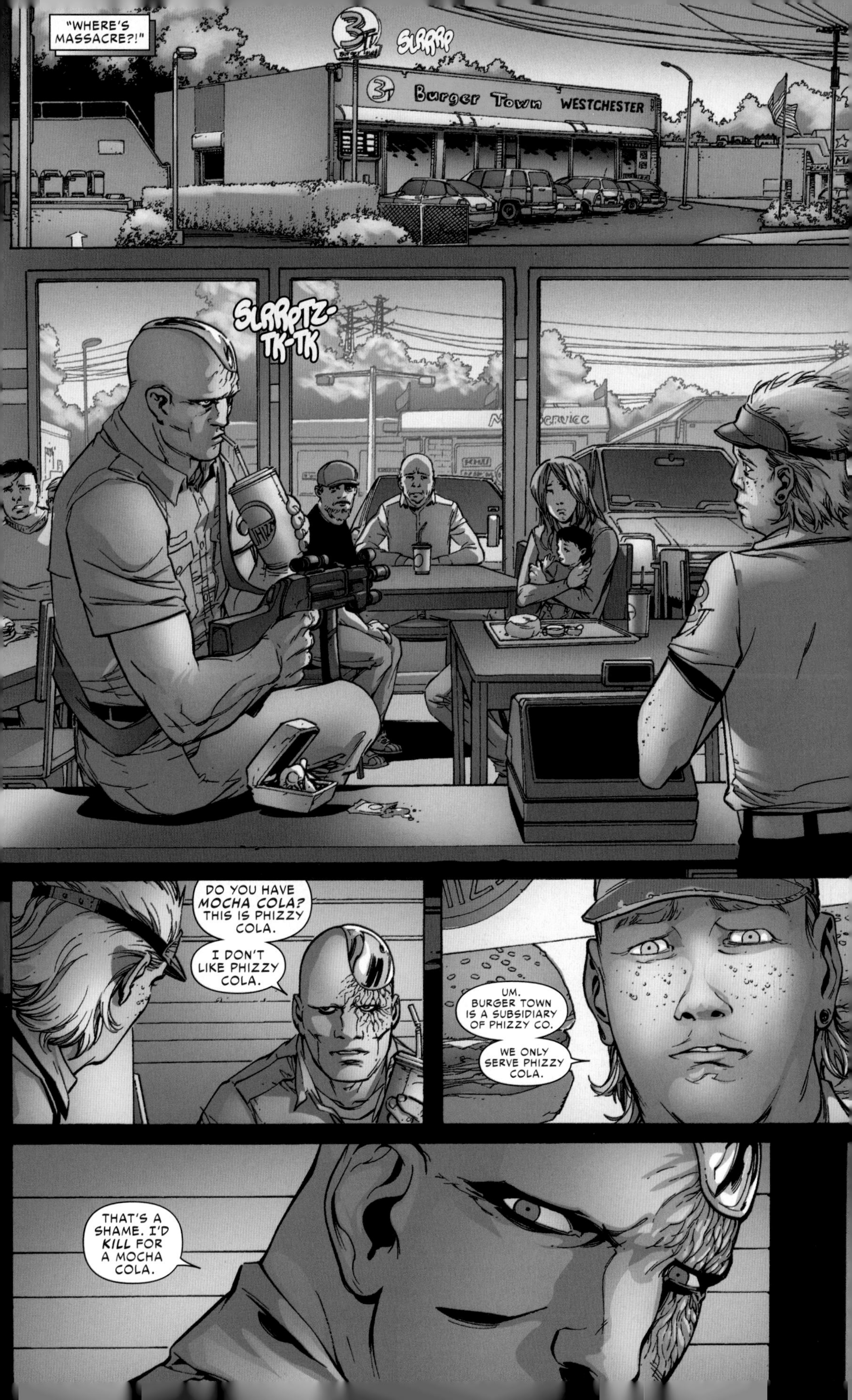
"WHERE'S MASSACRE?!"
SLRRRP
Burger Town WESTCHESTER
SLRRPTZ-TK-TK
DO YOU HAVE MOCHA COLA? THIS IS PHIZZY COLA.
I DON'T LIKE PHIZZY COLA.
UM. BURGER TOWN IS A SUBSIDIARY OF PHIZZY CO.
WE ONLY SERVE PHIZZY COLA.
THAT'S A SHAME. I'D KILL FOR A MOCHA COLA.

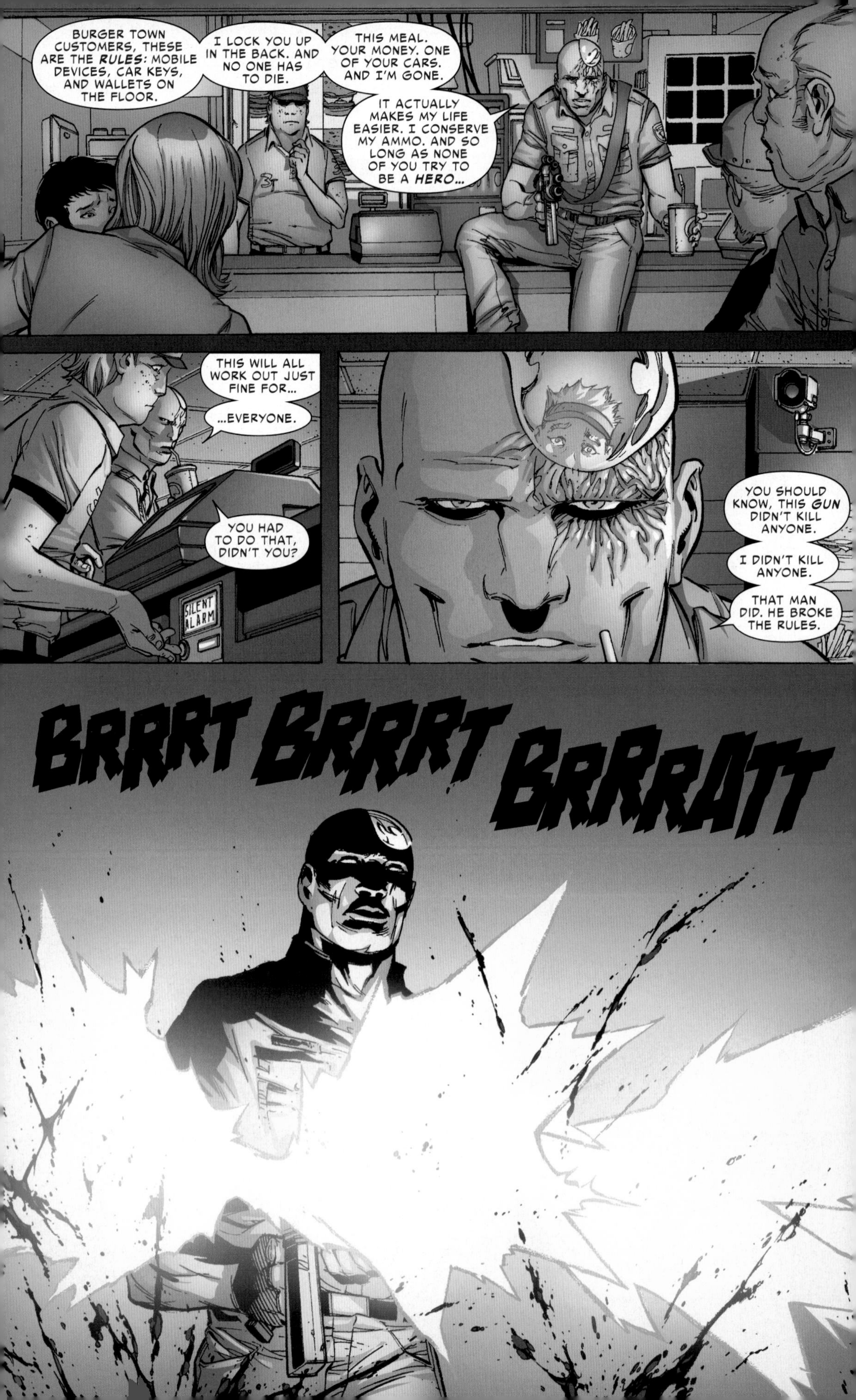
BURGER TOWN CUSTOMERS, THESE ARE THE RULES: MOBILE DEVICES, CAR KEYS, AND WALLETS ON THE FLOOR.
I LOCK YOU UP IN THE BACK. AND NO ONE HAS TO DIE.
THIS MEAL. YOUR MONEY. ONE OF YOUR CARS. AND I'M GONE.
IT ACTUALLY MAKES MY LIFE EASIER. I CONSERVE MY AMMO. AND SO LONG AS NONE OF YOU TRY TO BE A HERO...
THIS WILL ALL WORK OUT JUST FINE FOR...
...EVERYONE.
YOU HAD TO DO THAT, DIDN'T YOU?
SILENT ALARM
YOU SHOULD KNOW, THIS GUN DIDN'T KILL ANYONE.
I DIDN'T KILL ANYONE.
THAT MAN DID. HE BROKE THE RULES.
BRRRT BRRRT BRRRATT

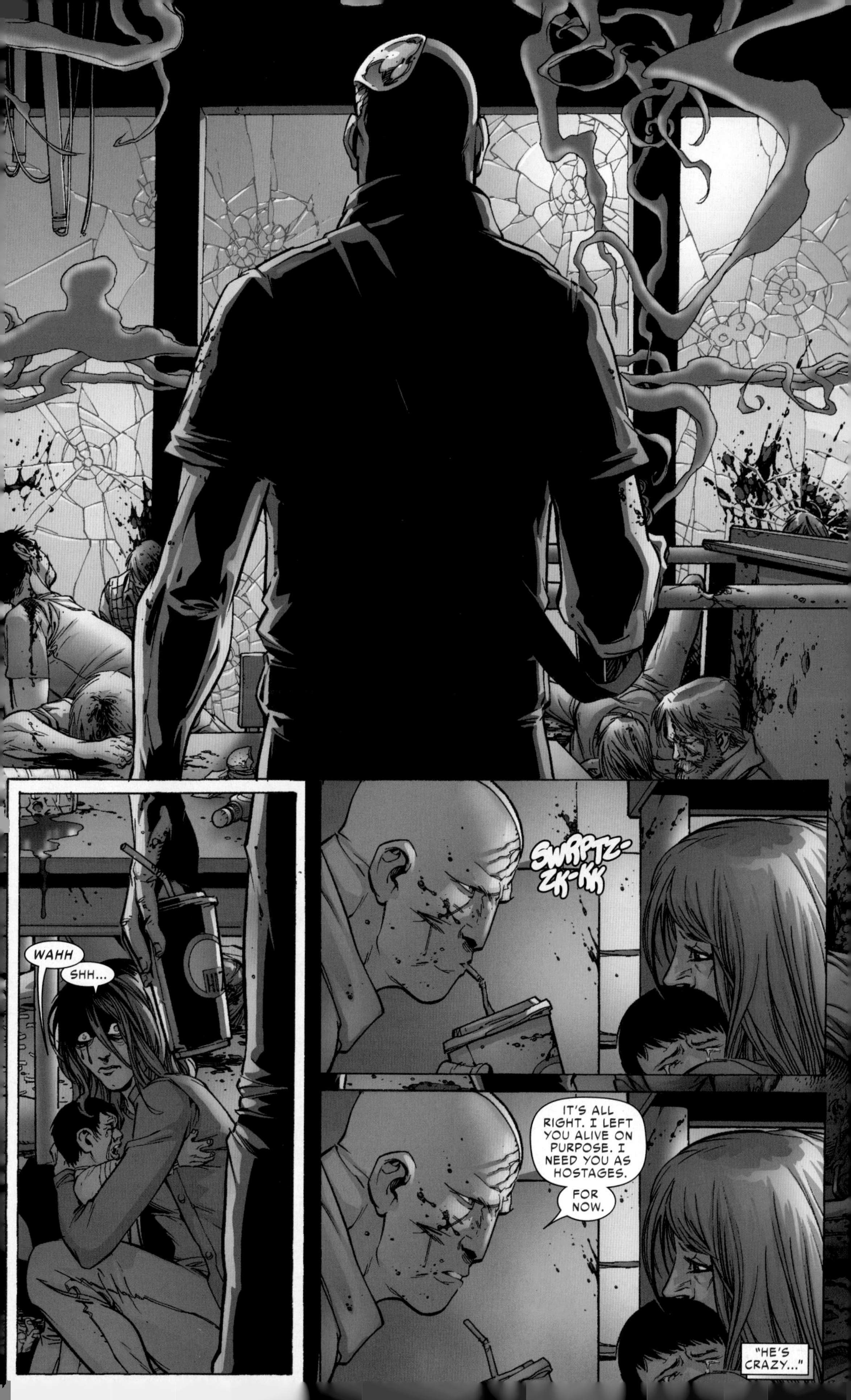
WAHH
SHH...
SWRPTZ-ZK-KK
IT'S ALL RIGHT. I LEFT YOU ALIVE ON PURPOSE. I NEED YOU AS HOSTAGES.
FOR NOW.
"HE'S CRAZY..."

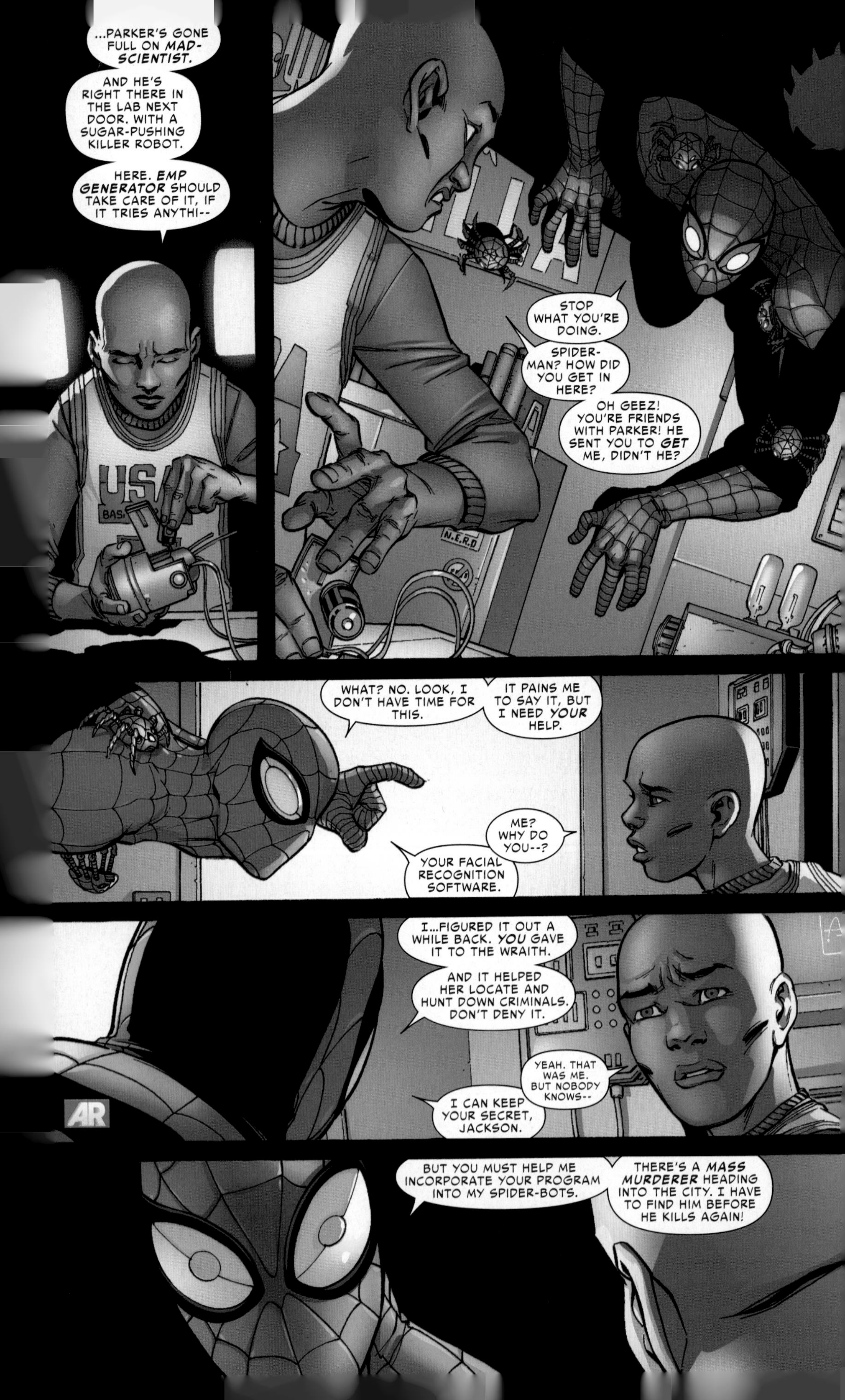

...PARKER'S GONE FULL ON MAD-SCIENTIST.
AND HE'S RIGHT THERE IN THE LAB NEXT DOOR. WITH A SUGAR-PUSHING KILLER ROBOT.
HERE. EMP GENERATOR SHOULD TAKE CARE OF IT, IF IT TRIES ANYTHI--
STOP WHAT YOU'RE DOING.
SPIDER-MAN? HOW DID YOU GET IN HERE?
OH GEEZ! YOU'RE FRIENDS WITH PARKER! HE SENT YOU TO GET ME, DIDN'T HE?
WHAT? NO. LOOK, I DON'T HAVE TIME FOR THIS.
IT PAINS ME TO SAY IT, BUT I NEED YOUR HELP.
ME? WHY DO YOU--?
YOUR FACIAL RECOGNITION SOFTWARE.
I...FIGURED IT OUT A WHILE BACK. YOU GAVE IT TO THE WRAITH.
AND IT HELPED HER LOCATE AND HUNT DOWN CRIMINALS. DON'T DENY IT.
YEAH. THAT WAS ME. BUT NOBODY KNOWS--
I CAN KEEP YOUR SECRET, JACKSON.
BUT YOU MUST HELP ME INCORPORATE YOUR PROGRAM INTO MY SPIDER-BOTS.
THERE'S A MASS MURDERER HEADING INTO THE CITY. I HAVE TO FIND HIM BEFORE HE KILLS AGAIN!

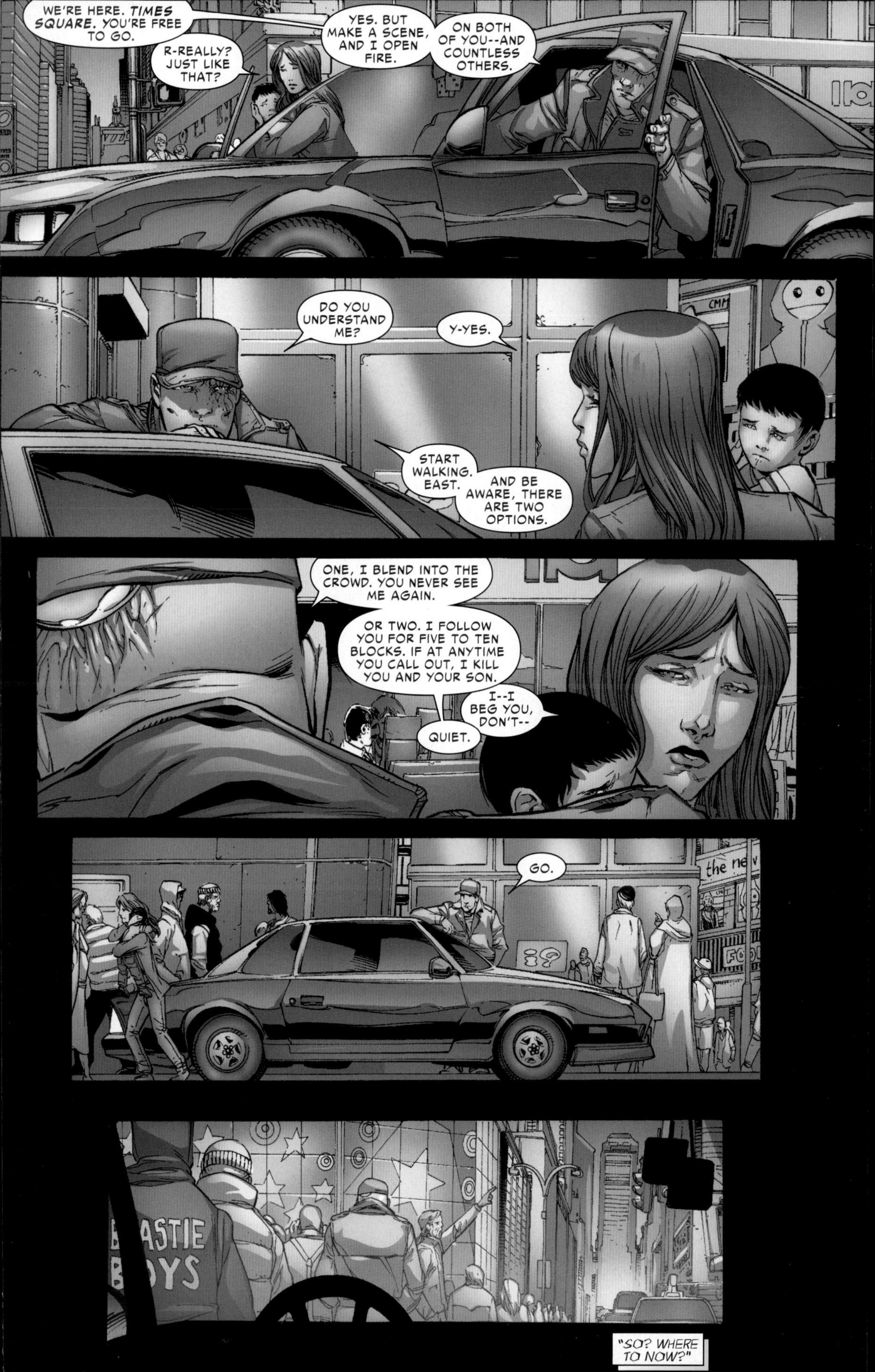

WE'RE HERE. TIMES SQUARE. YOU'RE FREE TO GO.
R-REALLY? JUST LIKE THAT?
YES. BUT MAKE A SCENE, AND I OPEN FIRE.
ON BOTH OF YOU--AND COUNTLESS OTHERS.
DO YOU UNDERSTAND ME?
Y-YES.
START WALKING. EAST.
AND BE AWARE, THERE ARE TWO OPTIONS.
ONE, I BLEND INTO THE CROWD. YOU NEVER SEE ME AGAIN.
OR TWO. I FOLLOW YOU FOR FIVE TO TEN BLOCKS. IF AT ANYTIME YOU CALL OUT, I KILL YOU AND YOUR SON.
I--I BEG YOU, DON'T--
QUIET.
GO.
BEASTIE BOYS
"SO? WHERE TO NOW?"

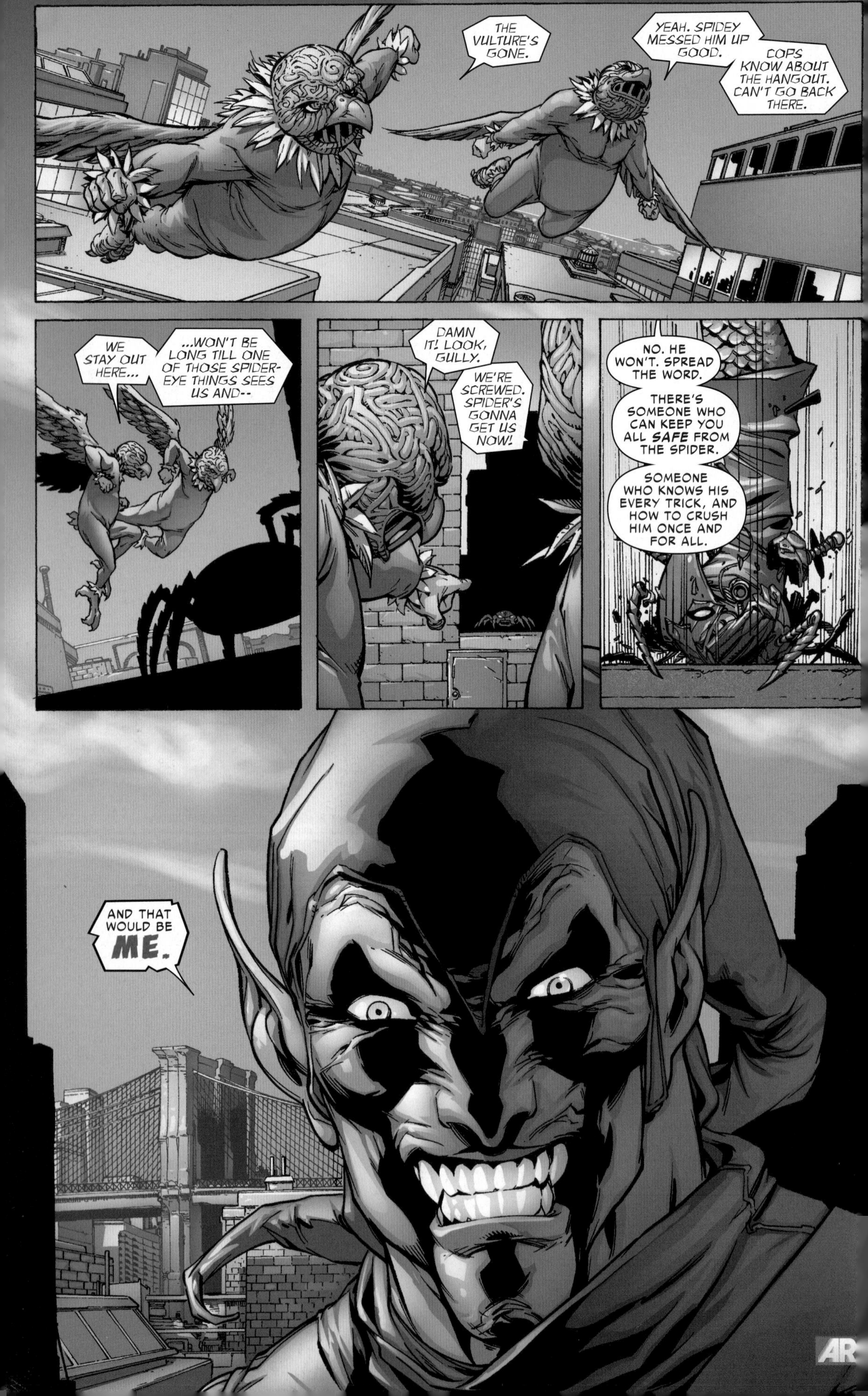
THE VULTURE'S GONE.
YEAH. SPIDEY MESSED HIM UP GOOD.
COPS KNOW ABOUT THE HANGOUT. CAN'T GO BACK THERE.
WE STAY OUT HERE...
...WON'T BE LONG TILL ONE OF THOSE SPIDER-EYE THINGS SEES US AND--
DAMN IT! LOOK, GULLY.
WE'RE SCREWED. SPIDER'S GONNA GET US NOW!
NO. HE WON'T. SPREAD THE WORD.
THERE'S SOMEONE WHO CAN KEEP YOU ALL SAFE FROM THE SPIDER.
SOMEONE WHO KNOWS HIS EVERY TRICK, AND HOW TO CRUSH HIM ONCE AND FOR ALL.
AND THAT WOULD BE ME.

5

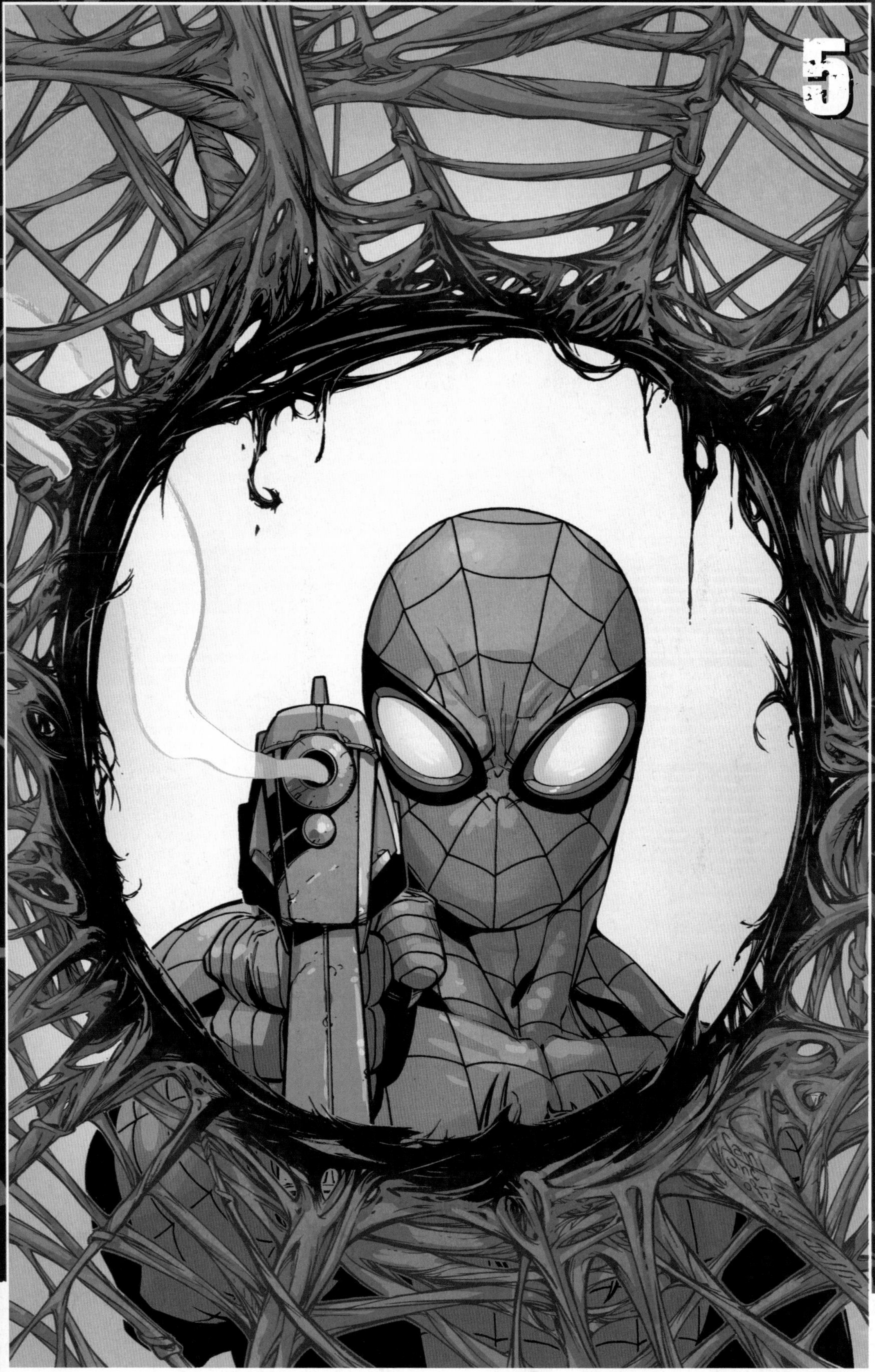

EMOTIONAL TRIGGERS

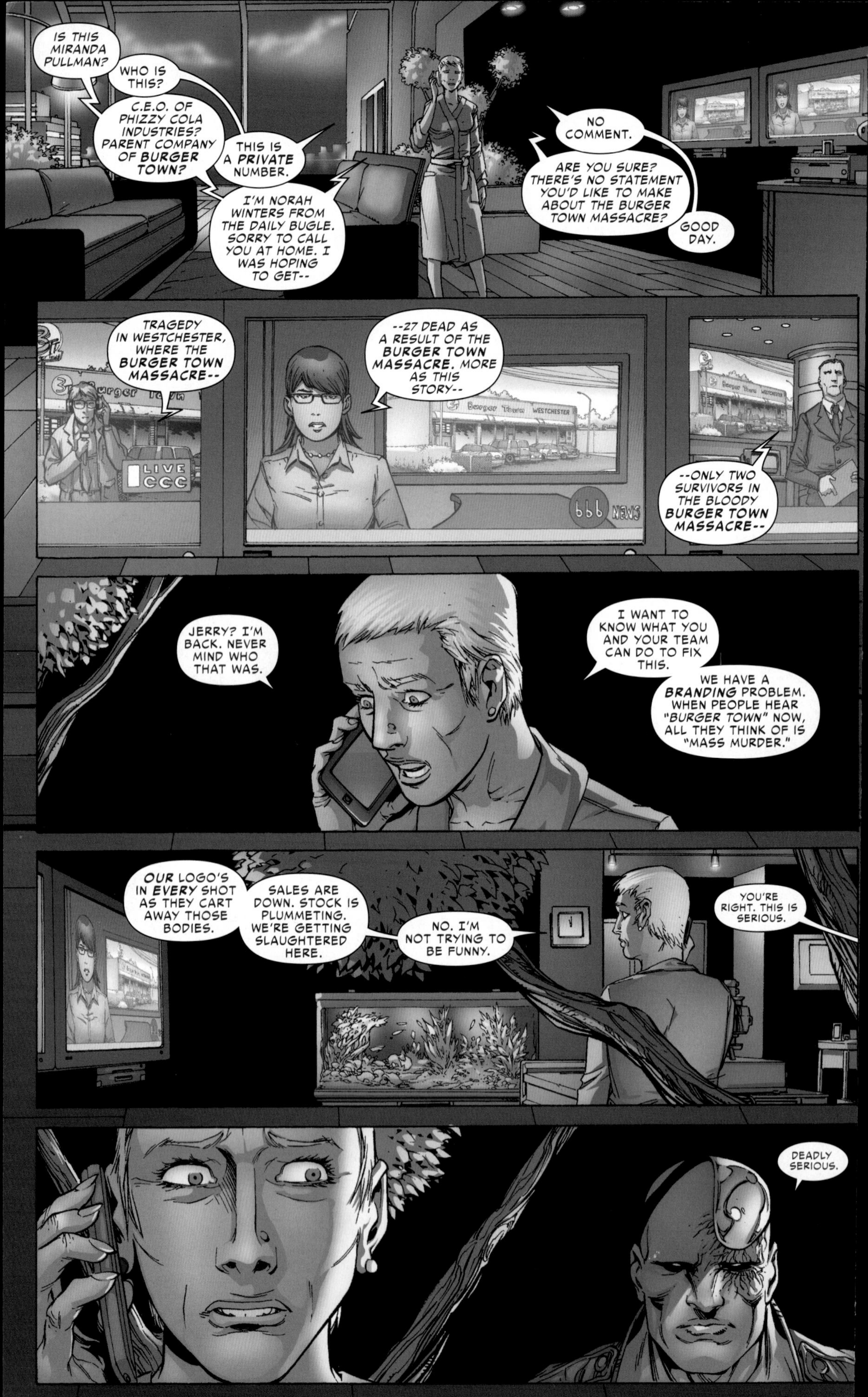
IS THIS MIRANDA PULLMAN?
WHO IS THIS?
C.E.O. OF PHIZZY COLA INDUSTRIES? PARENT COMPANY OF BURGER TOWN?
THIS IS A PRIVATE NUMBER.
I'M NORAH WINTERS FROM THE DAILY BUGLE. SORRY TO CALL YOU AT HOME. I WAS HOPING TO GET--
NO COMMENT.
ARE YOU SURE? THERE'S NO STATEMENT YOU'D LIKE TO MAKE ABOUT THE BURGER TOWN MASSACRE?
GOOD DAY.
TRAGEDY IN WESTCHESTER, WHERE THE BURGER TOWN MASSACRE--
LIVE
CCC
--27 DEAD AS A RESULT OF THE BURGER TOWN MASSACRE. MORE AS THIS STORY--
Burger Town WESTCHESTER
bbb NEWS
--ONLY TWO SURVIVORS IN THE BLOODY BURGER TOWN MASSACRE--
JERRY? I'M BACK. NEVER MIND WHO THAT WAS.
I WANT TO KNOW WHAT YOU AND YOUR TEAM CAN DO TO FIX THIS.
WE HAVE A BRANDING PROBLEM. WHEN PEOPLE HEAR "BURGER TOWN" NOW, ALL THEY THINK OF IS "MASS MURDER."
OUR LOGO'S IN EVERY SHOT AS THEY CART AWAY THOSE BODIES.
SALES ARE DOWN. STOCK IS PLUMMETING. WE'RE GETTING SLAUGHTERED HERE.
NO. I'M NOT TRYING TO BE FUNNY.
YOU'RE RIGHT. THIS IS SERIOUS.
DEADLY SERIOUS.

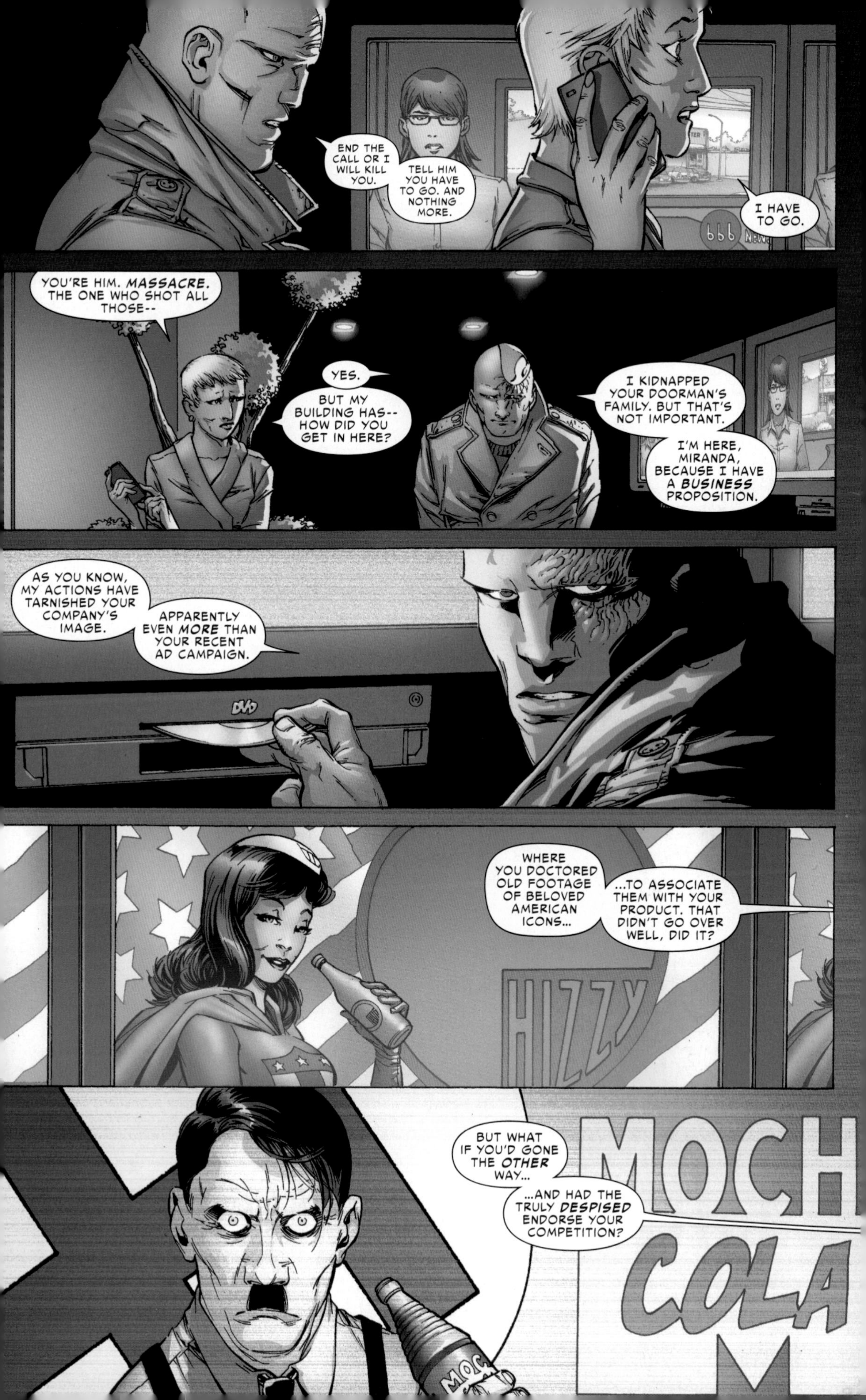

END THE CALL OR I WILL KILL YOU.
TELL HIM YOU HAVE TO GO. AND NOTHING MORE.
I HAVE TO GO.
YOU'RE HIM. MASSACRE. THE ONE WHO SHOT ALL THOSE--
YES.
BUT MY BUILDING HAS-- HOW DID YOU GET IN HERE?
I KIDNAPPED YOUR DOORMAN'S FAMILY. BUT THAT'S NOT IMPORTANT.
I'M HERE, MIRANDA, BECAUSE I HAVE A BUSINESS PROPOSITION.
AS YOU KNOW, MY ACTIONS HAVE TARNISHED YOUR COMPANY'S IMAGE.
APPARENTLY EVEN MORE THAN YOUR RECENT AD CAMPAIGN.
DVD
WHERE YOU DOCTORED OLD FOOTAGE OF BELOVED AMERICAN ICONS...
...TO ASSOCIATE THEM WITH YOUR PRODUCT. THAT DIDN'T GO OVER WELL, DID IT?
HIZZY
BUT WHAT IF YOU'D GONE THE OTHER WAY...
...AND HAD THE TRULY DESPISED ENDORSE YOUR COMPETITION?
MOCH
COLA

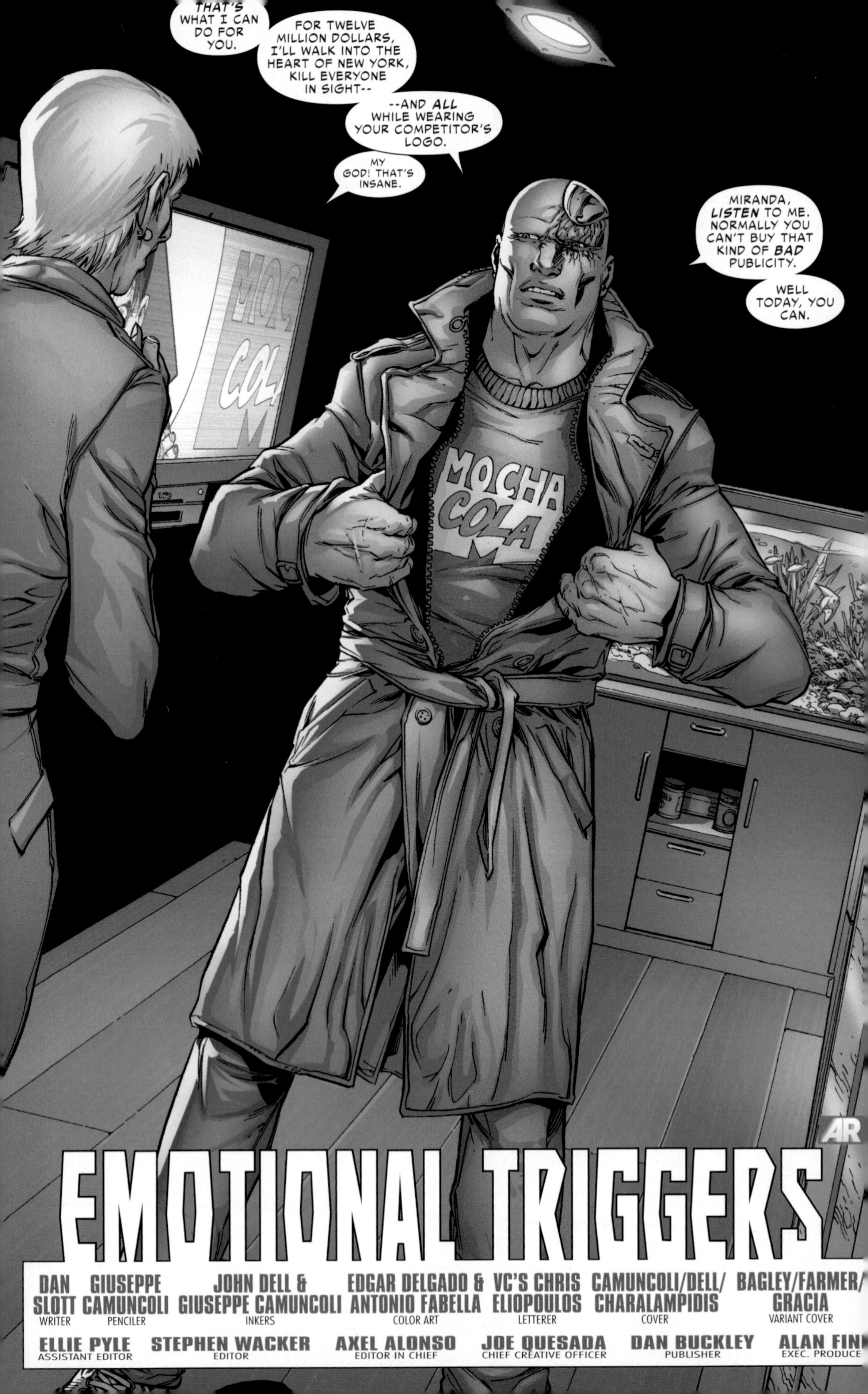
THAT'S WHAT I CAN DO FOR YOU.
FOR TWELVE MILLION DOLLARS, I'LL WALK INTO THE HEART OF NEW YORK, KILL EVERYONE IN SIGHT--
--AND ALL WHILE WEARING YOUR COMPETITOR'S LOGO.
MY GOD! THAT'S INSANE.
MIRANDA, LISTEN TO ME. NORMALLY YOU CAN'T BUY THAT KIND OF BAD PUBLICITY.
WELL TODAY, YOU CAN.
MOCHA COLA
AR
EMOTIONAL TRIGGERS
DAN SLOTT WRITER
GIUSEPPE CAMUNCOLI PENCILER
JOHN DELL & GIUSEPPE CAMUNCOLI INKERS
EDGAR DELGADO & ANTONIO FABELLA COLOR ART
VC'S CHRIS ELIOPOULOS LETTERER
CAMUNCOLI/DELL/ CHARALAMPIDIS COVER
BAGLEY/FARMER/ GRACIA VARIANT COVER
ELLIE PYLE ASSISTANT EDITOR
STEPHEN WACKER EDITOR
AXEL ALONSO EDITOR IN CHIEF
JOE QUESADA CHIEF CREATIVE OFFICER
DAN BUCKLEY PUBLISHER
ALAN FIN EXEC. PRODUCE

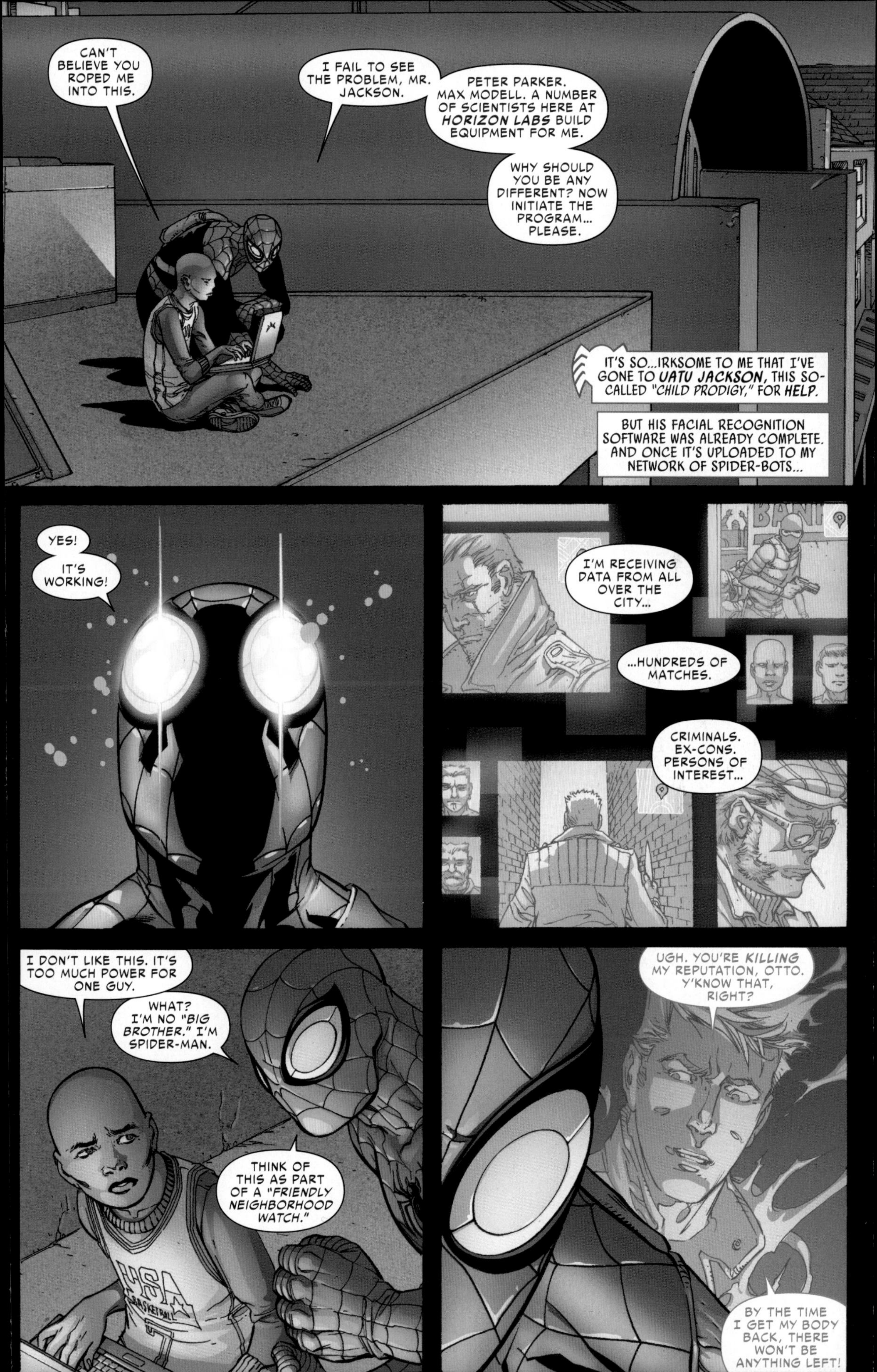
CAN'T BELIEVE YOU ROPED ME INTO THIS.
I FAIL TO SEE THE PROBLEM, MR. JACKSON.
PETER PARKER. MAX MODELL. A NUMBER OF SCIENTISTS HERE AT HORIZON LABS BUILD EQUIPMENT FOR ME.
WHY SHOULD YOU BE ANY DIFFERENT? NOW INITIATE THE PROGRAM... PLEASE.
IT'S SO...IRKSOME TO ME THAT I'VE GONE TO UATU JACKSON, THIS SO-CALLED "CHILD PRODIGY," FOR HELP.
BUT HIS FACIAL RECOGNITION SOFTWARE WAS ALREADY COMPLETE. AND ONCE IT'S UPLOADED TO MY NETWORK OF SPIDER-BOTS...
YES!
IT'S WORKING!
I'M RECEIVING DATA FROM ALL OVER THE CITY...
...HUNDREDS OF MATCHES.
CRIMINALS. EX-CONS. PERSONS OF INTEREST...
I DON'T LIKE THIS. IT'S TOO MUCH POWER FOR ONE GUY.
WHAT? I'M NO "BIG BROTHER." I'M SPIDER-MAN.
THINK OF THIS AS PART OF A "FRIENDLY NEIGHBORHOOD WATCH."
UGH. YOU'RE KILLING MY REPUTATION, OTTO. Y'KNOW THAT, RIGHT?
BY THE TIME I GET MY BODY BACK, THERE WON'T BE ANYTHING LEFT!

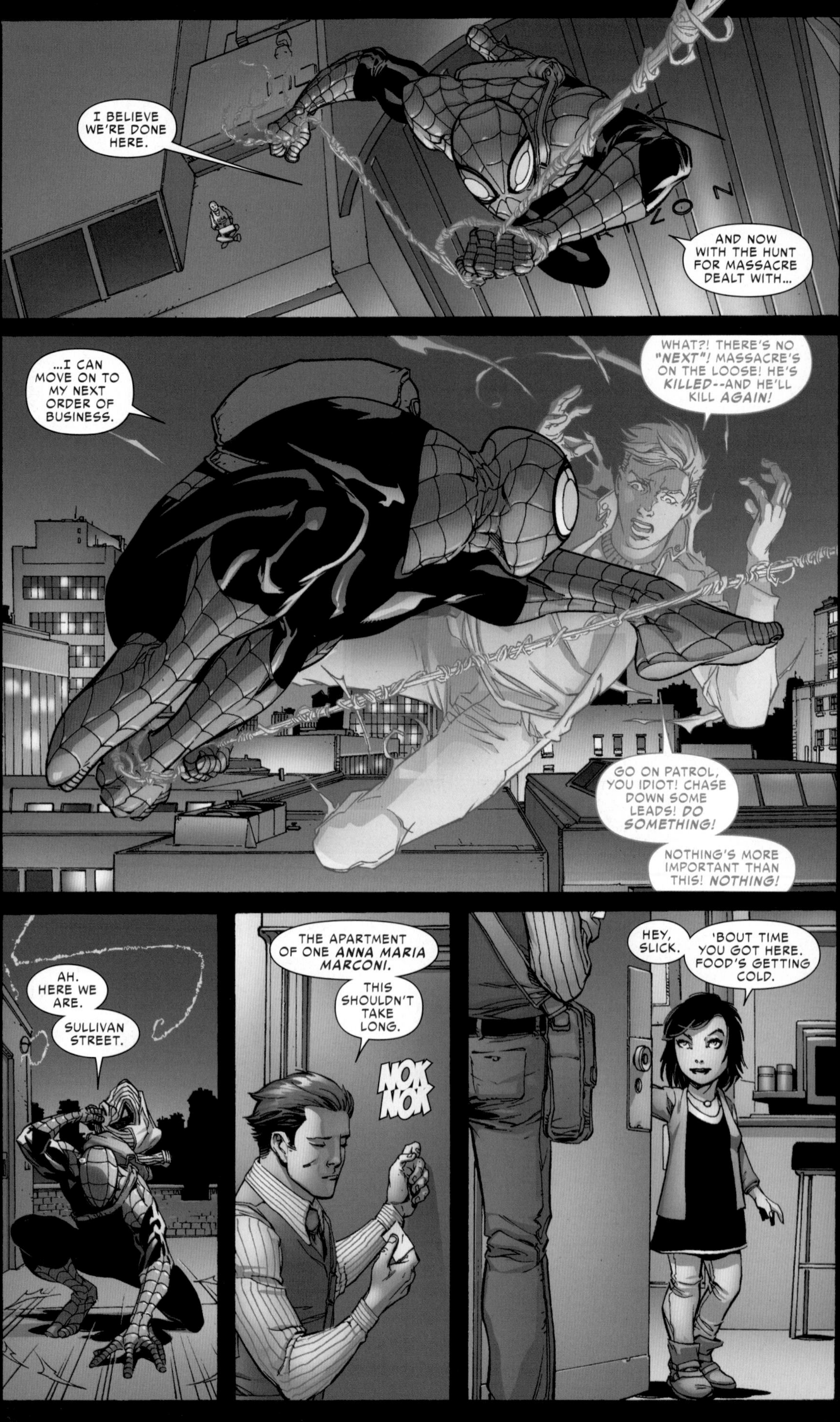
I BELIEVE WE'RE DONE HERE.
AND NOW WITH THE HUNT FOR MASSACRE DEALT WITH...
...I CAN MOVE ON TO MY NEXT ORDER OF BUSINESS.
WHAT?! THERE'S NO "NEXT"! MASSACRE'S ON THE LOOSE! HE'S KILLED--AND HE'LL KILL AGAIN!
GO ON PATROL, YOU IDIOT! CHASE DOWN SOME LEADS! DO SOMETHING!
NOTHING'S MORE IMPORTANT THAN THIS! NOTHING!
AH. HERE WE ARE.
SULLIVAN STREET.
THE APARTMENT OF ONE ANNA MARIA MARCONI.
THIS SHOULDN'T TAKE LONG.
NOK NOK
HEY, SLICK.
'BOUT TIME YOU GOT HERE. FOOD'S GETTING COLD.

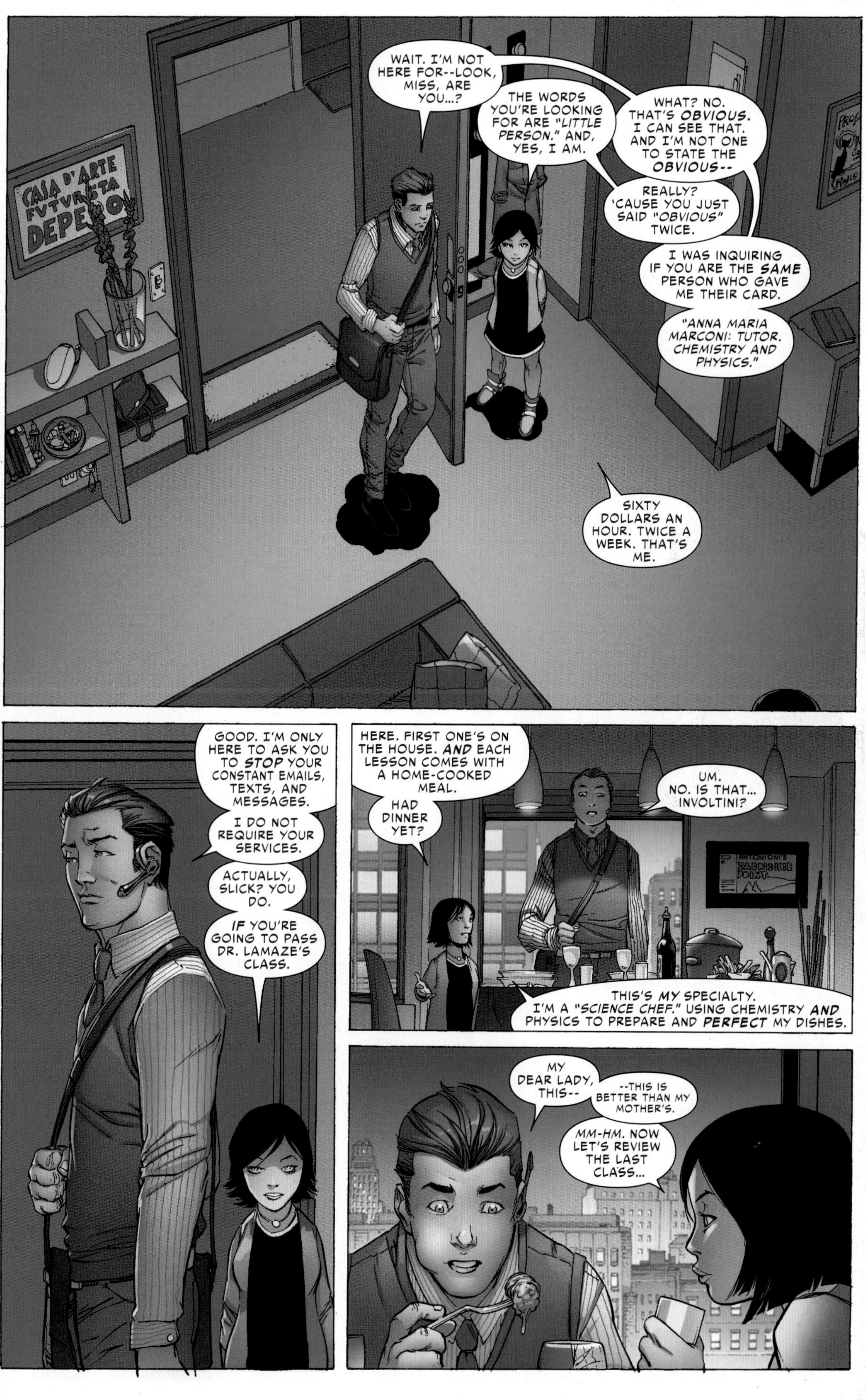
WAIT. I'M NOT HERE FOR--LOOK, MISS, ARE YOU...?
THE WORDS YOU'RE LOOKING FOR ARE "LITTLE PERSON." AND, YES, I AM.
WHAT? NO. THAT'S OBVIOUS. I CAN SEE THAT. AND I'M NOT ONE TO STATE THE OBVIOUS--
REALLY? 'CAUSE YOU JUST SAID "OBVIOUS" TWICE.
I WAS INQUIRING IF YOU ARE THE SAME PERSON WHO GAVE ME THEIR CARD.
"ANNA MARIA MARCONI: TUTOR. CHEMISTRY AND PHYSICS."
SIXTY DOLLARS AN HOUR. TWICE A WEEK. THAT'S ME.
GOOD. I'M ONLY HERE TO ASK YOU TO STOP YOUR CONSTANT EMAILS, TEXTS, AND MESSAGES.
I DO NOT REQUIRE YOUR SERVICES.
ACTUALLY, SLICK? YOU DO.
IF YOU'RE GOING TO PASS DR. LAMAZE'S CLASS.
HERE. FIRST ONE'S ON THE HOUSE. AND EACH LESSON COMES WITH A HOME-COOKED MEAL.
HAD DINNER YET?
UM. NO. IS THAT... INVOLTINI?
THIS'S MY SPECIALTY. I'M A "SCIENCE CHEF." USING CHEMISTRY AND PHYSICS TO PREPARE AND PERFECT MY DISHES.
MY DEAR LADY, THIS--
--THIS IS BETTER THAN MY MOTHER'S.
MM-HM. NOW LET'S REVIEW THE LAST CLASS...

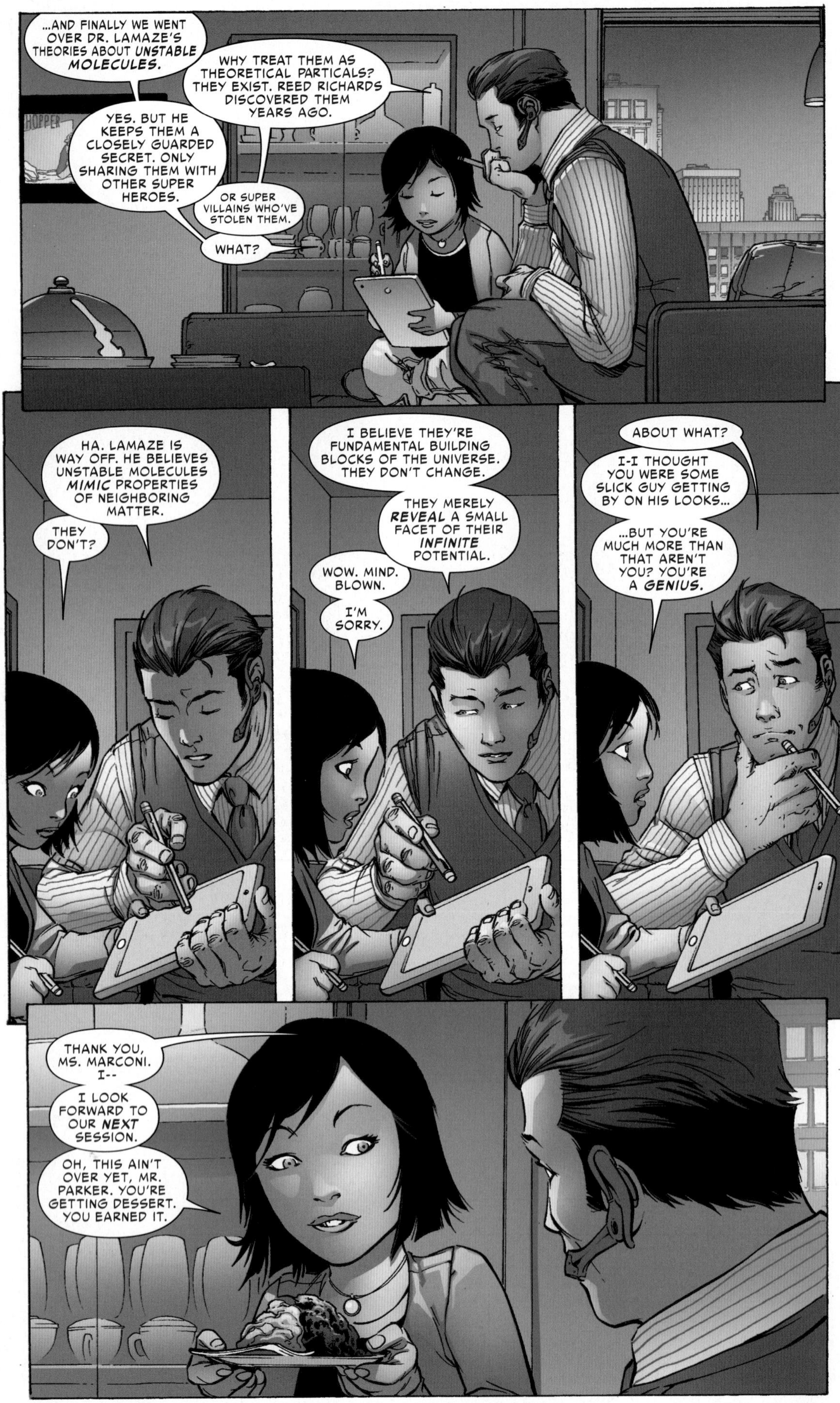
...AND FINALLY WE WENT OVER DR. LAMAZE'S THEORIES ABOUT UNSTABLE MOLECULES.
WHY TREAT THEM AS THEORETICAL PARTICALS? THEY EXIST. REED RICHARDS DISCOVERED THEM YEARS AGO.
YES. BUT HE KEEPS THEM A CLOSELY GUARDED SECRET. ONLY SHARING THEM WITH OTHER SUPER HEROES.
OR SUPER VILLAINS WHO'VE STOLEN THEM.
WHAT?
HA. LAMAZE IS WAY OFF. HE BELIEVES UNSTABLE MOLECULES MIMIC PROPERTIES OF NEIGHBORING MATTER.
THEY DON'T?
I BELIEVE THEY'RE FUNDAMENTAL BUILDING BLOCKS OF THE UNIVERSE. THEY DON'T CHANGE.
THEY MERELY REVEAL A SMALL FACET OF THEIR INFINITE POTENTIAL.
WOW. MIND. BLOWN.
I'M SORRY.
ABOUT WHAT?
I-I THOUGHT YOU WERE SOME SLICK GUY GETTING BY ON HIS LOOKS...
...BUT YOU'RE MUCH MORE THAN THAT AREN'T YOU? YOU'RE A GENIUS.
THANK YOU, MS. MARCONI. I--
I LOOK FORWARD TO OUR NEXT SESSION.
OH, THIS AIN'T OVER YET, MR. PARKER. YOU'RE GETTING DESSERT. YOU EARNED IT.

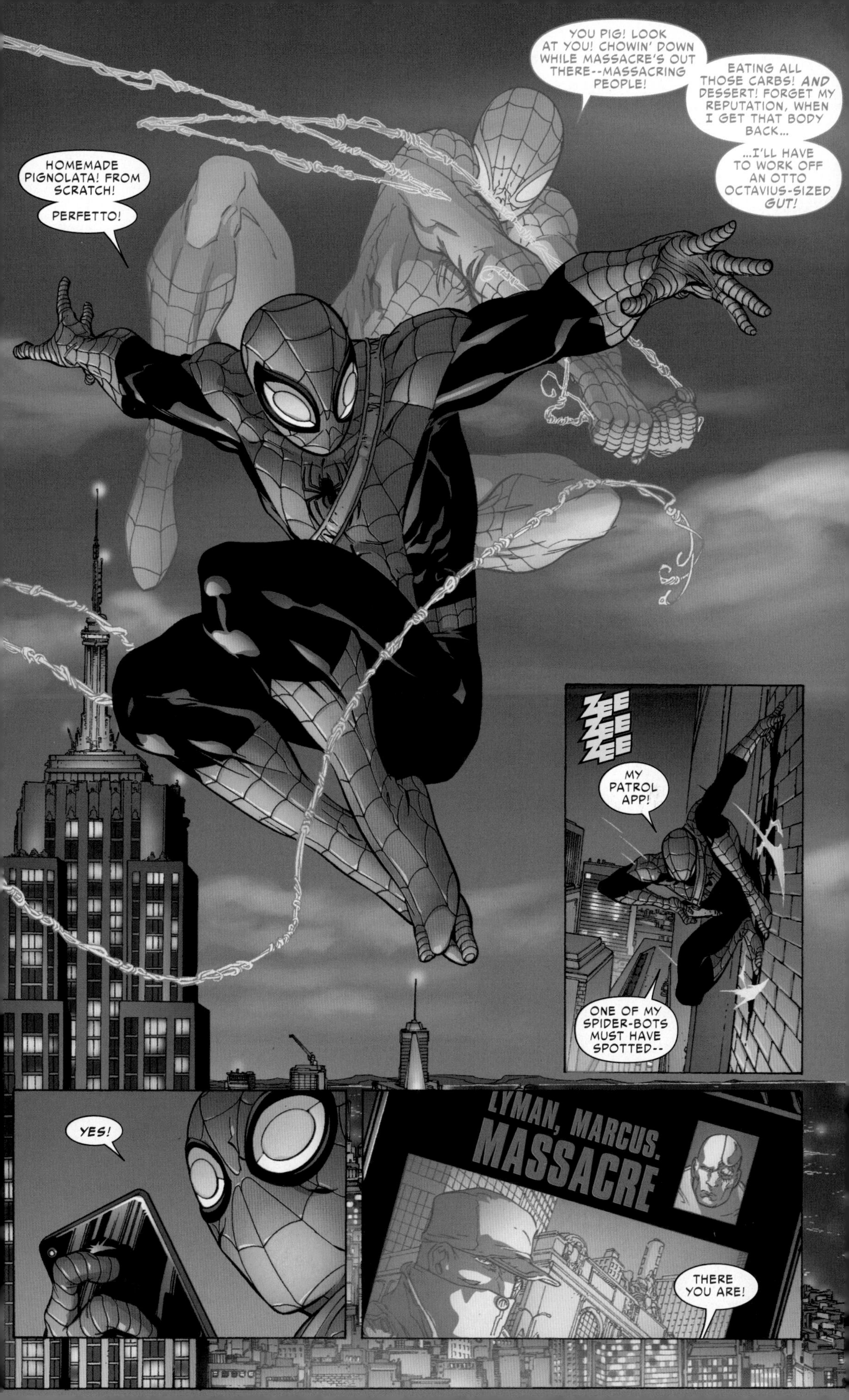
HOMEMADE PIGNOLATA! FROM SCRATCH!
PERFETTO!
YOU PIG! LOOK AT YOU! CHOWIN' DOWN WHILE MASSACRE'S OUT THERE--MASSACRING PEOPLE!
EATING ALL THOSE CARBS! AND DESSERT! FORGET MY REPUTATION, WHEN I GET THAT BODY BACK...
...I'LL HAVE TO WORK OFF AN OTTO OCTAVIUS-SIZED GUT!
ZEE ZEE ZEE
MY PATROL APP!
ONE OF MY SPIDER-BOTS MUST HAVE SPOTTED--
YES!
LYMAN, MARCUS.
MASSACRE
THERE YOU ARE!

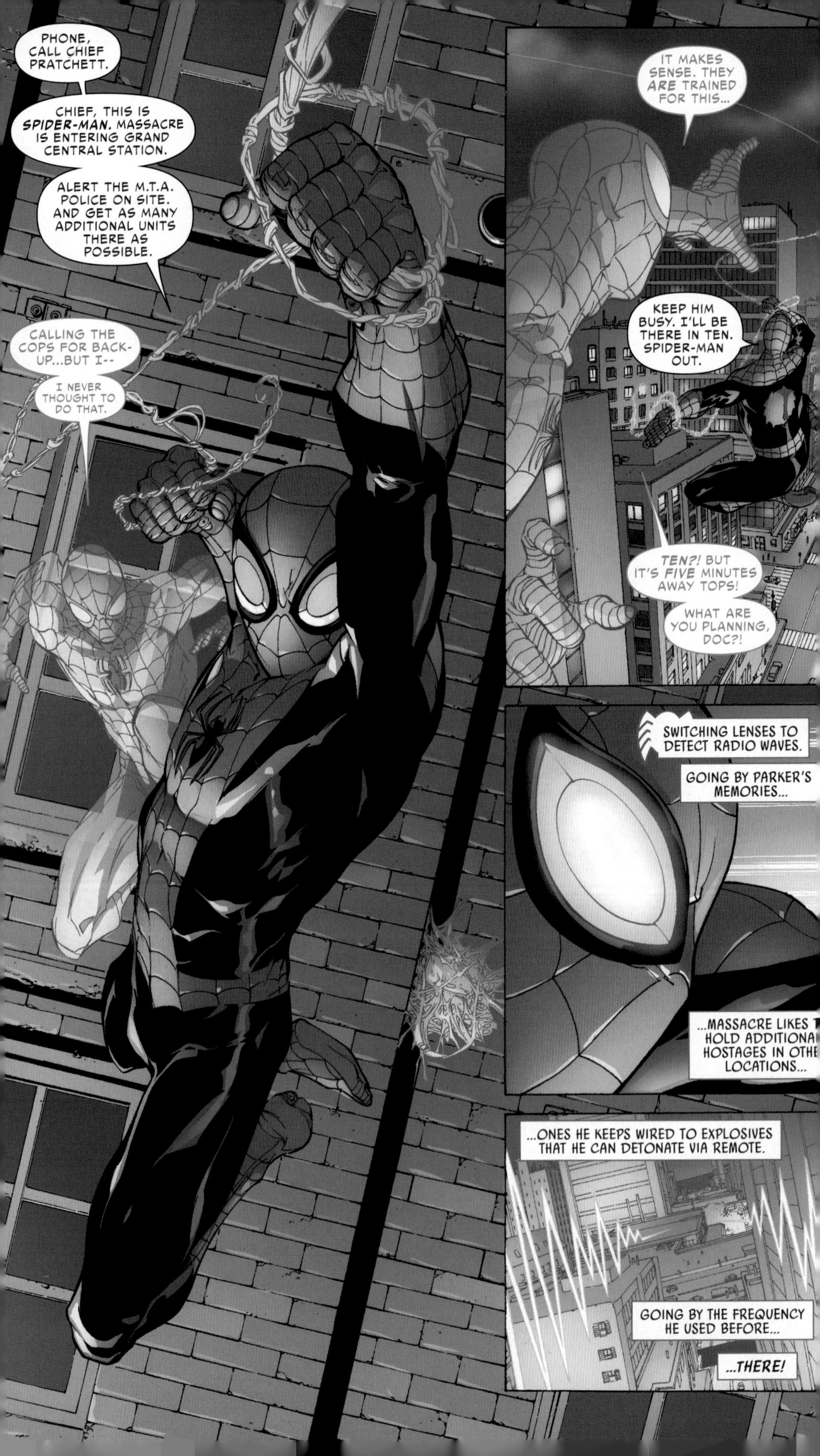
PHONE, CALL CHIEF PRATCHETT.
CHIEF, THIS IS SPIDER-MAN. MASSACRE IS ENTERING GRAND CENTRAL STATION.
ALERT THE M.T.A. POLICE ON SITE. AND GET AS MANY ADDITIONAL UNITS THERE AS POSSIBLE.
CALLING THE COPS FOR BACK-UP...BUT I--
I NEVER THOUGHT TO DO THAT.
IT MAKES SENSE. THEY ARE TRAINED FOR THIS...
KEEP HIM BUSY. I'LL BE THERE IN TEN. SPIDER-MAN OUT.
TEN?! BUT IT'S FIVE MINUTES AWAY TOPS!
WHAT ARE YOU PLANNING, DOC?!
SWITCHING LENSES TO DETECT RADIO WAVES.
GOING BY PARKER'S MEMORIES...
...MASSACRE LIKES T
HOLD ADDITIONA
HOSTAGES IN OTHE
LOCATIONS...
...ONES HE KEEPS WIRED TO EXPLOSIVES THAT HE CAN DETONATE VIA REMOTE.
GOING BY THE FREQUENCY HE USED BEFORE...
...THERE!

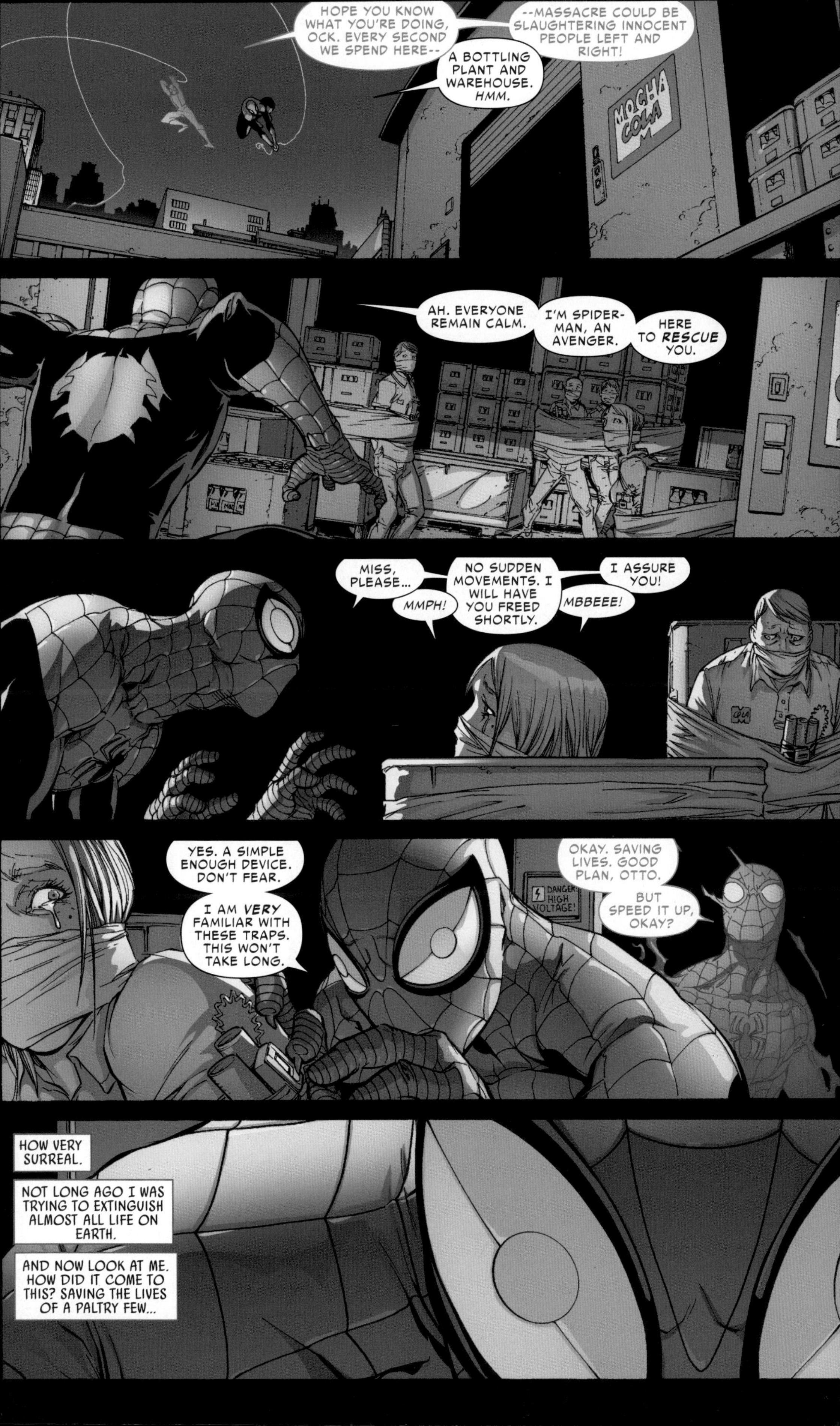
HOPE YOU KNOW WHAT YOU'RE DOING, OCK. EVERY SECOND WE SPEND HERE--
--MASSACRE COULD BE SLAUGHTERING INNOCENT PEOPLE LEFT AND RIGHT!
A BOTTLING PLANT AND WAREHOUSE. HMM.
MOCHA COLA
AH. EVERYONE REMAIN CALM.
I'M SPIDER-MAN, AN AVENGER.
HERE TO RESCUE YOU.
MISS, PLEASE...
MMPH!
NO SUDDEN MOVEMENTS. I WILL HAVE YOU FREED SHORTLY.
MBBEEE!
I ASSURE YOU!
YES. A SIMPLE ENOUGH DEVICE. DON'T FEAR.
I AM VERY FAMILIAR WITH THESE TRAPS. THIS WON'T TAKE LONG.
DANGER HIGH VOLTAGE!
OKAY. SAVING LIVES. GOOD PLAN, OTTO.
BUT SPEED IT UP, OKAY?
HOW VERY SURREAL.
NOT LONG AGO I WAS TRYING TO EXTINGUISH ALMOST ALL LIFE ON EARTH.
AND NOW LOOK AT ME. HOW DID IT COME TO THIS? SAVING THE LIVES OF A PALTRY FEW...

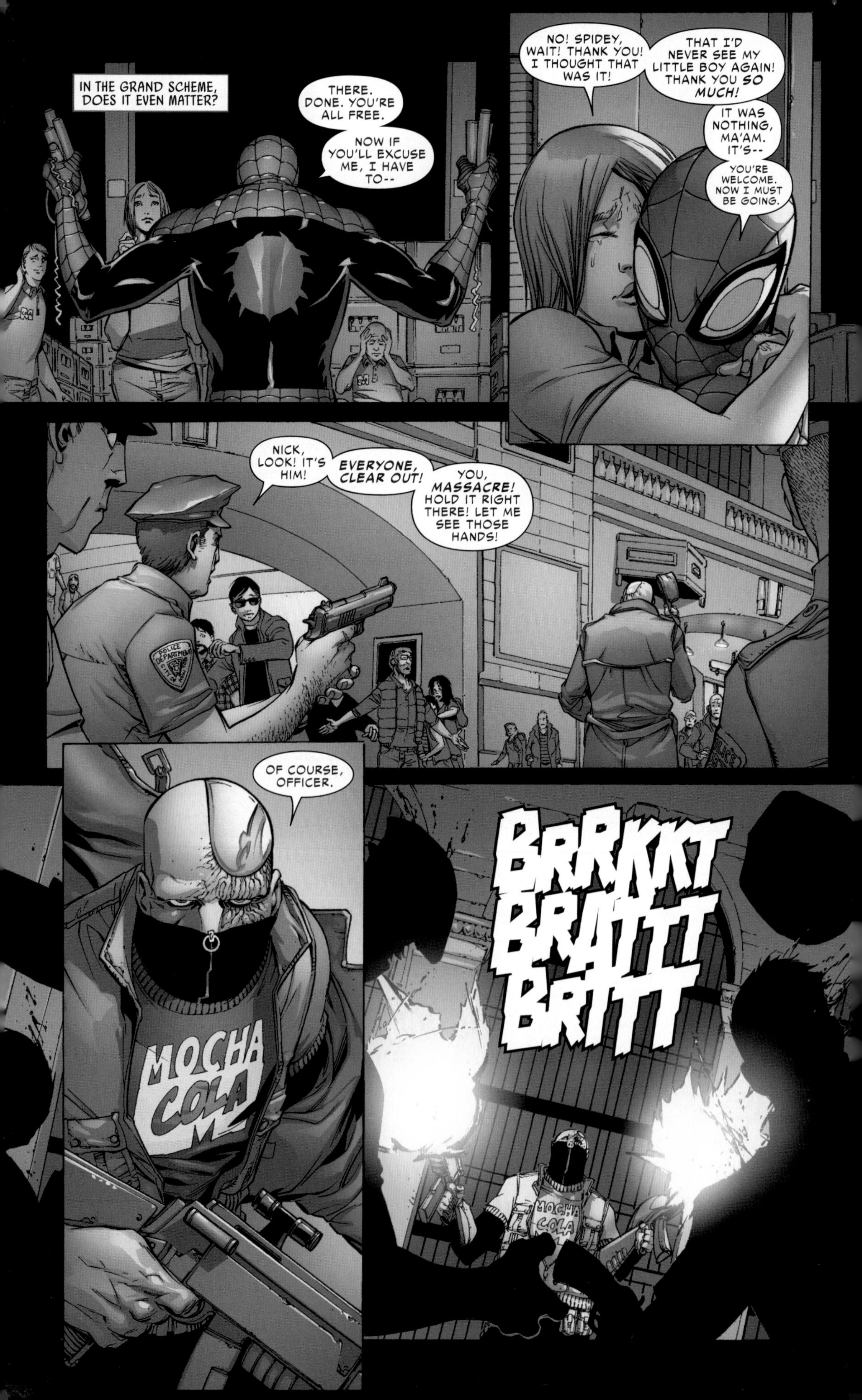

IN THE GRAND SCHEME, DOES IT EVEN MATTER?
THERE. DONE. YOU'RE ALL FREE.
NOW IF YOU'LL EXCUSE ME, I HAVE TO--
NO! SPIDEY, WAIT! THANK YOU! I THOUGHT THAT WAS IT!
THAT I'D NEVER SEE MY LITTLE BOY AGAIN! THANK YOU *SO MUCH!*
IT WAS NOTHING, MA'AM. IT'S--
YOU'RE WELCOME. NOW I MUST BE GOING.
NICK, LOOK! IT'S HIM!
EVERYONE, CLEAR OUT!
YOU, *MASSACRE!* HOLD IT RIGHT THERE! LET ME SEE THOSE HANDS!
OF COURSE, OFFICER.
MOCHA COLA
BRRKKT BRATTT BRTTT

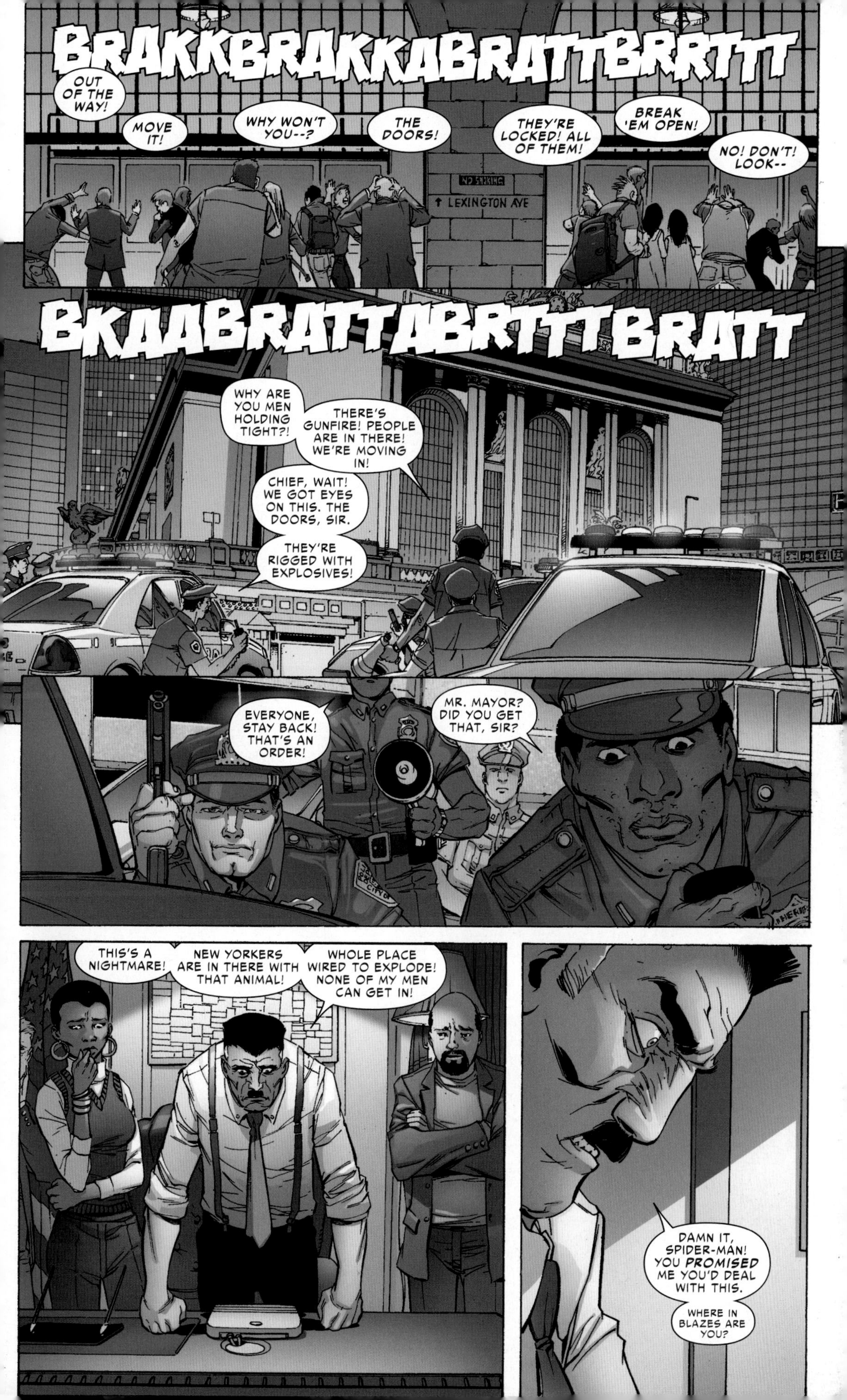
BRAKKBRAKKABRATTBRRTTT
OUT OF THE WAY!
MOVE IT!
WHY WON'T YOU--?
THE DOORS!
THEY'RE LOCKED! ALL OF THEM!
BREAK 'EM OPEN!
NO! DON'T! LOOK--
NO SMOKING
LEXINGTON AVE
BKAABRATTABRTTTBRATT
WHY ARE YOU MEN HOLDING TIGHT?!
THERE'S GUNFIRE! PEOPLE ARE IN THERE! WE'RE MOVING IN!
CHIEF, WAIT! WE GOT EYES ON THIS. THE DOORS, SIR.
THEY'RE RIGGED WITH EXPLOSIVES!
EVERYONE, STAY BACK! THAT'S AN ORDER!
MR. MAYOR? DID YOU GET THAT, SIR?
THIS'S A NIGHTMARE!
NEW YORKERS ARE IN THERE WITH THAT ANIMAL!
WHOLE PLACE WIRED TO EXPLODE! NONE OF MY MEN CAN GET IN!
DAMN IT, SPIDER-MAN! YOU *PROMISED* ME YOU'D DEAL WITH THIS.
WHERE IN BLAZES ARE YOU?

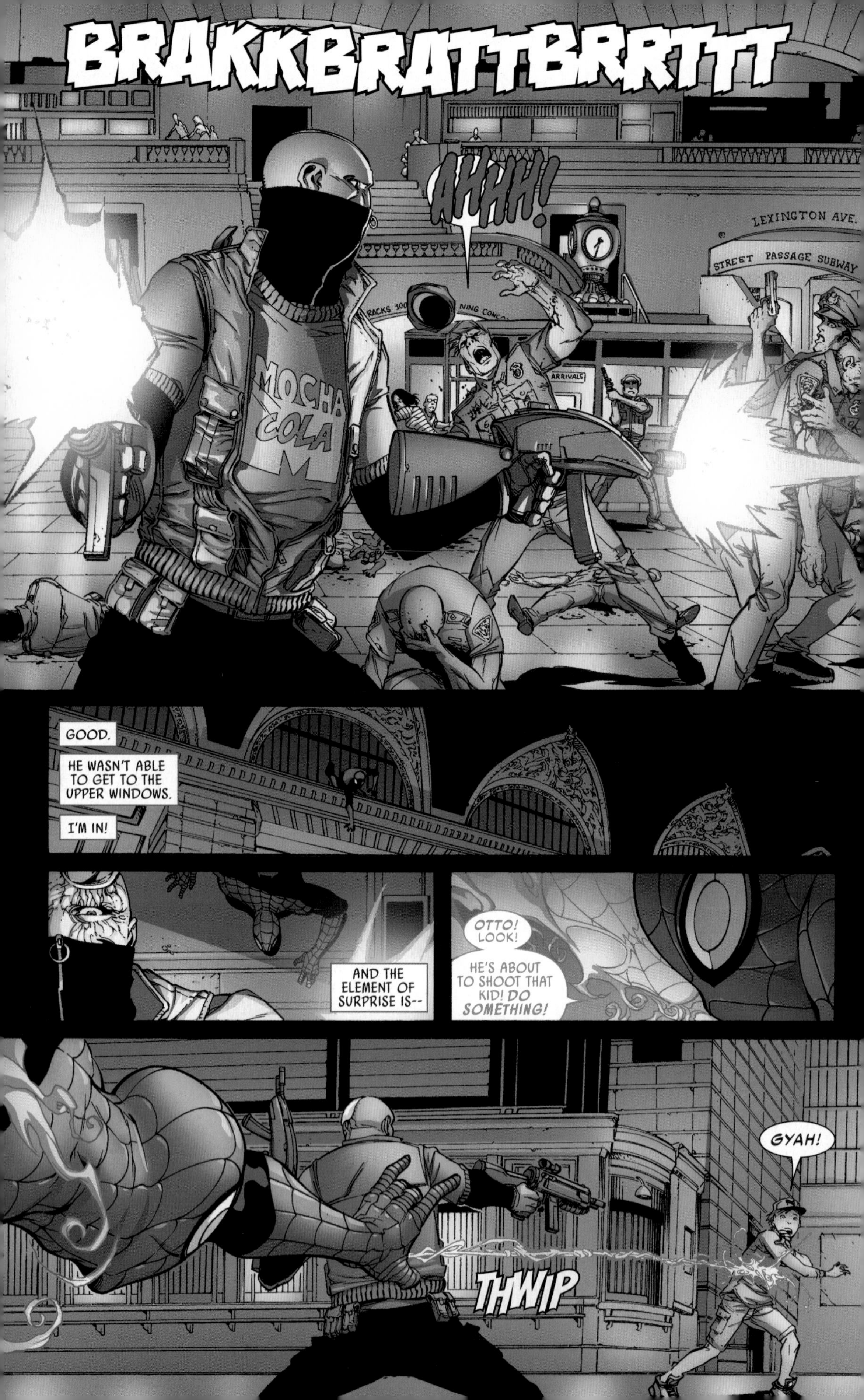
BRAKKBRATTBRRTTT
AHHH!
LEXINGTON AVE.
STREET PASSAGE SUBWAY
MOCHA COLA
ARRIVALS
GOOD.
HE WASN'T ABLE TO GET TO THE UPPER WINDOWS.
I'M IN!
AND THE ELEMENT OF SURPRISE IS--
OTTO! LOOK!
HE'S ABOUT TO SHOOT THAT KID! DO SOMETHING!
GYAH!
THWIP

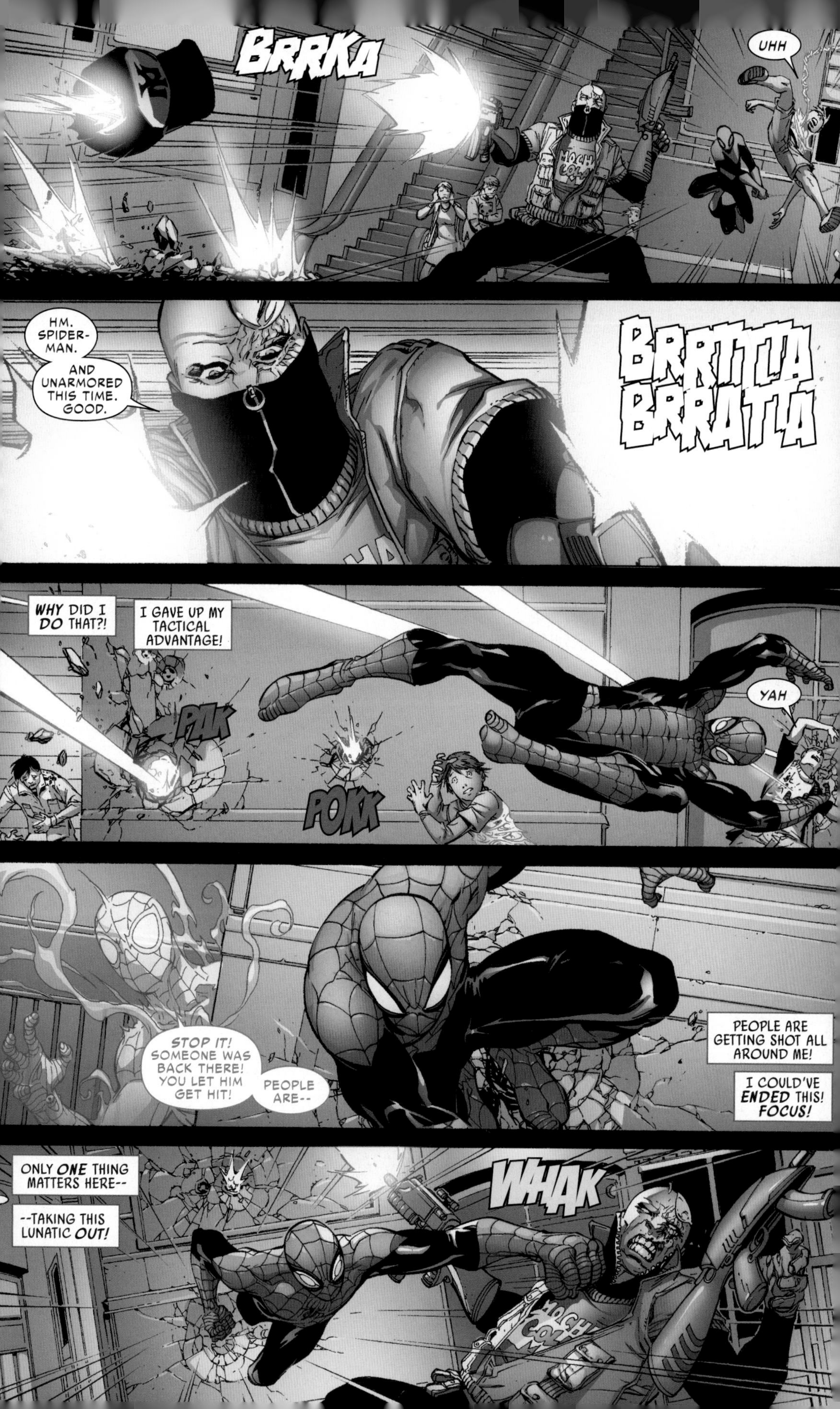
BRRKA
UHH
HM. SPIDER-MAN.
AND UNARMORED THIS TIME. GOOD.
BRRTTTA BRRATTA
WHY DID I DO THAT?!
I GAVE UP MY TACTICAL ADVANTAGE!
PAK
POKK
YAH
STOP IT! SOMEONE WAS BACK THERE! YOU LET HIM GET HIT!
PEOPLE ARE--
PEOPLE ARE GETTING SHOT ALL AROUND ME!
I COULD'VE ENDED THIS! FOCUS!
ONLY ONE THING MATTERS HERE--
--TAKING THIS LUNATIC OUT!
WHAK

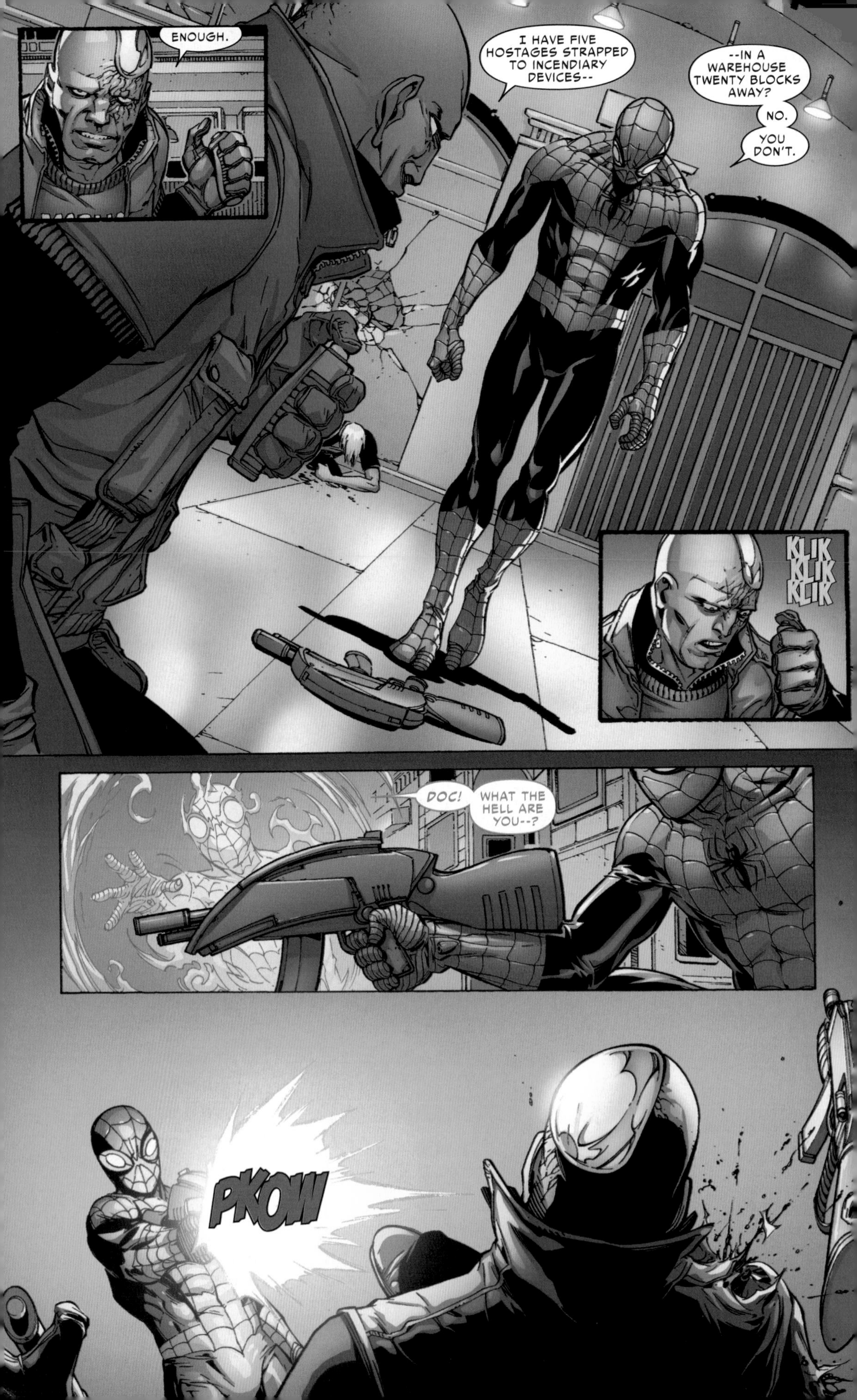

ENOUGH.
I HAVE FIVE HOSTAGES STRAPPED TO INCENDIARY DEVICES--
--IN A WAREHOUSE TWENTY BLOCKS AWAY?
NO.
YOU DON'T.
KLIK KLIK KLIK
DOC!
WHAT THE HELL ARE YOU--?
PKOW

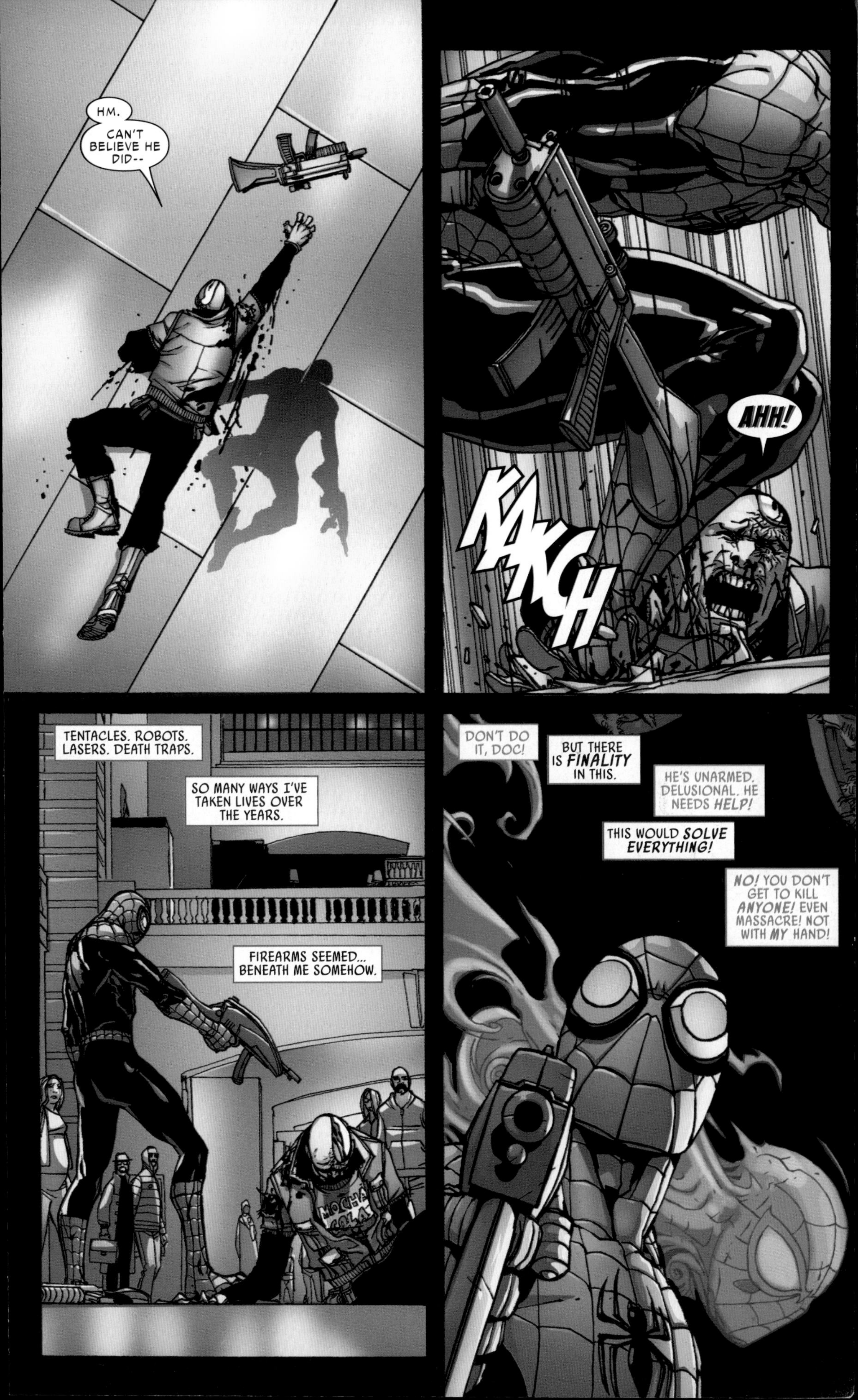
HM.
CAN'T BELIEVE HE DID--
AHH!
KAKCH
TENTACLES. ROBOTS. LASERS. DEATH TRAPS.
SO MANY WAYS I'VE TAKEN LIVES OVER THE YEARS.
FIREARMS SEEMED... BENEATH ME SOMEHOW.
MOCHA COLA
DON'T DO IT, DOC!
BUT THERE IS FINALITY IN THIS.
HE'S UNARMED. DELUSIONAL. HE NEEDS HELP!
THIS WOULD SOLVE EVERYTHING!
NO! YOU DON'T GET TO KILL ANYONE! EVEN MASSACRE! NOT WITH MY HAND!

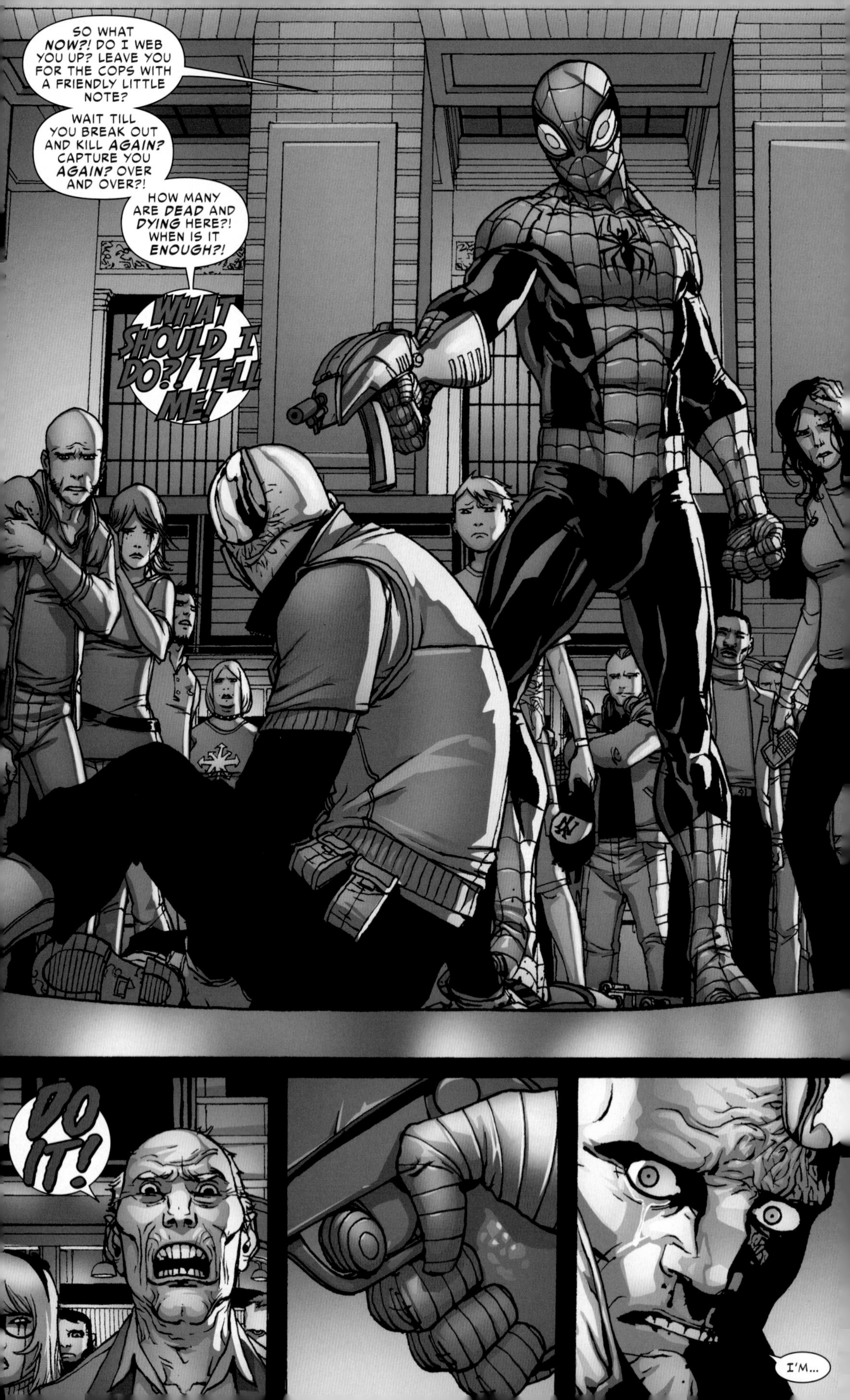
SO WHAT NOW?! DO I WEB YOU UP? LEAVE YOU FOR THE COPS WITH A FRIENDLY LITTLE NOTE?
WAIT TILL YOU BREAK OUT AND KILL AGAIN? CAPTURE YOU AGAIN? OVER AND OVER?!
HOW MANY ARE DEAD AND DYING HERE?! WHEN IS IT ENOUGH?!
WHAT SHOULD I DO?! TELL ME!
DO IT!
I'M...

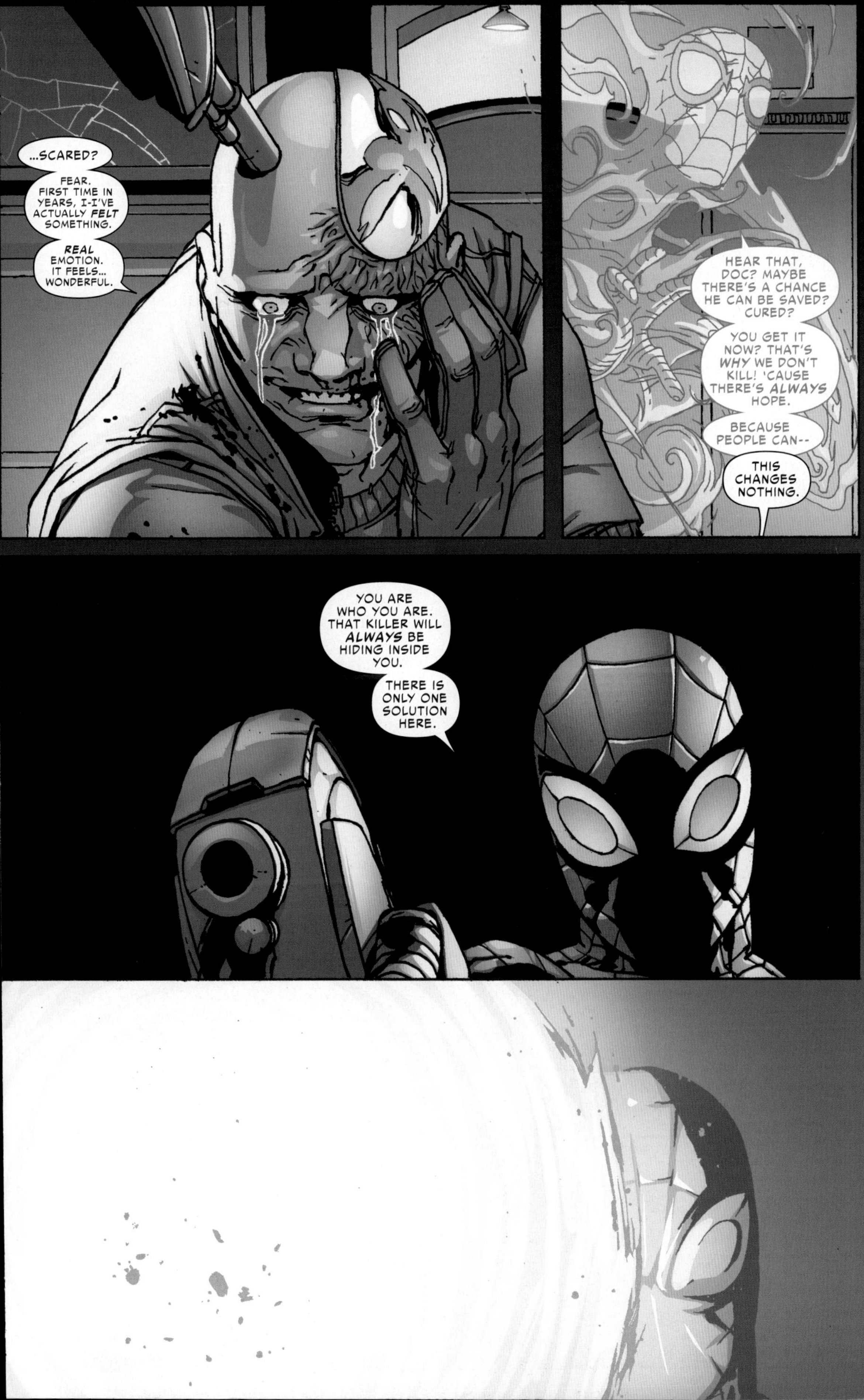
...SCARED?
FEAR. FIRST TIME IN YEARS, I-I'VE ACTUALLY *FELT* SOMETHING.
REAL EMOTION. IT FEELS... WONDERFUL.
HEAR THAT, DOC? MAYBE THERE'S A CHANCE HE CAN BE SAVED? CURED?
YOU GET IT NOW? THAT'S *WHY* WE DON'T KILL! 'CAUSE THERE'S *ALWAYS* HOPE.
BECAUSE PEOPLE CAN--
THIS CHANGES NOTHING.
YOU ARE WHO YOU ARE. THAT KILLER WILL *ALWAYS* BE HIDING INSIDE YOU.
THERE IS ONLY ONE SOLUTION HERE.

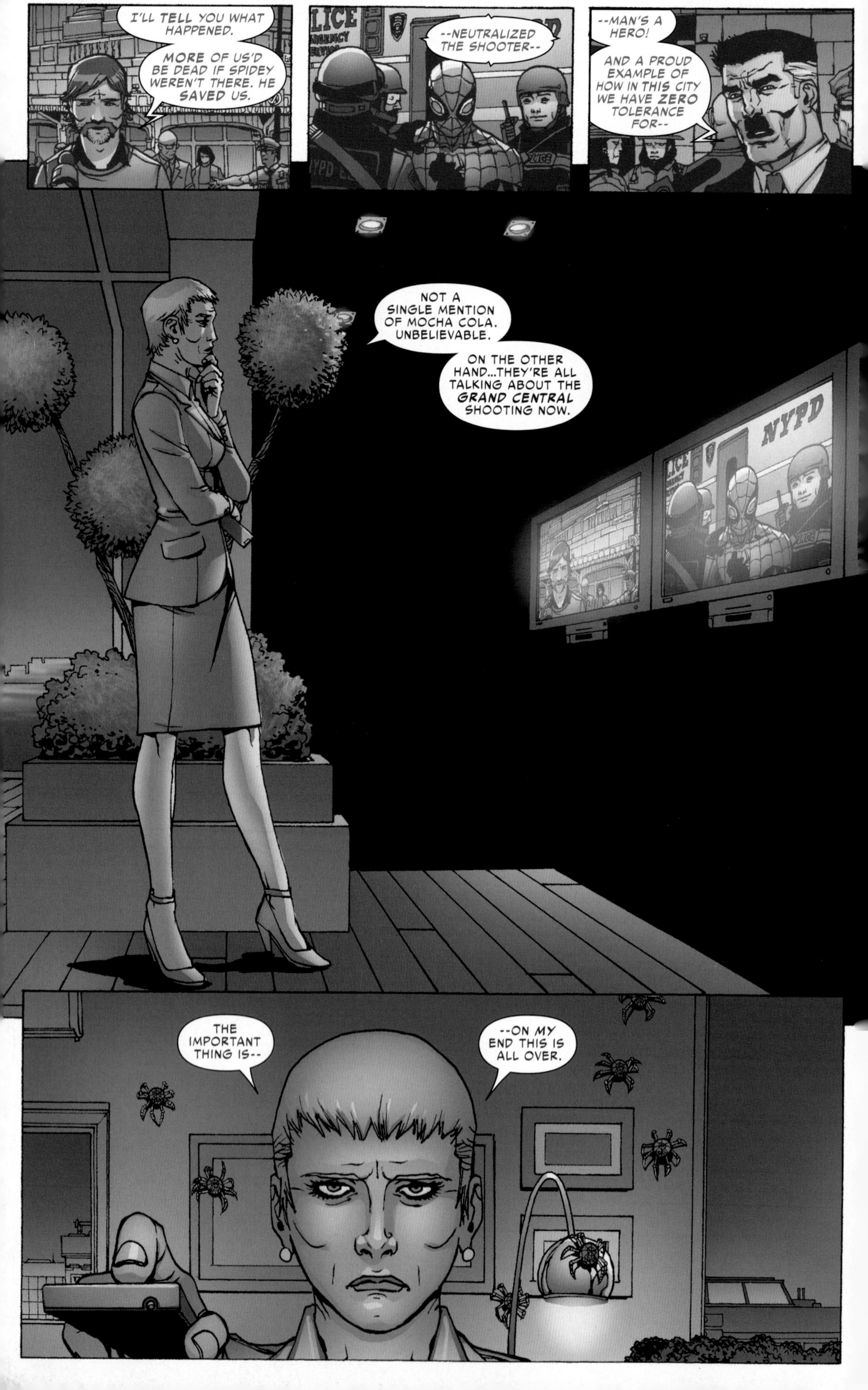
I'LL TELL YOU WHAT HAPPENED.
MORE OF US'D BE DEAD IF SPIDEY WEREN'T THERE. HE SAVED US.
--NEUTRALIZED THE SHOOTER--
--MAN'S A HERO!
AND A PROUD EXAMPLE OF HOW IN THIS CITY WE HAVE ZERO TOLERANCE FOR--
NOT A SINGLE MENTION OF MOCHA COLA. UNBELIEVABLE.
ON THE OTHER HAND...THEY'RE ALL TALKING ABOUT THE GRAND CENTRAL SHOOTING NOW.
NYPD
THE IMPORTANT THING IS--
--ON MY END THIS IS ALL OVER.

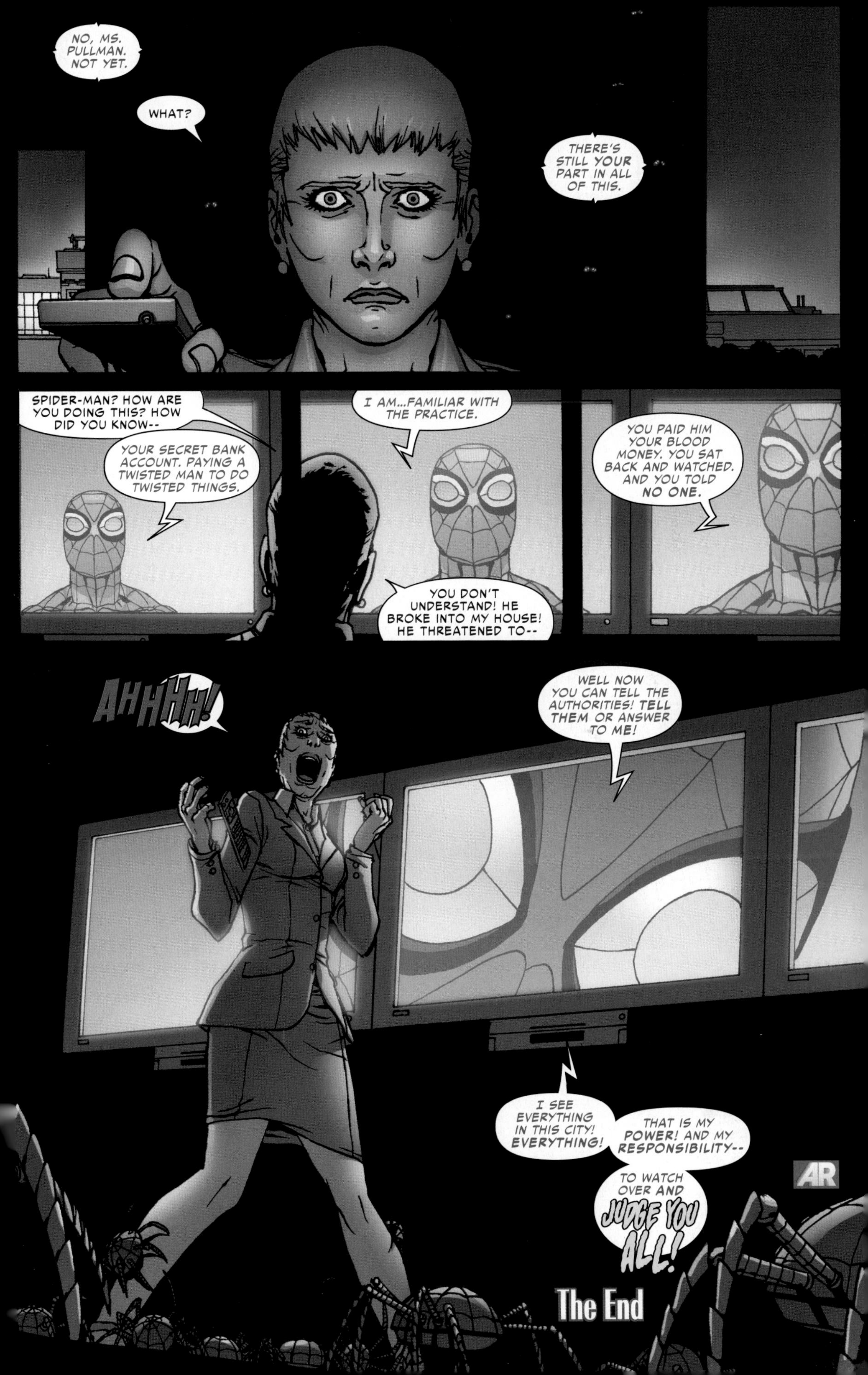
NO, MS. PULLMAN. NOT YET.
WHAT?
THERE'S STILL YOUR PART IN ALL OF THIS.
SPIDER-MAN? HOW ARE YOU DOING THIS? HOW DID YOU KNOW--
YOUR SECRET BANK ACCOUNT. PAYING A TWISTED MAN TO DO TWISTED THINGS.
I AM...FAMILIAR WITH THE PRACTICE.
YOU PAID HIM YOUR BLOOD MONEY. YOU SAT BACK AND WATCHED. AND YOU TOLD NO ONE.
YOU DON'T UNDERSTAND! HE BROKE INTO MY HOUSE! HE THREATENED TO--
AHHHH!
WELL NOW YOU CAN TELL THE AUTHORITIES! TELL THEM OR ANSWER TO ME!
I SEE EVERYTHING IN THIS CITY! EVERYTHING!
THAT IS MY POWER! AND MY RESPONSIBILITY--
TO WATCH OVER AND JUDGE YOU ALL!
AR
The End

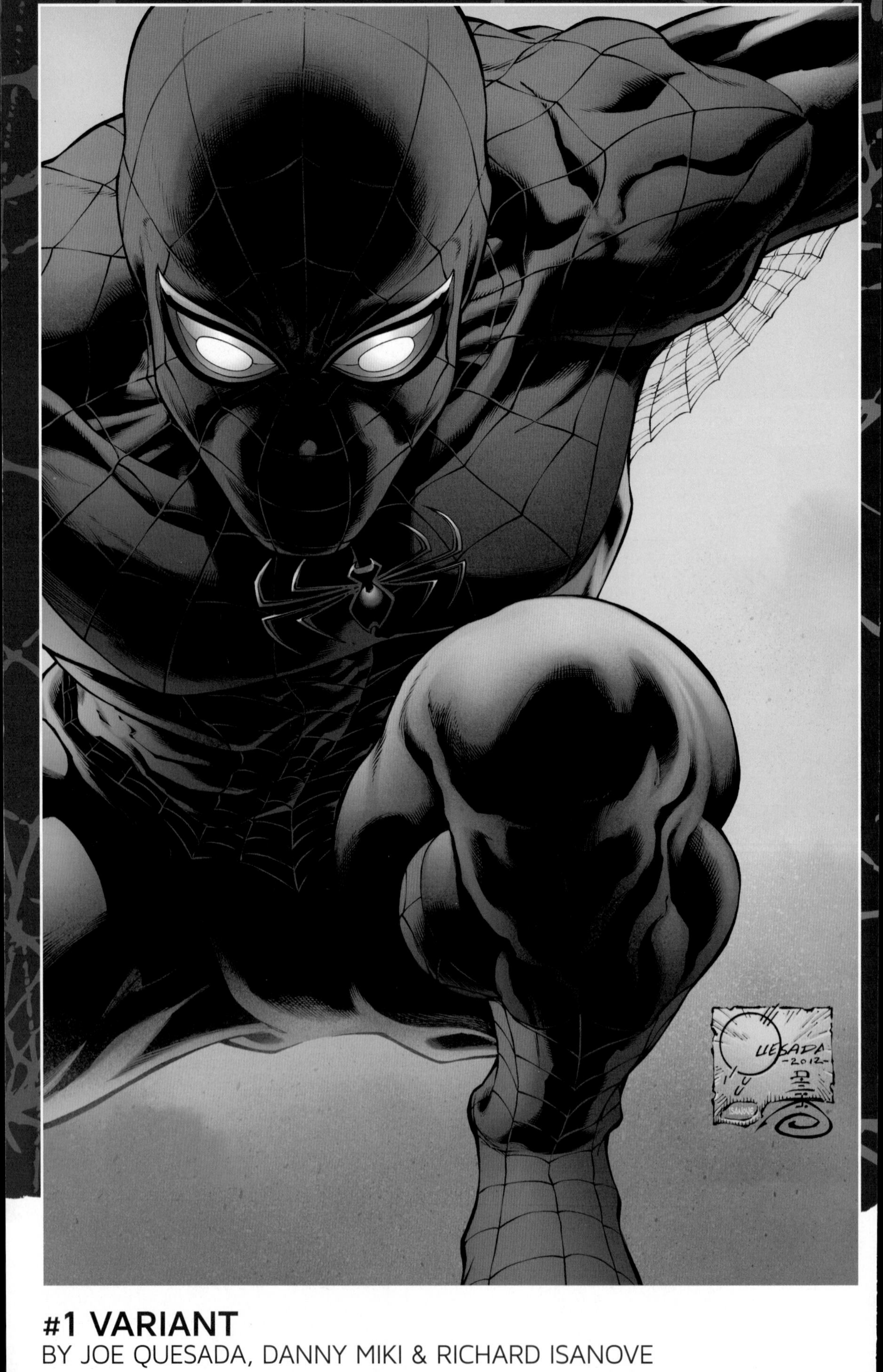

#1 VARIANT
BY JOE QUESADA, DANNY MIKI & RICHARD ISANOVE

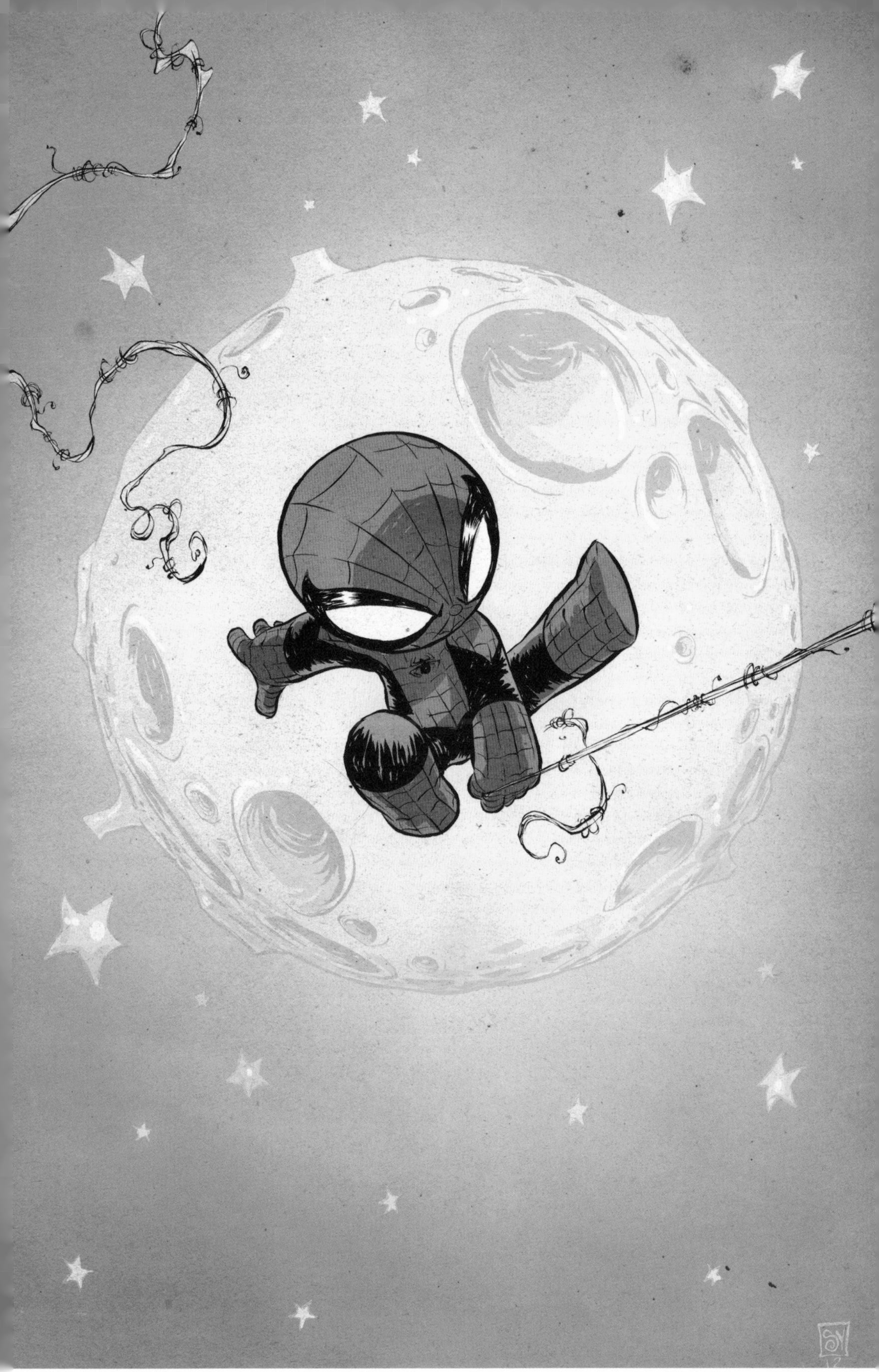

#1 VARIANT
BY SKOTTIE YOUNG

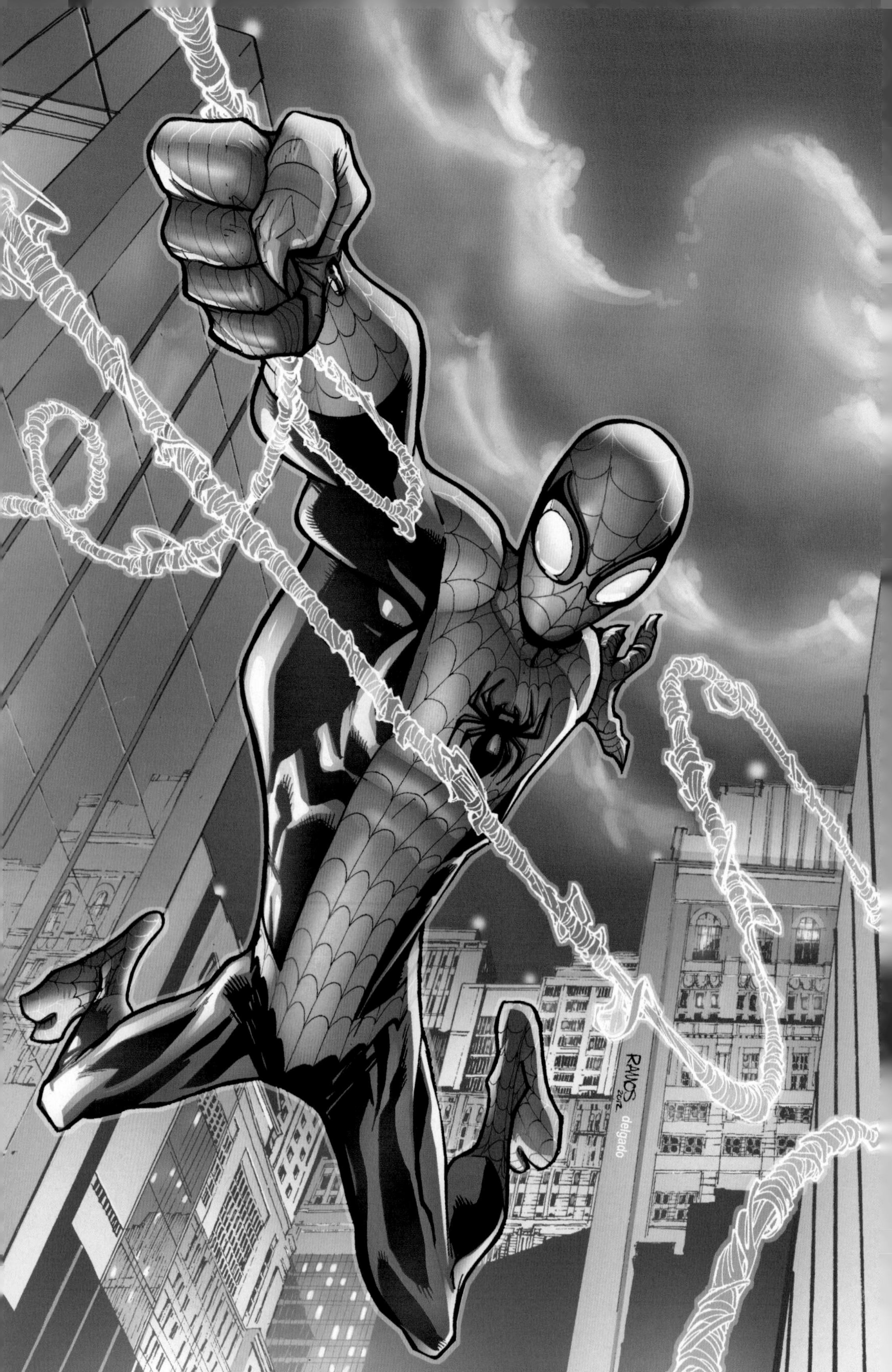
RAMOS
2012
delgado

#1 VARIANT
BY HUMBERTO RAMOS & EDGAR DELGADO

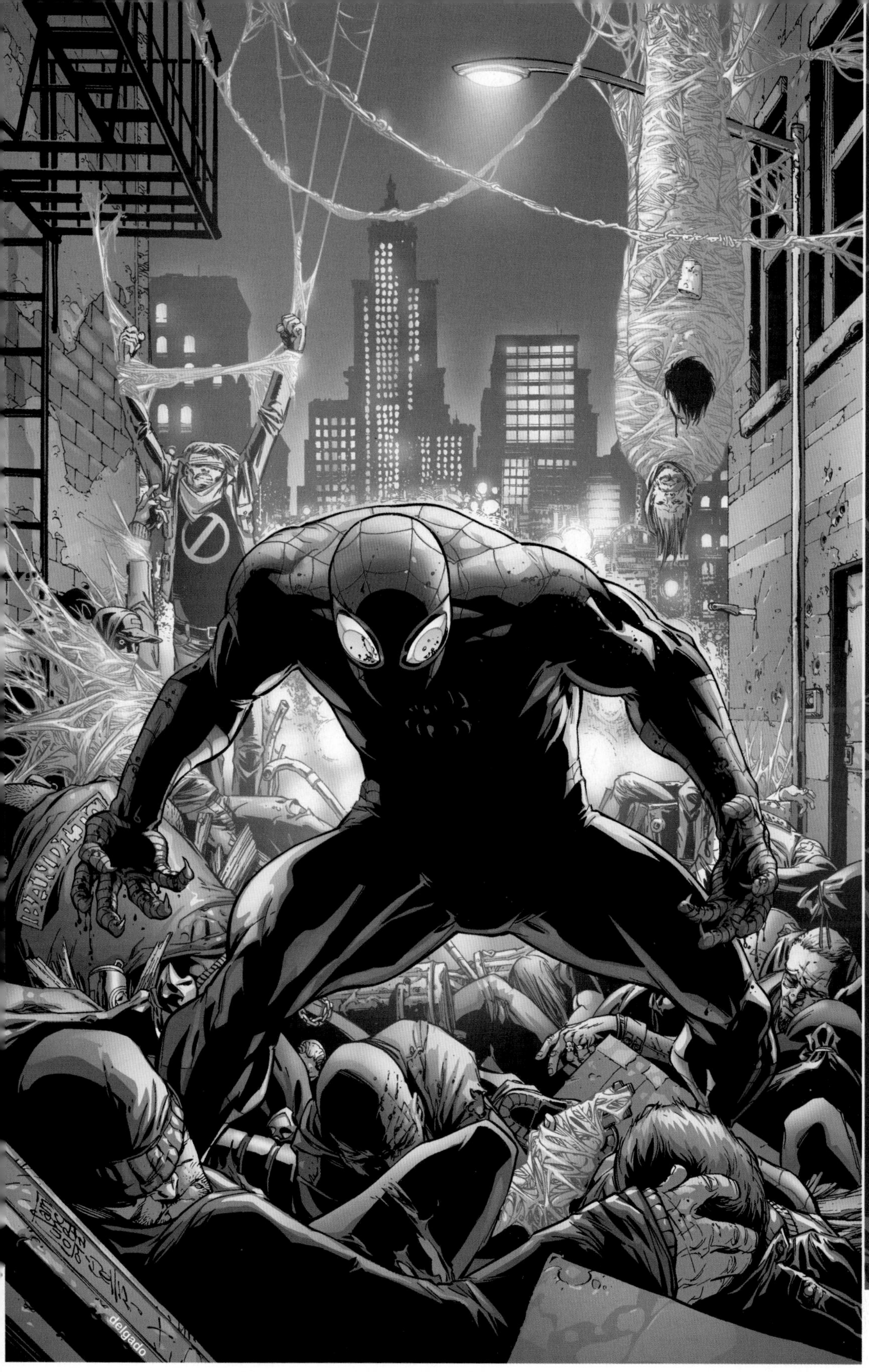
delgado

#1 VARIANT
BY GIUSEPPE CAMUNCOLI, JOHN DELL & EDGAR DELGADO

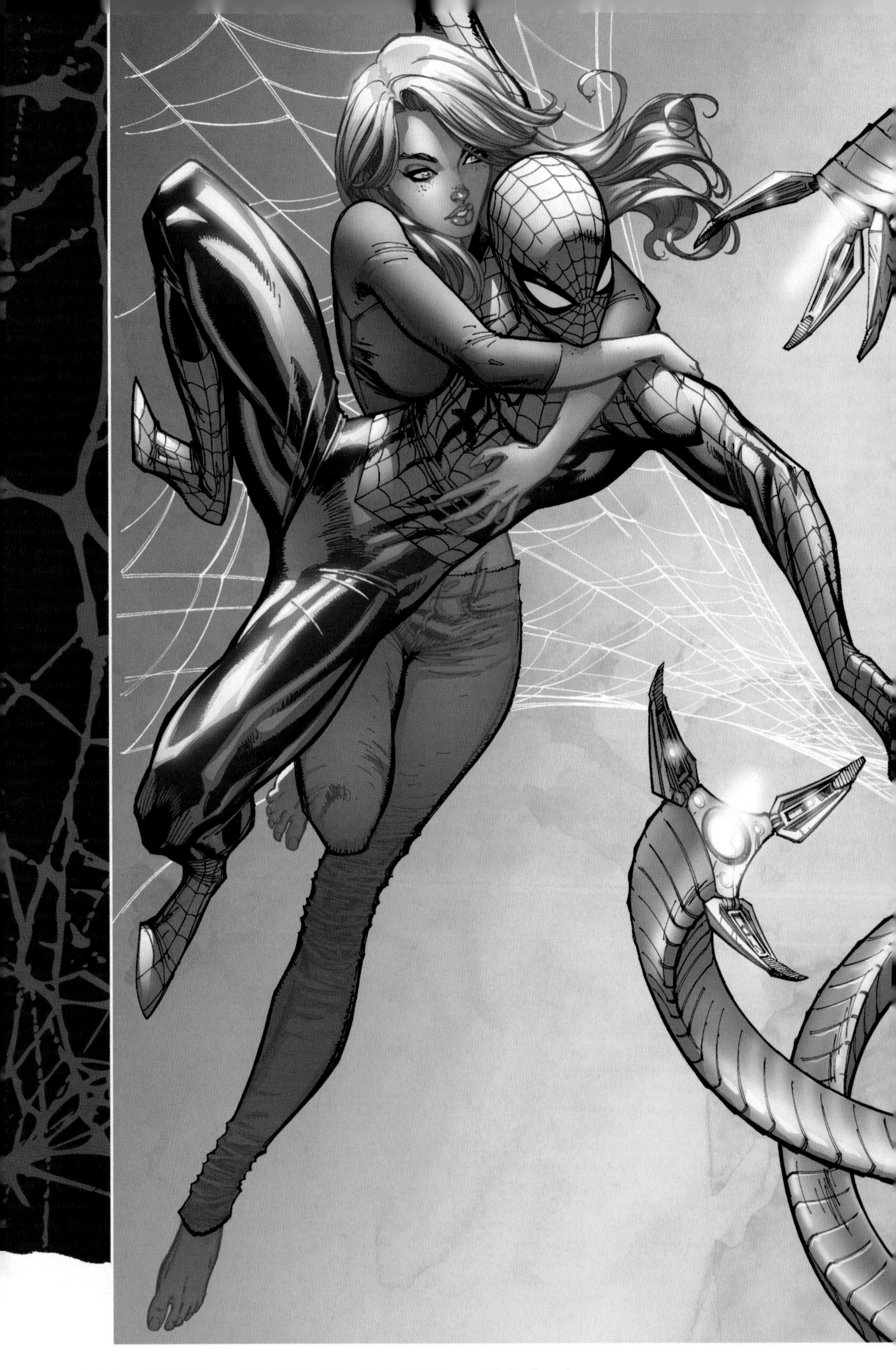

AMAZING SPIDER-MAN #700 &
SUPERIOR SPIDER-MAN #1 COMBINED VARIANTS

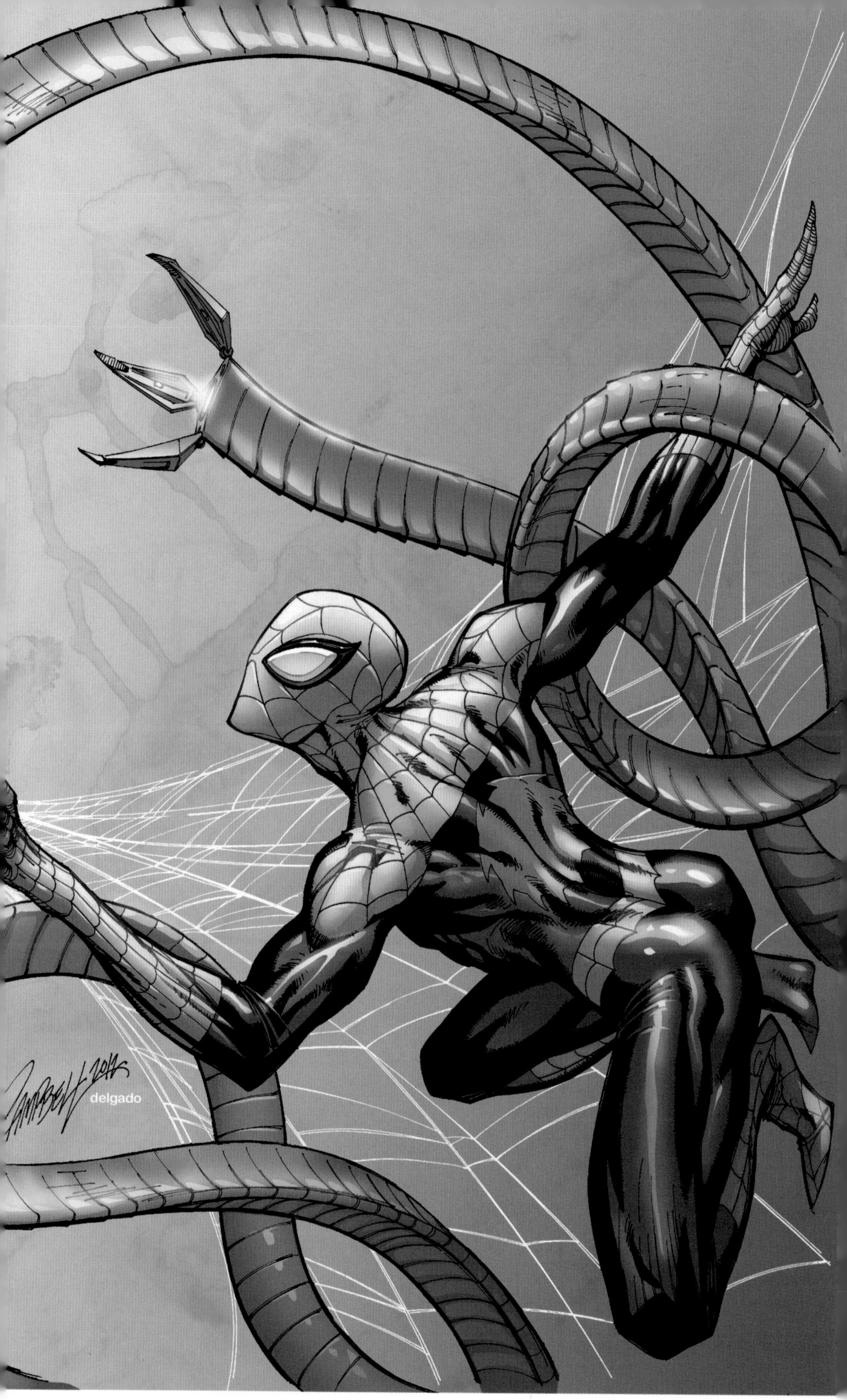
delgado

BY J. SCOTT CAMP
& EDGAR DEL

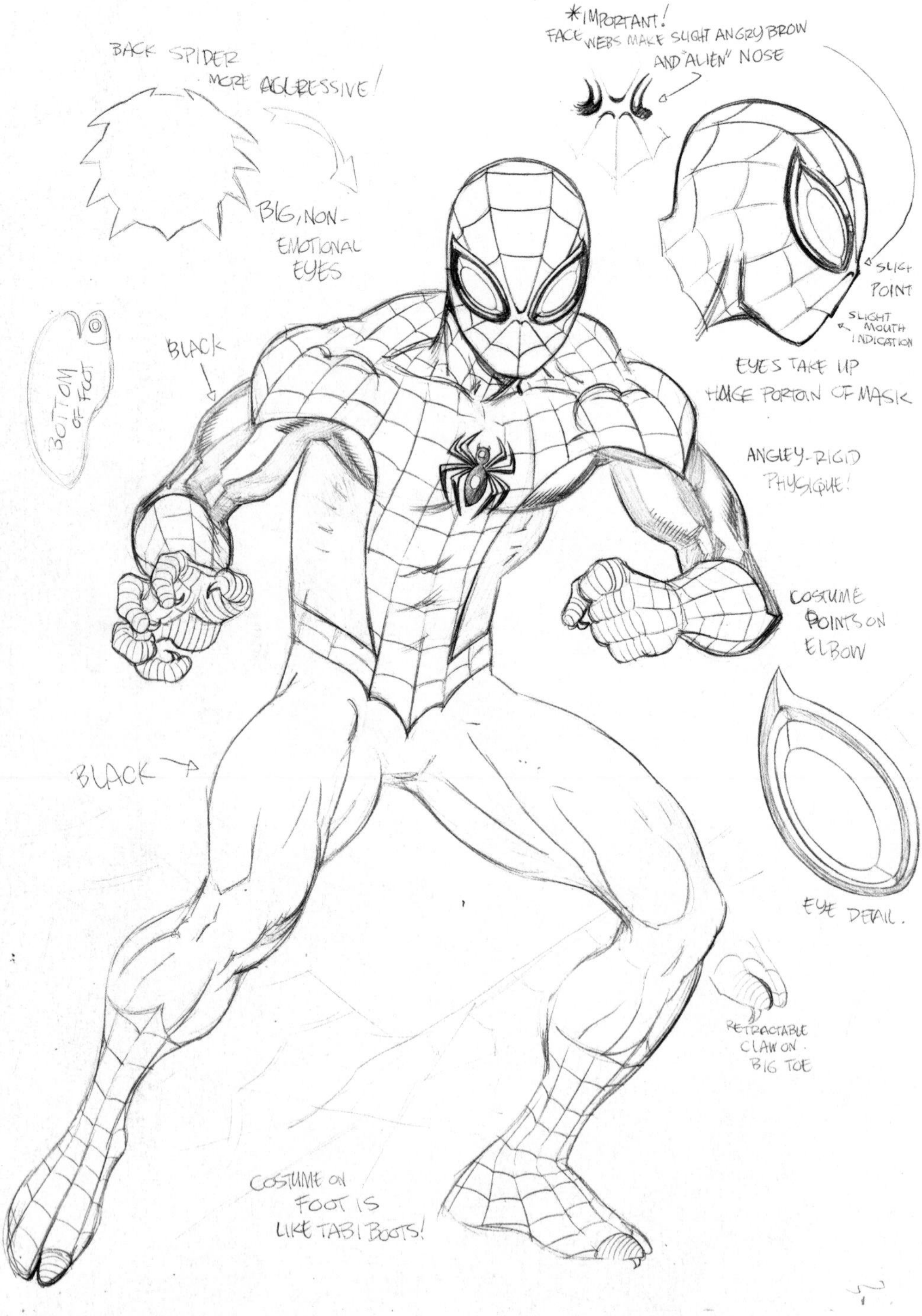
*IMPORTANT! FACE WEBS MAKE SLIGHT ANGRY BROW AND "ALIEN" NOSE
BACK SPIDER MORE AGGRESSIVE!
BIG, NON-EMOTIONAL EYES
SLIGHT MOUTH INDICATION
EYES TAKE UP HUGE PORTION OF MASK
BLACK
BOTTOM OF FOOT
ANGLEY-RIGID PHYSIQUE!
COSTUME POINTS ON ELBOW
BLACK
EYE DETAIL.
RETRACTABLE CLAW ON BIG TOE
COSTUME ON FOOT IS LIKE TABI BOOTS!

#1 DESIGN VARIANT
BY ED McGUINNESS

#1 HASTINGS VARIANT
BY MIKE DEODATO & RAIN BEREDO

#1 LONDON CON VARIANT
BY ADI GRANOV

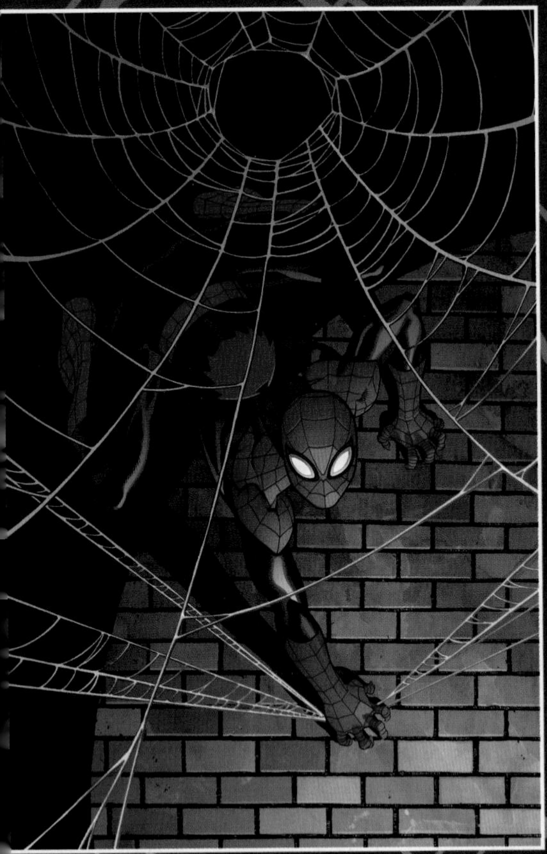

#2 VARIANT
BY ED McGUINNESS & MARTE GRACIA

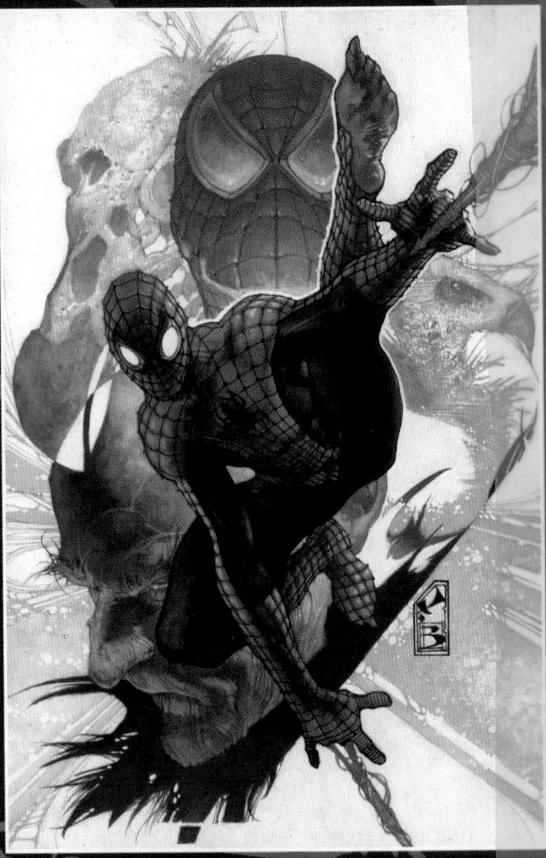

#3 VARIANT
BY SIMONE BIANCHI & SIMONE PERUZZI

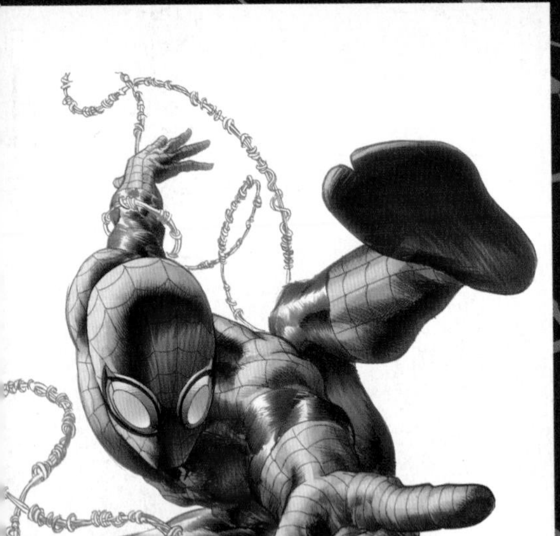

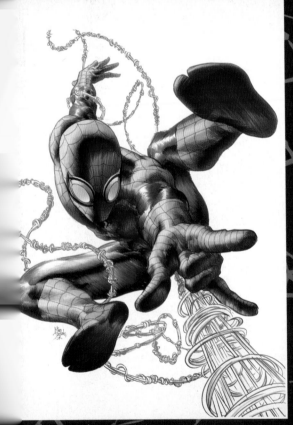

#4 VARIANT
BY MIKE DEODATO & RAIN BEREDO

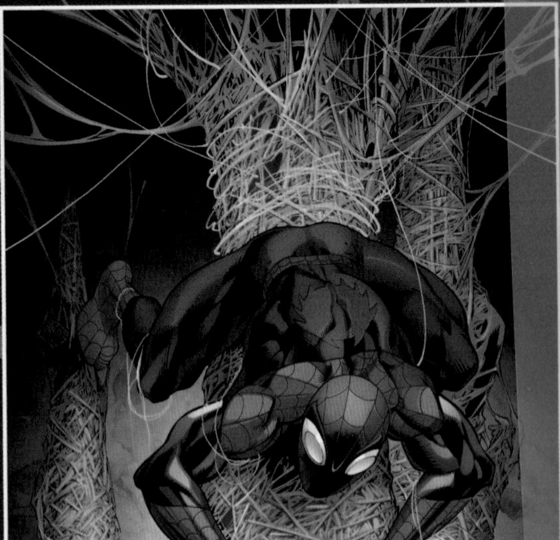

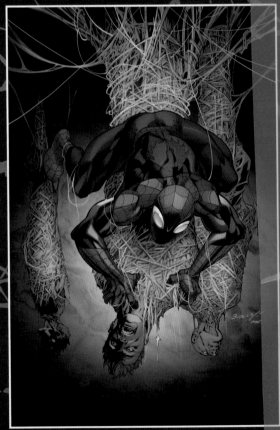

#5 VARIANT
BY MARK BAGLEY, MARK FARMER & MARTE GRACIA

THE SUPERIOR SPIDER-MAN

AR

INDEX